A JOURNEY OF SERVANT LEADERSHIP

LEADING
in the
LORD'S
WAY

A JOURNEY OF SERVANT LEADERSHIP

LEADING
in the
LORD'S WAY

ERNEST LEE DAVIS

CFI
An imprint of Cedar Fort, Inc.
Springville, Utah

© 2024 Ernest Lee Davis
All rights reserved.

No part of this book may be reproduced in any form whatsoever, whether by graphic, visual, electronic, film, microfilm, tape recording, or any other means, without prior written permission of the publisher, except in the case of brief passages embodied in critical reviews and articles.

This material is neither made, provided, approved, nor endorsed by Intellectual Reserve, Inc. or The Church of Jesus Christ of Latter-day Saints. Any content or opinions expressed, implied or included in or with the material are solely those of the owner and not those of Intellectual Reserve, Inc. or The Church of Jesus Christ of Latter-day Saints." Permission for the use of sources, graphics, and photos is also solely the responsibility of the author.

Paperback ISBN 13: 978-1-4621-4852-3
eBook ISBN 13: 978-1-4621-4853-0

Published by CFI, an imprint of Cedar Fort, Inc.
2373 W. 700 S., Suite 100, Springville, UT 84663
Distributed by Cedar Fort, Inc., www.cedarfort.com

Library of Congress Cataloging Number: 2024947516

Cover design by Shawnda Craig
Cover design © 2024 Cedar Fort, Inc.
Printed in the United States of America

10 9 8 7 6 5 4 3 2 1

Printed on acid-free paper

CONTENTS

Author's Note vii

Introduction ix

CHAPTER 1
Emulating Jesus Christ: A Call to Serve and Love 1

CHAPTER 2
Walking in the Light of Christ: A Journey of Faith, Leadership,
    and Service 11

CHAPTER 3
The Path of Servant-Leadership 21

CHAPTER 4
Calloused Hands and Fusing of Servant-Leadership 33

CHAPTER 5
Servant-Leadership: Bearing the Burden of the Cross.......................... 43

CHAPTER 6
A More Excellent Way.. 51

CHAPTER 7
Agape: How Unconditional Love Conquers All 67

CHAPTER 8
Cultivating Greatness 83

CHAPTER 9
Rising from the Margins: The Talented Tenth as Servant-Leaders   93

Preface to Characteristics of Servant Leadership 103

CHAPTER 10
Empathy: Illuminating a Path of Healing.. 113

CHAPTER 11
Navigating Leadership with Listening 125

CHAPTER 12
Change with Healing, Love, and Wholeness...........................135

CHAPTER 13
A Journey of Awareness: From the Streets to
    Servant-Leadership...145

CHAPTER 14
Persuasive Leadership and the Illumination of Ideals 157

CHAPTER 15
Envisioning the Promised Land: A Journey toward Servant-Leadership
    and Conceptualization 167

CHAPTER 16
Overcoming and Leading with Foresight 179

CHAPTER 17
The Sea of Galilee: Stewardship and Service...........................189

CHAPTER 18
 Leadership Growth: Navigating Troubled Waters toward Service...........199

CHAPTER 19
Building the Beloved Community 211

FINAL WORDS..225

ABOUT THE AUTHOR 229

BIBLIOGRAPHY 231

Author's Note

Growing up in Los Angeles, our family's last residence was on West Slauson Ave. Blue marks the colors represented on the block of Slauson. As a color, Blue has no negative words associated with its significance and represents the unpredictable beauty that still exists in the world. The cover of this book denotes Blue—a spirit of faith and love that encourages a meaningful appreciation toward the heavens above. In this book, I choose to use the color Blue as a metaphor for leadership, drawing inspiration from Jesus Christ as the epitome of servant-leadership, blessing of our lives with the dew of heaven. As children of God, the light of Christ is ever-present in our lives. Our belief in the atoning power of Christ will allow us to overcome adversity faithfully, for God will enlarge our steps so that our feet will not slip.[1] Imbued with Blue's serene essence, I aspire to weave together and relay a beautiful message of experiences marked by hope, altruism, and love, a vision first presented to us in Martin Luther King's famous "I Have a Dream" speech.

---

1. Old Testament, 2 Samuel 22:37.

Introduction

The streets bear the scars of despair. A liquor store stands outside Days Inn, its entrance surrounded by homeless individuals clutching tightly to a fading semblance of the American dream. The neighboring areas pulsate with unyielding tension as rival factions, bearing the names of Crips and Bloods, vie for control, driven by a relentless pursuit to reclaim the identity denied them by history. A pornography store beckons to the right, enticing bystanders toward a treacherous path of unending addiction. And a few blocks to the left, a strip club thrives, systematically degrading the dignity of women. Whichever direction one turns, the reality is bleak, eroding any trace of the once-promising dreams of the civil rights movement. It is a harrowing journey where hopelessness vibrates like a never-ending nightmare.

At a young age, my daughter Athena said to me, "Daddy, everyone in jail looks like you; they're all Black." The gospel of Jesus Christ provided me with a different path. My journey from the LA streets began with love and the belief that I was a child of God. My heart swells with gratitude for the faithful individuals who walked beside me, gradually leading me toward a path of salvation, one step at a time.

Inequality, so blatantly evident on the streets of Los Angeles and other marginalized communities, severely limits the possibility of a better life. Growing up off West Slauson Avenue in South Central Los Angeles, I witnessed firsthand the harsh realities of life on the margins of society. In high school, my report card painted an unpromising picture, with Ds lining the columns and the threat of failure looming over me. I read "in danger of failing" on every other line. Rather than succumbing to disappointment, however, I refused to accept defeat. It was during this time, long before I fully grasped the concept of God's grace, that I was constantly on my knees, waiting for the right moment to rise into a better version of myself. I prayed for the faith to foresee opportunities that would allow me to walk upright and be more confident in my potential.

Week after week I gazed out the bus window as I traversed the diverse neighborhoods, witnessing countless stories of fragmented gang cultures etched upon the corners. At each bus stop scars inflicted by gun violence bore a stark reminder that, for me, the privilege of attending football practice was a life-saving gift, despite the wounds inflicted by a merciless world bleeding relentlessly under the cover of my uniform and pads.

I found beauty in stories of strength and determination all around me. Amidst this disheartening backdrop, a mother tirelessly placed herself at the forefront, determined to shield her sons from treading their father's path. From LA Southwest Community College, I saw a football coach dedicating himself to preventing young Black men from succumbing to deterministic statistics that society insists they cannot transcend. Crossing the streets of South Central, I was comforted by the devoted faith of best friends prioritizing each other's needs, offering mutual reassurance and unconditional love despite the bleakness of the way forward. Unsung heroes like these served selflessly to renew my hope and the hopes of others like me. Their support and encouragement empowered us to rise above life's difficulties.

As a young man, I had gleaned the essence of leadership from the LA streets, where young and old individuals outside the margins led their communities using a blend of resilience and street smarts. My leadership aspirations had initially propelled me toward the Gangsta Crips, yearning to make my mark. The streets, however, overshadowed any notion of meaningful leadership, trapping me in a cycle of desperation, unable to see beyond the struggles of homelessness. I stumbled and persevered for five years, unaware of God's guiding influence. Gratefully, along the way, I had best friends who blessed me with God's love: Eric, my supportive twin brother, and Ruth, my beloved eternal companion. They sustained me, serving and leading, having my back when I needed to go forward. Their untiring support gave me a sense of unconditional love, a rare treasure when I traversed the streets shaded with Crip Blue.

Even in the sweltering grip of poverty, I discovered beauty amid brokenness through the faith-filled leaders who gave me confidence. I now could visualize possibility, like a resilient rose breaking through concrete. Despite the previously impenetrable shadows of hopelessness and scarcity, the Light of Christ illuminated for me the possibility of happiness through God's tender mercies. My journey to lead in the Lord's way began with redemption in Christ, allowing me to forgive my experiences on the streets of Los Angeles and leave behind resentment toward my past life.

As I began to embark on my journey, I realized that I needed to shift my perspective of what it means to lead. The underlying ideals of servant-leadership inspire me. They captivate my attention in the same way a husband looks deeply into the faithful eyes of his beloved, knowing that they are equally yoked and bound together in God's love, believing with confidence that timeless devotion to the word of God will bless their lives. When we marry ourselves to these ideals of leadership, our eyes open to the limitless depths of human potential, and those we lead feel God's love through us.

Reflecting on my journey as a leader, I have come to cherish every experience, for each has helped to teach me life's lessons. In leadership, there is often an assumption that those with the highest intellectual capacities, most impressive credentials, and privilege are naturally best suited to lead. However, it was through failure and hardship that I truly honed my leadership abilities.

Questions often arise: What qualifies you for leadership? What qualifies you to write a book? When the chances of success appear low and the possibility of failure is high, what inspires you and eventually leads you to triumph?

My response is straightforward: life itself has qualified me. It was those days when I walked the streets of Slauson Avenue with nothing, surviving the harsh realities marked by homelessness, that molded me. Before I realized it, God had already equipped me with the strength to persevere, preventing me from failing and inspiring me to keep pressing forward.

When asked about his education and qualifications for leadership, Frederick Douglass enthusiastically replied, "My degree is written on my back."[1] He reflected on living multiple lives in one, drawing inspiration from overcoming generational obstacles and striving to become

1. Nelson and London, *Becoming Frederick Douglass.*

the fullest expression of himself. His qualifications for leadership were evident in the lines etched on his face, reflecting his determination to outlast every experience.

A book, at best, is simply an additional aid for the vast and often uncharted quest for purposeful leadership. On our leadership journey, we can stay safely on the traditional path and vicariously savor the adventures lying beyond the horizon. However, if we seek genuine experience, learning, and cultivation of the desire to make a significant contribution, we must embrace life's opportunities to fail so that we may discover new paths for ourselves and others.

Each day affords us a new opportunity to narrow the broad road that leads to defeat by helping others discover the promise-laden path leading to God's love. Through our faith in Christ, we feel unwavering love and support, strengthening our resolve to forge ahead even when faced with challenges others may have viewed as impossible. Obstacles will always be present in life, but with love, we can strive to remove the barriers that may obstruct the Light of Christ from illuminating the lives of others.

Some of us may not appear to possess the qualifications to lead, write, or achieve remarkable success. Yet, life qualifies you and me through sheer determination and the trials we have prevailed. In moments of adversity, I remain steadfast in my leadership responsibilities. I have crossed the streets of Los Angeles and faced a hotel manager demanding payment for the night's stay. I have stared down the avenues of depression and managed to find a glimmer of faith. While searching for a companion, I met the love of my life. These moments have qualified the person who was once in "danger of failing" for leadership. My leadership journey began when I was sitting at a bus stop awaiting the number 42 bus, hoping I could one day lead those facing obscurity to more meaningful lives.

As I studied Jesus's path, I realized that He faced the same challenges we traverse. While we may find difficulty on our path, we can also find happiness in loving service toward one another. His words become our promise: "In the world you shall have tribulation: but be of good cheer; I have overcome the world."[2] We embark on this journey together, drawing inspiration from Jesus's example. In the fol-

2. John 16:33.

Introduction

lowing pages, we will witness the painting of a vivid picture of a world celebrated by possibility, wonder, and imagination.

Each chapter serves as a conversation with seekers who have wrestled with the difficulty of choosing the right path and have committed themselves to following Christ's lead. As testimony fills my heart and touches the hearts of my readers, together we will share in the joy of witnessing the beloved community described by Dr. Martin Luther King Jr. come to life before our eyes.

CHAPTER 1

Emulating Jesus Christ: A Call to Serve and Love

Our ability to lead and our capacity to serve are not measured by where we were born, the color of our skin, our gender, or socioeconomic status. Some of you have been homeless. Some of you have risked family rejection to pursue your dreams. Many of us have lain awake at night wondering how we were going to support our children while still paying rent, the mortgage, or monthly bills. Many of us know what it is like to live not just month-to-month or day-to-day but meal-to-meal. Never be embarrassed by those struggles. We should never view our challenges as a disadvantage. Instead, we can faithfully understand that our experience of facing and overcoming misfortune is one of our most significant advantages. I know this because I experienced it myself as I traversed the streets of Los Angeles.

During my tenth grade year of high school, I faced suspension due to some poor choices—missing class, walking the hallways with the Eight Trey Gangsta Crips, and shooting dice (street craps). In response, my mom sent me to the park rather than letting me stay home. There was a park with a basketball court nearby, and I spent the entire day there. As I left the park, I encountered missionaries from The Church of Jesus Christ of Latter-day Saints. We spoke briefly, and they gave me scriptures as another testament to Jesus Christ. Despite my lack of faith at the time, I remember feeling no resistance to the sincerity of their message. I recall praying, albeit unsure of how to do so, asking for spiritual confirmation about the truthfulness of the words I had read in the Book of Mormon. I anticipated a profound response that would unequivocally confirm or deny its truth. However, I did not receive an immediate answer. Truth didn't come to me in a moment of clarity; it unfolded gradually through life's experiences, strengthening my testimony over time. Years later, during my senior year of high school and my time at Los Angeles Southwest Community College, I found myself homeless, feeling demoralized and resentful toward life.

Despite life's challenges, through Christ, we can emerge victorious through unfavorable circumstances with an indomitable will to finish. God has given us the gift of Christ's Atonement, making us unbeatable under the weight of adversity. We become leaders when we go about life doing good with love toward all people, emulating the reverent steps of Christ. Testifying of His goodness, Dr. King said:

I know a man—and I want to talk about him a minute, and you will discover who I'm talking about as I go down the way because he was a great one. And he just went about serving. He was born in an obscure village, the child of a poor peasant woman. And then he grew up in still another obscure village, where he worked as a carpenter until he was thirty years old. Then for three years, he just got on his feet, and he was an itinerant preacher. And he went about doing some things. He did not have much. He never wrote a book. He never held an office. He never had a family. He never owned a house. He never went to college. He had never visited a big city. He never went two hundred miles from where he was born. He did none of the usual things the world would associate with greatness. He had no credentials but himself. He was only thirty-three when the tide of public opinion turned against him. . . . Today, he stands as the most influential figure that ever-entered human history. . . .

All of the armies that ever marched, all the navies that ever sailed, all the parliaments that ever sat, and all the kings that ever reigned put together have not affected the life of [people] on this earth as much as that one solitary life. His name may be a familiar one (Jesus). Today I can hear them talking about him. Every now and then somebody says, He's King of Kings. And again, I can hear somebody saying, He's Lord of Lords. Somewhere else I can hear somebody saying, In Christ there is no East nor West. And then they go on and talk about, In Him there's no North and South, but one great Fellowship of Love throughout the whole wide world. He did not have anything. He just went around serving and doing good. . . . You can be on his right hand and his left hand if you serve.[1]

When I felt displaced, had no words to express myself, and had no worldly influence whatsoever, I learned to sing "I Am a Child of God," which strengthened me when my burdens got too heavy. Through the life of Jesus Christ, there is a "balm of Gilead to heal the soul."[2]

When we live the gospel of Jesus Christ, we will have peace flowing from us like a river. My passage of life, like a river, has had many stoppages. The way forward was hedged up, but with every blockage, I was determined to dig out a path that would allow water to flow through seamlessly. One vivid memory stands out as I reflect on traveling across the river of life—a trip with my wife and children to Lower Lewis Falls. As we finally reached our destination after hours of travel, we rested, frozen by the breathtaking sight of the waterfall. After a while, we ventured across the river's edge, eager to explore the hidden wonders on the opposite side of the cascading waters. We had never before sought to cross a river or to witness the beauty of a waterfall up close, and we soon began to feel rocks and boulders concealed under the water hidden by the sun's reflection. While other families crossed the river quickly, some families did not. The path across the river grew increasingly difficult as we reached the midway point, causing our children to contemplate retracing their steps.

Undeterred, we pressed on, determined to conquer the obstacles before us. Obstacles, however, are problems, and problems are opportunities to improve and grow. Each attempt to cross proved challenging as our feet struggled for stability on the slippery rocks. The splashes and our apprehension grew larger with each stumble, and, unaccustomed to such challenging circumstances, our daughter Athena stopped. Overwhelmed by the obstacles before her, she cried out for assistance. At that moment, as parents, we found ourselves navigating the dangerous terrain beneath our feet while extending our hands toward the children, helping them over the rocks. That is what friends and family do; they help each other over the rocks when one person cannot do it alone. Servant-leadership encompasses the heartfelt desire to help others

---

1. King and Washington, *A Testament of Hope*, 266.
2. Jeremiah 8:22.

overcome their obstacles, reaching with sincere concern, like parents reaching out to their children. Unaided, some challenges may seem impossible, but together—as friends, leaders, and followers—we can overcome the formidable rocks that stand in our way.

I also traversed the broken roads of inequality before reaching the river's edge as a teenager. When I had arrived, there was not a clear pathway easily marked for me, and the vision of a daunting river unfolded before me. As I overlooked that metaphorical river ahead of me, I failed to realize the immediate blessings that protected me daily while traversing the streets of Los Angeles.

Broken Dreams and Renewed Faith

As I navigated the river of life, I eventually found myself in Moscow, Idaho, with Eric at the University of Idaho, on an athletic scholarship with unforeseen opportunities and challenges ahead of me, with deprivation behind me. The summer of my second year at U of I, however, I ruptured my patellar tendon while at football practice. As I rounded the corner, sprinting at full speed, a sudden snap echoed through my right knee, sending me tumbling to the ground. I looked down at my leg as my kneecap rolled into my thigh like a window shade. Desperation surged through me as I pounded the ground repeatedly with my fists. I could no longer move my leg. My brother Eric and friends carried me off the football field. I remember lying on the table, the team doctor coming to me and telling me, "Ernest, you tore the tendon connecting your leg. Your season is over, and maybe your career." Tears welled up instantly as I glanced at my brother, who shared in my sorrow.

At that moment, my world shattered. The pain I experienced was beyond words. How could this happen? I had invested tremendous time and effort in overcoming my obstacles on and off the field. The consequences of my injury meant the end of my college football journey. Football had helped me overcome homelessness; it had given me identity when the world did not notice me. This career-ending injury seemed unendurable and was a trial of my faith.

During my time of need, I could not hear the voice of the Lord saying, "I love you. You did your best. I am here for you. Be faithful."

When I injured my knee, negative thoughts whirling around fear and anxiety encompassed my mind, and I felt trapped by walls of depression, blocking the Light of Christ.

Over the next year, however, I faithfully studied the scriptures with my beloved Ruth and became a member of The Church of Jesus Christ of Latter-day Saints. I realized that I had additional obstacles to overcome and needed to see another path forward despite my pain. The gospel of Jesus Christ was my ensign after navigating a mountain of challenges. Learning that Christ could atone for my pain and shortcomings allowed me to be hopeful in my immediate future, illuminating my darkest moments of depression. Once I realized God's love for me, I could recognize it like trees easily seen from far distances. I recall the voice of the Lord finding me in the dark and reassuring me. Knowing I was a son of God gave me the drive I needed to succeed without football, venturing into new opportunities afforded me by following the path of Christ. As I looked upward, I felt the heavens open. Gradually, I began to smile, and my joy was full.

Ruth and I first met through mutual friends at a college party at Washington State University. At the time, I was selling weed to make extra money and had my last twenty-ounce sack to sell. So, I went to the party with my friends while hosting U of I recruits. I remember that night clearly. I had a backpack on, tightly secured to my back. Inside I had my weed supply and a couple of old English 40-ounce beer bottles. As I arrived at the party, I noticed Ruth exiting another car. She was the designated driver for her friends. Our eyes met as we entered the party.

When I got Ruth's phone number, I didn't have a phone, so I used my friend's instead. Rather than saving her number, I called the number so that it would be recorded in his phone's outgoing call history. The following day, I frantically searched through the phone's call history. All the numbers called on the phone had a similar 509 area code for Pullman, Washington. Fortunately, I picked the correct number. Unsure it was Ruth's number, I left her a voicemail. When she called me back the next day, she shared with me that she was a member of The Church of Jesus Christ of Latter-day Saints. Coincidentally, our paths had crossed numerous times at the University of Idaho before that fateful night. I would often see Ruth from a distance, not knowing it was her studying. Her best friend was dating my roommate, giving us a shared social circle. We both originally lived in the Los Angeles area, a commonality that allowed our relationship to grow.

I have found myself in circles, environments, and a family where we took Ls (losses) without a second thought—navigating life without fatherly leadership, enduring the cold, harsh walls of incarceration within the justice system, facing the relentless grip of scarcity, and wandering the unforgiving streets of LA, where homelessness painted our days with shades of unhappiness. I define taking an L as allowing life's circumstances to overwhelm you, causing you to lose the determination or hope to achieve when progress stops. As children of God, any failure will eventually become a significant blessing if we wait upon the Lord, allowing His tender mercies to give us victory. In my adolescence, I took Ls daily for years until I encountered Christ's unconditional love.

The Apostle Peter, when speaking of trials, said, "Beloved, think it not strange concerning the fiery trial which is to try you, as though some strange thing happened unto you: But rejoice, inasmuch as [we] are partakers of Christ's [atonement]; that, when his glory shall be revealed, [we] may be glad also with exceeding joy."[3] Until the spirit of Christ, the comforter, fell upon me, what had initially appeared to be a significant trial during that time eventually became the most profound blessing, affording me a strong testimony of Jesus Christ. I immersed myself in the life-giving waters of the gospel in July 2005.

Ruth helped me prepare for baptism through her example and by sharing her testimony of the gospel. Her influence allowed me to feel the gospel light and find hope while navigating life to find personal meaning beyond the streets and blades of grass. During this time, I decided to "bury my weapons of war,"[4] setting aside my aspirations of playing professional football to follow a different path. I chose to follow Christ and found more happiness in going to school, spending time with Ruth, and attending church.

Initially, I didn't have church clothes. I wore my blue Converse, Snoop Dogg pants with the blue rage imprint, and a white button-up shirt. Over time, Ruth bought me church clothes, which made me feel more comfortable attending church each week, allowing me to see myself in a different light—the Light of Christ.

3. 1 Peter 4:12–13.
4. See Alma 24.

At the age of twenty-two, I emerged from the waters of baptism. My hope for freedom seemed to sweeten, and the spirit of Christ made me glow from within. As I studied the path of Christ, I realized that He was indeed a man of rare endowments—a child of God—guilty of no crime but His unconditional love toward everyone, even me. With hope, His ability to lead with love can become our possibility to live life more purposefully.

Elder Maxwell once wrote, "What may seem now to be mere unconnected pieces of tile will someday, when we look back, take form to reveal a pattern, and we will realize that God was making a mosaic. There is in each of our lives this kind of marvelous design, this pattern, this purpose that is in the process of becoming, which is continually before the Lord but which, for us, looking forward, is sometimes perplexing."[5] Growing up in Los Angeles, California, the vibrant yet challenging environment of the City of Angels exposed me, a person of color, to the harsh realities of poverty, crime, and social mistreatment. In such circumstances, individuals up and down the blocks of Los Angeles did not flaunt their faith in God; it was respected and understood. Faith could determine whether one veered toward trouble or chose a path of righteousness amidst the allure of gangs and neighborhood affiliations.

Throughout urban communities, particularly among people of color, there was a prevailing reliance on faith in God. The concept was straightforward: did this faith lead individuals away from trouble or prepare them to navigate the difficulties and challenges of their surroundings? My baptism into The Church of Jesus Christ of Latter-day Saints came without the weight of judgment from my family and neighborhood. Having already experienced life on the fringes, I consciously decided to pursue a better path rather than persisting in a direction that would inevitably lead to a dead end. In my community, the measure of success wasn't so much about making perfect choices as it was about avoiding the dire consequences of incarceration or violence.

Jesus was no mere teacher of scripture. He walked with people in need, witnessing the masses parched by the drought of depravity, with joints swollen from uncompromising labor. Jesus stood side-by-side with the downtrodden, empathizing fully with God's children as they

5.   Maxwell, *But for a Small Moment*, 3–4.

suffered in the throes of poverty. He strengthened those whose arms were made heavy by hopelessness, as He witnessed the stony countenance of the enslaved and the hopeful smiles generated by an initial encounter with His redeeming love. Christ stood by me, as well—the crutch restoring my broken spirit.

I felt His embrace when missionaries from The Church of Jesus Christ of Latter-day Saints visited me after my knee surgery because they knew I needed the encouragement of their kind words. I sat in a room with no doors, only walls. Excessive bandages wrapped my knee. No one was to the left of me, my fears were to the right of me, and my anguish paralyzed me. I sat on a couch alone, only me and my thoughts. I had occasional visitors. Eric and my friends would bring me food from football camp when they had free time. Still, at night when the shadows of depression grew, it was only me. My injury upended my aspirations, and my loneliness was at its peak. When I traversed the formidable streets of Los Angeles, Eric helped me find a path forward, but this time, the challenge was different; it was me, myself, and I.

As the gospel of Jesus Christ gradually broadened my perspective, I became captivated and deeply moved by the allure of its beauty. I realized that the loveliness of the gospel could ignite the imagination, flashing inspiration before my eyes that allowed me to navigate the streets of loneliness without fear or sorrow. I discovered beauty in the truth that I was a *child of God*, made in His image with potential to achieve any aspiration. After a long drought of belief in my potential, nothing could have been more wondrous than beginning to believe in myself, after drinking from the life-giving waters of the gospel of Jesus Christ. With each step forward, I realized I could overcome the trial of my faith through Him. I grew as a man, became spiritually nourished, more autonomous, and free to choose the path I would travel.

Regarding the necessity of our experiences, Elder Neal A. Maxwell said, "To be untested and unproved is also to be unaware of all that we are" to become. If we do not know our potential as children of God, we will risk forgoing unforeseen blessings. Elder Maxwell continued:

> Could we in ignorance of our capacities trust ourselves? Could others then be entrusted to us? . . . [God] will not allow the cutting short some of the brief experiences we have. To do so would be to deprive us of everlasting experiences and great joy. . . . Do we really want immunity

from adversity? Especially when certain kinds of suffering can aid our growth in this life. . . . To deprive ourselves of those experiences, much as we might momentarily like to, would be to deprive ourselves of the outcomes over which we shouted with anticipated joy when this life's experiences were explained to us so long ago, in the world before we came here.[6]

Had I not struggled on the streets of Los Angeles or withstood the loss of my football dreams, I would not fully appreciate Christ's redeeming love for me as I do now. As we navigate our journeys in life, we influence the world around us by our ability to serve, and writing this work was an opportunity to serve. We have the opportunity for enormous success with no limits, but the most significant choices begin and end with us believing that we are children of God.

---

6. *Maxwell, All These Things Shall Give Thee Experience, 27–28.*

CHAPTER 2

Walking in the Light of Christ: A Journey of Faith, Leadership, and Service

To build the faith that defines leadership, we must remain composed and open to inspiration even amid tension or pressure. In our quiet moments, we can experience the creativity that gives us the impulse and boldness to go forward with strength. Like the faith I discovered after my knee surgery, we must constantly build walls of faith to hold back the floods of fear in our minds. Through faith, we understand that the word of God framed the world. By faith, the walls of Jericho fell. Faith provides the determination not to be overwhelmed by opposition and to breed creative self-affirmation when faced with adversity.

Jesus Christ was so internally conditioned and prepared that He became a flawless representation of both of faith and leadership. His ideals, rooted in His teachings and message, carried influence that would change the calendar, redirect the world's thinking, determine the course of history, and infuse life with a new rhythm. When we, too, fully appreciate His ideals, we can step back and allow those ideals to direct our every action. Then, as the underlying characteristics of servant-leading begin to take hold, we can stand back and say, "Now, let it work."

If Christ had not suffered to build the bridge between us and God's love, how different might our stories have been over the past two thousand years? Through Jesus Christ's Atonement, I overcame the desperation of homelessness and the tragedy of knee surgery. My aspirations for a better life often seemed distant and uncertain. However, I eventually discovered a source of renewal above and beyond football.

Often, transformative experiences go unnoticed as we navigate the unfamiliar path, moments when we are deeply changed by an unexpected meeting with people who change our way of thinking or inspire us. Faithfully following the path the Lord sets before us, we will find ourselves on the margins of society, sharing the words of Christ with those whom society all too often overlooks.

Jesus's message carries the same invitation to choose that He imparted to Peter: "Come, follow me,"[1] bidding us in various and equivalent ways to venture as Peter did, "walking on the water."[2] If we are serious about our discipleship, Jesus will eventually request each of us to do the things most difficult for us to do, just as He challenged the wealthy young man to "sell all that thou hast and give it to the poor."[3] Christ challenges us because He loves us; real growth is no more random than easy.

As we strive to draw closer to God's love, we will bear Christ's burdens, ministering to those in need as He did. The greatest of all objectives is to love one another as we love Him, and then we may stand back and watch it unfold. When we find ourselves out on the margins, there are no words or scripts to follow Christ's example, only a drive to restore significance and hope into the lives of others. There are no guarantees of help along the way; we cannot rely on others to continually rescue us. Sometimes, we must take the initiative to envision our aspirations, evaluate our circumstances, and determine what steps will allow us to go forward.

The life of Jesus Christ is an experience that emboldens us to take the necessary faithful steps toward what we perceive as the unknown. We can look back across the never-ending vista of time to see that we would have not come thus far, "if not for the word of Christ and our unshaken faith in Him . . . who is mighty to save."[4]

Christ did not tell us that only a few are called; He taught that many are called. He did not teach that a few things were possible to those who believed; He said that all things are possible when we have faith. A sacred

---

1. Matthew 4:19.
2. Matthew 14:29.
3. Matthew 19:21.
4. 2 Nephi 31:5–25.

song sings, "I walked today where Jesus walked."[5] While it may not be practical to walk today where Jesus walked, we can embrace His teachings and reflect today on what Jesus believed. We can fill our minds and approach life with the very attitudes that made Him the Redeemer of the world. We are all aware of the truth that Jesus died for us. We are not always conscious that He also lived for us. By reliving His life, we can aim to impart His thoughts and motivations into our own journey.

With reverent steps, we walk today, emulating the steps of Christ, but walking reverently along the path of Christ requires patience to follow in His footsteps. Sometimes we will find ourselves lost, sunk in discouragement, and surveying the unimaginable distance between where we are and the goals we aim to achieve. Every experience requires faith to actively work toward worthwhile goals and avoiding discouragement when results appear slowly. Those moments are the birthplace of leadership. Elder Neal A. Maxwell advocated, "Patience is a willingness, in a sense, to watch the unfolding purposes of God with a sense of wonder and awe, rather than pacing up and down within the cell of circumstance."[6] Thus, every setback, every trial, and every moment of doubt ultimately shapes us into the leaders God intends for us to become.

Walking the leadership path, we align ourselves with the gospel of love, led by Jesus Himself, who helps to move us in the right direction at the appropriate pace. Some paths we traverse may be rough and unpaved, while others are smooth and discernible. Nonetheless, the greatest of life's rewards come from walking along the covenant path.

The most significant sermon ever spoken consisted of three words. Jesus said, "Come follow me."[7] One of the most important decisions we ever have to make is how we will we follow and emulate Christ's steps. Can we develop the leadership skills to make that accomplishment possible? If so, how? What should be our attitude, and how do we determine the appropriate steps we take?

As we walk the paths of life, there come dark seasons of doubt, opposition, and disappointment. In such circumstances, few see ahead by the light of faith, but many stumble in the darkness and

---

5. "I'll Walk with You," *Children's Songbook*, no. 140.
6. Maxwell, "Patience," 2.
7. Matthew 4:19.

even become lost for a time. When we emulate Christ's steps, the Spirit touches our hearts, pointing us in the right direction. And with faith, whether recognized or not, we take a few guarded steps until our stride lengthens into a brighter vista. The challenge faced by every follower of Christ is to take the next step, accept the responsibility to which they are all called, live the experiences they are given, and faithfully fulfill every opportunity with the expectation that God will light the way before them. President Gordon B. Hinckley encourages us, "We take one step at a time. In doing so, we reach toward the unknown, but faith lights the way. If we will cultivate that faith, we shall never walk in darkness."[8]

A man once said to Jesus, "Lord, I will follow thee whithersoever thou goes."[9] Jesus warned him to think about what was involved. How will we respond when the winds of opposition begin to blow? Jesus cautioned the man about indecision's troubles: "He who hesitates is lost" and "no man having put his hand to the plow and looking back, is fit for the kingdom of God."[10]

If we are to move along the covenant path in the right direction, we must faithfully look ahead of us, with Christ leading the way. So frequently, we find reasons for wavering, side-stepping, or turning back. Jesus allows us to decide how to follow Him. We determine the pace in how we will follow. Servant-leaders waste no energy on doubts, fears, or reconsiderations, leaving no stone unturned in the pursuit of the anticipated outcome. We should always have a definite answer to how and when we will achieve our goals, never looking back over our shoulders. When a challenging set of circumstances confronts us, we can spiritually follow Christ, and He will show us the next faithful step.

In Bethabara beyond the Jordan, John the Beloved and two of his disciples gazed upon Jesus as He walked. John proclaimed, "Behold the Lamb of God!"[11] Filled with admiration and curiosity, being moved by beauty and an undeniable calling, the two disciples stepped onto the road to follow the path of Christ. With genuine warmth in His

---

8. Hinckley, *We Walk by Faith*, 8.
9. Matthew 8:19.
10. Luke 9:62.
11. John 1:36.

eyes, Jesus turned toward them and asked, "What seek ye?"[12] In that sacred moment, their hearts spoke more eloquently than words, and they humbly asked, "Where do you live?" Without hesitation, Jesus responded, "Come and see." Welcoming them into His world, He embraced them with the promise of discovery for the day—a transformative journey leading them toward a path of servant-leadership. In the presence of the Savior, they absorbed profound teachings and lessons that left an indelible mark on their lives.

As the sun dipped below the horizon, Jesus bestowed upon them a vision of the incredible journey ahead: a path illuminated with wondrous experiences, where the heavenly bonds between service and love would testify of the heavenly connections between humanity and God's love. They were in awe as they witnessed the angels of God ascending and descending upon the Son of Man.[13]

In the Book of Mormon, after teaching His gospel to the Nephites in the land of Bountiful, Jesus ascended into heaven, and the people dispersed before it was dark. The multitude witnessed Jesus ministering to them, and He promised to appear again the following day.

After Jesus's ascension, the people gathered together, separating into twelve large groups, and did not vary from His teachings. Those chosen by Jesus were baptized and filled with the Holy Ghost, and they began to pray to God in the name of Christ.

As they prayed, angels descended out of heaven, encircling them with love. While the angels ministered to the people, Jesus came and stood in the midst, ministering to them also. As they continued to pray, Jesus left the group, bowed toward the earth, and prayed:

Father, I thank thee that thou hast given the Holy Ghost unto these whom I have chosen; and it is because of their belief in me that I have chosen them out of the world.

Father, I pray thee that thou wilt give the Holy Ghost unto all of them that shall believe in their words.

Father, thou hast given them the Holy Ghost because they believe in me; and thou seest that they believe in me because thou hearest

---

12. John 1:37–39.
13. John 1:50–51.

them, and they pray unto me; and they pray unto me because I am with them.[14]

At the end of His humble prayer, Jesus said, "I am with them," testifying that He will be with us during our trials and redeem us from every failure. When He returned to His disciples a second time and witnessed them continuing to pray without stopping, Jesus blessed them. His countenance shone upon them, and His light shone brightly through their faith. Inspired, Jesus went a little way off and bowed Himself to the earth for a second time, praying:

> Father, I pray not for the world, but for those whom thou hast given me out of the world, because of their faith, that they may be refined in me, that I may be in them as thou, Father, art in me, that we may be one, that I may be glorified in them.[15]

The multitude heard and bore record; Jesus's words opened their hearts, and they understood His love for them. The words Jesus prayed were so profound and awe-inspiring that they cannot be adequately written down or fully expressed—a beautiful representation of God's love.

Christ's Example of Service

Devotedly, Jesus teaches us, "I am the light of the world . . . he that followeth me shall not walk in darkness but shall have the light of life."[16] The Son of God offered His most eloquent message not by what He said but by the example He set through action as a devout man, lover of life, and champion for humanity. During His earthly ministry, Jesus taught a more excellent way by painting a picture of grace, mercy, and love for all to see, regardless of caste or creed, binding us all within the warm embrace of God's love. Elder Bruce C. Hafen wrote, "The Savior's gift of grace to us is not necessarily limited in time to 'after' all we can do. We may receive his grace before, during, and after the time when we expend our own efforts."[17] When we love

---

14. 3 Nephi 2–22.
15. 3 Nephi 19:23–29.
16. John 8:12.
17. Hafen, *The Broken Heart*, 155.

God with all our might, mind, and strength, His grace is sufficient for us, and we become perfected by His tender mercies.

How do we serve God with our hearts? With our devotion, love, and obedience. How do we serve God with our might? By using our determination and courage. How do we serve God with our minds? By making a firm, solid decision, and saying, "This is where I stand." Serving God with our minds means to study, think, and plan by faith. How do we serve God with our strength? By using physical activity to serve one another and follow through with our aspirations to uplift one another, we become perfected in Christ.

Elder John S. Robertson explained in a BYU devotional that our understanding of the word *perfect* has changed over time. Whereas in the present day we use perfect as a synonym for flawless, its Latin root means something closer to finished. In Hebrew, the word translated as *perfect* in the Bible is more accurately expressed as *complete*. Elder Robertson remarked:

> Perfection for us, is not about becoming flawless; it is about becoming finished. Our Heavenly Father is the author and designer of our lives and [aspires] that we finish each pursuit with diligence.[18]

The healing influence of Christ's Atonement remedies scrapes, bruises, and the brokenness of the challenging journeys behind and in front of us. The testament of Jesus represents a promise between God and humanity, signifying the continuance of heavenly blessings.

While ministering along the coasts of Judea, after He had blessed the children, a man came running, knelt before Jesus, and asked Him, "Good Master, what shall I do that I may inherit eternal life?" Then, Jesus, beholding him, loved him and said, "One thing thou lackest: go thy way, sell whatsoever thou hast, and give to the poor, and thou shalt have treasure in heaven: and come, take up the cross, and follow me."[19]

Elder Steven L. Lund encouraged us with his assurance that "life often presents itself as an incessant [dreary] wall stretching off into nowhere, but here and there, if [we] watch for them, flickering assurances of God's love for us will become evident."[20] Service toward one another can reveal those flickering assurances of God's love. The most

18. Luke 14:28–30.
19. Matthew 16:24.
20. Lund, "Flashes of Light."

significant influence we can have on anyone is expressing the words "I love you." When we were in college, Ruth spoke those affectionate words affirming God's love for me. Through her words, the Light of Christ shone brightly. When we follow Christ, we speak words of love and affirmation that are unconditional so that, over time, anyone will feel that they can achieve, finish, or complete any goal through belief in themselves.

Along the journey of servant-leadership, we discern the contours of leadership and finally grasp that it is through the experiences of Jesus Christ's unconditional love that we understand the characteristics of service. First, Jesus exemplified a greater purpose far beyond personal ambition. He showed commitment to the well-being of His disciples by investing time and effort in their needs. Inspired by Jesus's leadership, Elder Mark A. Bragg recounted that in the Book of Mormon, "His first day with the Nephites is one of recorded history's most significant days of leadership teaching. Think of it: [Jesus] had precious little time, given He had other sheep to visit. He had to be concise, clear, powerful, and inspired in His limited time. So, what did He do? Where was His focus? How did He teach? What can we learn about leadership principles, and how does His leadership in that single day stack up to leadership concepts taught today?"[21]

Jesus invited the multitude—all 2500—to come unto Him "one by one."[22] He healed the sick and afflicted that same day.[23] He later "took their little children, one by one, and blessed them, and prayed . . . for them."[24] He ministered to and ordained the twelve disciples individually. Jesus invested time in everyone according to their needs. Words did not confine His leadership, for He walked the path He paved, working and sharing life experiences with His followers.

Second, Jesus embodied the essence of leadership by setting a personal example of what others should follow. He preached and practiced, offering His best to others while expecting the best from them. Elder Bragg explained that in the one-day account of Jesus with the Nephites, the Savior at least ten times turned to the twelve disciples

---

21. Bragg, *A Master Class in Leadership,* 3.
22. 3 Nephi 11:15.
23. 3 Nephi 17:9.
24. 3 Nephi 17:21.

He had called to teach them specifically about their responsibilities.[25] He taught them how to lead and how they could bless the lives of the people. He modeled what they were to do. He patiently taught them how to baptize, how to bless the sacrament, and how to confer the gift of the Holy Ghost. At one point the Savior turned to the multitude and said, "Blessed are ye if ye shall give heed unto the words of these twelve whom I have chosen from among you to minister unto you, and to be your servants."[26] Imagine the disciples' emotions as they received their callings directly from the Savior, followed by His public acknowledgment and endorsement of their leadership positions.

Jesus testified openly, unequivocally, and unabashedly about leading through service. His servant's heart and humility were hallmarks of His leadership, as He had advocated for selfless giving, a concept reflected in the Gospel of Matthew. His message was simple, yet profound: perform acts of kindness and compassion without seeking acknowledgment, and God will endow us with the blessings we bestow upon others.

Before His Crucifixion, Christ washed His Apostles' feet. In those days, washing a visitor's feet was a gesture of praise and was usually done by a servant. Jesus did it as an embodiment of love and service. When we embody the love of Christ, we walk in truth that we are all children of God, offering succor to those in need and providing love to those who require it.

Visualize Jesus rendering service to uplift the blind beggar. With purposeful intent, Jesus mixed spit and mud, applying it to the man's eyes, instructing, "Go wash [your face] in the pool of Siloam."[27] The love of Christ, even with our bare hands, a little spit, and some dirt is sufficient to make a difference. Jesus went beyond a checklist approach, allowing the blind man to exercise his faith independently. Instead of merely performing a miracle, Jesus took a chance and through His service, we witness the healing touch of our Savior.

Devoid of any predefined assignment, Jesus had serendipitously crossed paths with the blind man. Recognizing the needs of others, Jesus exhibited empathy, acknowledging the dreams, weaknesses, and strengths of people living on the margins. He invited the man to participate in his own healing journey. Each day presents unique chances

---

25. Bragg, *A Master Class in Leadership*, 3–4.

26. 3 Nephi 12:1.

27. John 9:1–7.

for us to aid others in discovering their purpose, to be, like Jesus, an encourager, a helper, and a comforter.

In the words of Nephi from the Book of Mormon, we "talk of Christ, we rejoice in Christ, [and] we preach of Christ,"[28] who led with a heart attuned to a symphony of love. The essence of leadership is to witness the possibility of human potential by walking the ways of Christ. Like the sun and stars lighting the terrain of our lives, the Light of Christ provides direction so that we might learn to embody service.

May the Spirit of God awaken our minds to such an extent that we are fully possessed by the ideals and aspirations of the gospel, compelling us to act with such intensity that we will endure until we safely reach what Paul referred to as the "glory of the sun."[29]

By following in the footsteps of Christ, we embark on a journey of purpose, with kindness and a commitment to edifying others. As we strive to emulate His selfless example, may we find the courage to lead with goodness, the knowledge to serve with grace, and the strength to make a favorable difference in the lives of those around us.

---

28. 2 Nephi 25:26.
29. 1 Corinthians 15:41.

CHAPTER 3

The Path of Servant-Leadership

Throughout history, we have felt the discontent of disillusionment throughout our communities when those in power abuse their authority and perpetuate inequality. We have felt that deep sense of frustration as we have witnessed the tangible and sometimes detrimental consequences resulting from decisions made by selfish leaders seeking only personal gain. At other times, we have been inspired by selfless leaders who became instruments in the hands of God, sacrificing for the good of others. It is then that our hearts are infused with optimism, propelling us toward shared accomplishments.

When the future is unclear or ambiguous, I have often mused on the profound words of Robert Greenleaf: "I aim to serve and strengthen those who will work to build community wherever people are gathered so that the weak will be supported and the ill will be healed."[1] Greenleaf centered the concept of servant-leadership on the unique idea that cultivating individuals with a servant-minded approach is the most effective way to address societal problems. When we strive to embrace and accept all individuals for who they are and who they can become, pressing issues such as poverty, racial tensions, and social injustices will find resolution by following the teachings of Christ.

The influence of servant-leadership in the lives of the underprivileged is analogous to a track meet with two runners. The first runner is well-equipped with track shoes and runs on a smooth track, while the second runner is barefoot and runs on a sandy path. As the race starts, it is clear that the first runner has a significant advantage, easily

---

1. Greenleaf, *The Servant-Leader Within*, 123.

outdistancing the second runner. The servant-leader provides shoes to the second runner and ensures that both runners have the same track conditions. This intervention allows each runner to compete on equal footing, highlighting the potential and possibilities of both runners while removing barriers that prevent a fair and competitive race. Through these actions, servant-leadership ideals demonstrate how providing equal opportunities and addressing inequities can pave the way for everyone to reach their full potential.

Greenleaf coined the term *servant-leader* in his 1970 essay "The Servant as Leader," in which he hyphenated "servant-leadership," paving the way for a new paradigm of leadership. Traditionally written as "servant leadership," Greenleaf deliberately placed a hyphen between the words to emphasize the paradox in the traditional understanding of the terms, establishing a new way of thinking about the meaning, purpose, and methods of leading.

Greenleaf's essay provides us with the steps necessary to begin our servant-leadership journey:

> It begins with the natural feeling that one wants to serve, to serve first. Then conscious choice brings one to aspire to lead. . . . The difference manifests itself in the care taken by the servant-first to make sure that other people's highest-priority needs are being served.[2]

Our contemporary problem is that the words *serve* and *lead* have become overused, often with negative connotations, implying the degradation of servitude and unearned privilege of leadership. Today, Greenleaf would contend that "despite the negative connotations due to saturation of use, not everything old and worn, or even corrupt, can be thrown away." Some of it must be rebuilt and used again. So, it is, with the words *serve* and *lead*.[3]

Servant-leadership has always been something of an oxymoron. Greenleaf himself asked, "Servant and leader. Can these two roles be fused in one real person, in all levels of status or calling?" The fusing of servant and leader appears at first dangerous: for a servant to become a leader, for a leader to become a servant, and for followers

---

2. Greenleaf, *The Servant as Leader*, 7.
3. Greenleaf, *The Servant-Leader Within*: 31.

The Path of Servant-Leadership

to insist that a servant lead them. John Henry Horsman, a leadership academic at Gonzaga University, remarked:

> Serving and leading are almost interchangeable; being a servant allows an individual to lead, and being a leader implies that a person serves. The paradoxical nature of servant-leadership can go against our intuition. . . . The togetherness of follower and leader, linked by a hyphen between servant and leader, encompasses the integration of ideals and imagination that emerge out of devotion toward the well-being of one another.[4]

When we hyphenate servant and leader, the two words become a unified term representing the agreement of those who serve and lead with one accord. Jesus Christ exemplified the term: He washed His disciples' feet, epitomizing love, respect, and agreement among those who walked the path of service with Him.

Booker T. Washington spoke of the gospel of service, a concept that did not immediately resonate with the hearts and minds of people of color. He believed that people too often applied the notion of degradation to the word *service* relating it to the idea of having power over someone. He asserted that every individual serves another in some capacity or should aspire to serve humanity. Washington recounted, "In proportion as one renders service, they become great. . . . In one way or another, every individual who amounts to anything is a servant."[5] When we humbly acknowledge any misconceptions and fully commit to helping others, we clarify our misunderstandings accompanying the words *servant, serve,* and *service.*

President Lorenzo Snow counseled that, to become as God would wish us, we must accustom our minds to rejoicing in seeing others prosper and fulfill their responsibilities. He compared the gospel of Christ to a great building, with individual leaders as part of that building, saying that "we should never feel too proud to be sometimes cut down, squared, scratched, and hewed to be fitted into the place we are to occupy in the spiritual building."[6] Washington strove to teach students at Tuskegee how to "see and appreciate the practical value of

---

4. Horsman, *Perspectives of Servant-Leadership and Spirit in Organizations,* 20–21.
5. Washington, *Character Building,* 113.
6. *Teachings of Presidents of the Church: Lorenzo Snow,* 218.

the [gospel] of Christ."[7] Like President Snow, Washington perceived service not as a burden but as a responsibility and privilege we should aim to uphold—not in a far-off, imaginary way but in a humble, intimate way, with the spirit of Christ as our constant companion.

Washington concluded that all people who embrace the gospel of service should know that "[faith in Christ] makes you happier, brighter, and more hopeful."[8] He urged believers to "get hold of the spirit of wanting to help somebody else. Seeking every opportunity to make somebody happy and comfortable."[9] As we fulfill the responsibilities within our families, communities, organizations, and places of worship, we can strive to emulate the selfless, loving, yet empowering example of Jesus Christ.

Navigating the Crucible of Purpose

When we shake hands with one another, our experiences interweave, creating agreement and oneness, forcing us to truly gaze into one another's eyes. The melding together of servant and leader lifts the heads that hang low. The praise given by a leader can inspire every member of a marginalized group to escape from the shackles of oppression and poverty. Whether we like it or not, being a leader means being freighted with the mantle of responsibility, representing the aspirations of the underprivileged we aspire to lead. Elder Boyd K. Packer remarked, "The mantle is far, far greater than the intellect of traditional leadership standards." He concluded that it is a privilege to help others witness the mantle worn by the servants of the Lord "in every hour and every moment of existence the almighty hand of God."[10]

In February 1834, a group of Latter-day Saints who called themselves Zion's Camp marched more than nine hundred miles to recover stolen land from local mobs in Jackson County, Missouri. The camp members walked long distances daily, covering between twenty and forty miles, often in torrid conditions with inadequate food and water to sustain them. Their close association with one another over several

---

7. Washington, *Character Building*, 163.
8. Washington, *Character Building*, 163.
9. Washington, *Character Building*, 164.
10. Packer, "The Mantle Is Far, Far Greater Than the Intellect," 259–278.

weeks of travel, as well as their bone-deep weariness and hunger, led camp members to argue and criticize the trip's leaders.

President George A. Smith recounted that camp leader Joseph Smith "took a full share of the fatigues of the entire journey. . . . He walked most of the time and understood blistered, bloody, and sore feet . . . while most of the men in the Camp complained to him of sore toes, blistered feet, long drives, and scanty provisions."[11] Despite facing numerous challenges and illnesses, including cholera outbreaks, Joseph Smith taught camp members indispensable leadership principles throughout the journey. They never relented from their mission to restore displaced Saints to their rightful homes and provide protection against further persecution. Wilford Woodruff, a member of Zion's Camp, later recalled that "we gained an experience that we never could have gained in any other way. We had the privilege of beholding the face of the Prophet, traveling a thousand miles with him, and seeing the workings of [faith] in the Spirit of God and the revelations of Jesus Christ unto him."[12]

Joseph Smith had created the appropriate conditions to lead by serving the less fortunate as he faithfully led Zion's Camp on a strenuous journey. Despite the murmuring of Camp members, their leaders learned to bear the chastisement with patience. They became more optimistic, highlighting the power of prayer with undeterred faith in God, as they witnessed and experienced miraculous healing along the journey. Their faith lightened the hearts of other camp members as they placed the concern for the welfare of the Church on the mantle of responsibility. With a willingness to lay down their lives, if necessary, their experience with the Prophet Joseph Smith taught these brethren to lead in the Lord's way.[13]

Leadership often demands walking alongside those who endure hardship with the path ahead obscured by physical discomfort and criticism. Notwithstanding harsh conditions—impending attacks from militias, thunderstorms, and sicknesses—Joseph Smith served, offering blessings upon those who suffered from sicknesses, providing food sufficient for the needs of his people, and proclaiming God's word to

---

11. *Church History in the Fulness of Times*, 24.
12. Woodruff, *Deseret New: Semi-Weekly*, 1.
13. *Teachings of Presidents of the Church: Joseph Smith*, 281–284.

members when their faith wavered. The journey of servant-leadership requires patience; leaders must be willing to wander into the fog of the unknown while holding onto hope, with faith becoming the lamp.

When we follow Christ along the path of servant-leadership, enduring is more than just surviving; it means avoiding complaints in the trough of our difficulties. We can find peace knowing that our adversities and afflictions "shall be but a small moment."[14] If we endure them well, God shall bless us with His tender mercies. Enduring "well" means passing the breaking point without breaking, having cause to be bitter—without being bitter. Joseph Smith's readiness to lead Zion's Camp required faith, patience, and boldness as he committed to the journey, submitting to "all things the Lord [saw] fit to inflict upon him."[15]

What initially appeared to be a failure evolved into a journey of faith. Elder Neal A. Maxwell believed that the challenging experiences faced by the brethren of Zion's Camp were developmental, stating, "All these things afforded those brethren vital experiences that were for their good—and for the latter good of those who chose to follow these tempered leaders."[16] The lessons learned by future leaders of The Church of Jesus Christ of Latter-day Saints emerged from the seeming furnace of affliction, teaching us today that the crucibles of life are an essential element in the process of becoming a leader. In the sweat and toil, through shared struggles and triumphs, we can truly grasp the essence of leading in the Lord's way. Like Zion's Camp embarking on their arduous journey, traversing countless miles to reach their promised destination, we, too, must labor diligently, our efforts fortified by a foundation of love, as we strive to become servant-leaders.

We live in a time of singular opportunity, wherein we face countless tests of faith and heartbreaking journeys. The Apostle Paul, who passed through various trials, observed, "For I reckon that the sufferings of this present time are not worthy to be compared with the glory which shall be revealed in us."[17] Within a crucible of despair, crisis, and doubt, leaders may feel overwhelmed by discomfort and anguish.

---

14. Doctrine & Covenants 121:7.
15. Doctrine & Covenants 121:8.
16. Maxwell, *All These Things Shall Give Thee Experience*, 121.
17. Romans 8:17–18.

However, their resilience will allow them to emerge from hopelessness and open themselves to introspection that may catalyze their growth and community breakthroughs.

Paul said, "All things work together for the good of them that love God."[18] We must learn that every experience can be our benefactor, that night is as necessary as day, and that struggle can have as rich a purpose as the satisfaction of accomplishment. One set of experiences teaches us what to avoid, while the other teaches us what to continue. Concerning tribulations, President John Taylor said, "Followers of Christ can rejoice in their afflictions, for they are necessary to humble and prove us, that we may comprehend ourselves, become acquainted with our weaknesses and challenges; and rejoice when we triumph over them because God answers our prayers."[19]

The trek of Latter-day Saint pioneers was a difficult journey that involved backbreaking labor, crossing rough terrain, and traveling long distances on foot while carrying supplies on handcarts. As I read about their experience, I often mused, "If only there were modern highways to traverse the valleys of rugged terrain." In leadership, quick-fix solutions keep us from testing and building our faith in ourselves and others. For Zion's Camp, the difficult journey served as a test to determine who was prepared to serve in positions of leadership. Servant-leaders must be willing to lead despite adversity, avoiding the spotlight to put forth the effort where the needs of their people are greater than the accomplishments of leadership. The crucible of leadership is not solely about overcoming problems but overcoming them while ensuring that all of one's companions also reach their destinations safely.

Throughout history, servant-leaders have faced the daunting task of maintaining strength, positivity, and confidence despite their own continual doubts. They have searched intently for the light within others, relying on that light to navigate their own paths while pointing others in the right direction. Often, and unbeknownst to them, those who began as followers have often become shining examples and eventual leaders themselves, inspiring and illuminating the way for others.

---

18. Romans 8:28.
19. *Teachings of Presidents of the Church: John Taylor*, 207–208.

Drum Majors for Good

The lack of unity that marks our time will impede the generations after us unless society envisions and believes in our shared humanity with one accord, one heart, and determined faith in one another. All too frequently, people aspire to move themselves into the forefront, seeking recognition for their efforts, rather than sharing the glory with those who also labored toward the goal. Even James and John, disciples of Christ, expressed their desire to sit by Jesus's side once God established the kingdom of God on Mount Zion. Jesus said to James and John, "Whosoever will be great among you shall be your servant, and whosoever of you will be the chiefest shall be a servant of all. For even the son of [God] came not to be ministered unto, but to serve."[20]

Two millennia later, Dr. Martin Luther King Jr. embodied this spirit, declaring that a person's fame, fortune, or achievements do not measure greatness. In one of his final sermons, "Drum Major Instinct," given only two months before his assassination, Dr. King responded to humanity's search for praise and the desire to be first:

> If you want to be important—wonderful. If you want to be recognized—wonderful. If you want to be great—wonderful. But recognize that he who is greatest among you shall be your servant. That's a new definition of greatness. . . . That definition of greatness means that anyone can be great because anyone can serve. You don't have to have a college degree to serve. You don't have to make your subject and your verb agree to serve. You don't have to know about Plato and Aristotle to serve. You don't have to know Einstein's theory of relativity to serve. You don't have to know the second theory of thermodynamics in physics to serve. You only need a heart full of grace, a soul generated by love. And you can be that servant.[21]

Dr. King contended that deep down within all of us, there is a drum major instinct—a desire to lead the parade and be first in line; an instinct that says, "I must be first; I must be supreme"— overshadowing the collective good for all people. We must break free from selfish ambition by identifying this instinct and channeling it toward serving others. He continued:

---

20. Mark 10:43–45; Luke 14:28–30.
21. King and Washington, *A Testament of Hope*, 259–267.

The drum major instinct can lead to exclusivism in one's thinking and can lead one to feel that because [they] have some training, [they're] a little better than that person that doesn't have it, or because [they] have some economic security, that's a little better than the person who doesn't have it. And that's the uncontrolled, perverted use of the drum major instinct.[22]

Dr. King's view encapsulates the very essence of servant-leadership. Developing a mindset centered on service allows us to utilize our talents and strength to express God's love, echoing King's call to action, "If you want to say that I was a drum major, say that I was a drum major for justice, peace, and righteousness. The shallow things will not matter." He affirmed that "no individual or nation can be great if they do not have a concern for 'the least of these.'"[23] We honor our families by aspiring to be drum majors for Christ, striving to embody His goodness in our lives.

The marginalized are undernourished, ill-housed, and have no houses or beds to sleep. Yet, we sometimes shut out of our minds those who encounter deprivation and are driven from the mainstream of society because we have allowed them to become invisible. Our discontent with one another and the inequality that marginalizes people of color, women, people with disabilities, and people experiencing poverty emerges from the drum major instinct—to be first.

Dr. King presented an alternative by paraphrasing Jesus's response to James and John's request to sit at His right and left hand in the kingdom of God. King recounted that Christ understood their request, saying, "Oh, I see you want to be first. You want to be great. You want to feel important. Well, you ought to feel that way. As children of God, we are all important. If you want to be my disciple, you must be." However, to be drum majors for good, King explained that Christ had redefined their priorities and concept of being first, imparting His knowledge: "Don't give up, keep feeling the need for being important. Keep feeling the need to be first, but I want you to be first in love. I want you to be first in moral excellence. I want you to be first in generosity. That's what I want you to do."[24]

---

22. King and Washington, *A Testament of Hope*, 259–267.
23. King and Baldwin, *In a Single Garment of Destiny*, 121.
24. King and Washington, *A Testament of Hope*, 265–266.

King reminded his listeners that Jesus changed our ideals of being first with a new definition of greatness. Paraphrasing Christ's words, he concluded, "And you know how he said it? Jesus said, 'Brethren, I cannot give you greatness. And really, I cannot make you first. You must earn it. True greatness comes not through favoritism, but by fitness. And the right hand and the left are not mine to give; they belong to those who are prepared."[25] In life, we often find ourselves under the heel of unfavorable circumstances that create in our hearts a powerful determination to rise above others, but our Heavenly Father did not intend for anyone to be first or last.

The drum major instinct can lead to exclusivism in one's thinking, causing individuals to become satisfied with their privilege. Unearned privilege, according to King, leads to *-isms*—classism, racism, sexism, and ableism. Leaders fail to understand the needs of their people when they feel that they are better than the communities or people they steward. When we believe that others or even ourselves are deficient in dignity, we pervert the love God has for us. I felt excluded from popularity when I sat at the bus stop in front of LA Southwest. However, God's love is all-embracing, not excluding anyone from the Light of Christ.

Elder Boyd K. Packer likened Christ's light to the sun.[26] Sunlight is familiar to everyone; it is present everywhere in life. Like sunlight, the Light of Christ is given to everyone equally without discrimination. It is always there for us in times of need and will never leave us, diminish, or fade away, offering comfort throughout life's journey. Stumbling blocks exist in the dark but become stepping stones in the Light of Christ. Like the appearance of the rainbow in the cloud after the rain, so is the appearance of brightness near our stepping stones.

When my weaknesses seemed to mock, expose, and challenge my leadership abilities, I realized that every weakness held a hidden strength within it. It was as though my vulnerabilities collected in my mind, like water dammed up, until the pressure became a force capable of breaking through obstacles. My off-the-field life had been the same each day after a victory or loss following LA Southwest football games. Most days I felt like merely a paving stone in a concrete jungle. Desperation for survival

---

25. King and Washington, *A Testament of Hope*, 265–266.
26. Packer, *Mine Errand from the Lord*, 112–113.

never diminished, and the numbers on the door of what we called home changed weekly, from La Quinta to Days Inn and Extended Stay.

I remember the nights when Eric and I had our friends drop us off at random apartments to keep others from knowing we were living in hotels each night. Imagine star football players bunking together every night, barely able to fit on the mattress, occasionally sharing a bed with their mom—that was our reality. Despite excelling in sports and leading on the field, I still felt myself to be inadequate and short of accomplishment due to my lack of privilege. Inside those hotel rooms, all of us held tightly to our dreams.

During the day, I projected an image of accomplishment and contentment. Still, each evening, I found myself back in that room, its walls invisible but suffocating, my pillow weighed down by the burden of discouragement. Working day and night while playing football allowed me to survive the streets of Los Angeles mentally and physically; however, I tried to control my life each night by visualizing every step required to leave behind my old life. In leadership, every experience is an opportunity to learn and transform difficulty into inspiration.

Dr. King urged us to transform our drum major instinct into an aspiration for good. At LA Southwest, I wanted to be first and sought praise instead of being overlooked and overshadowed by street living. I was determined because I was tired of always being last. My resentment toward life stemmed from my unrefined drum major instinct, seeking praise to boost my ego, rather than embracing the humble circumstances of every hotel room. For Eric and me, our reality was far from glamorous; it involved black garbage bags filled with food to disguise our living circumstances, feelings of embarrassment, and a sense of endurance etched onto our faces.

The clamor for victory should not have been our demand; even Jesus was not handed victory, nor should it have been bestowed upon us. I began to realize that no one would bestow leadership upon me, but that growing into leadership was a necessity for my survival. We had to figure out daily how to persevere from week to week. Serving was not optional; it was an obligation to one another to ensure that we did not sink deeper into the shadows of those hotels. In those shadows stood individuals battling addiction, women trying to evade their abusers, and desperation culminating in violence. Christ's teachings empower us to triumph over even the most horrific circumstances, where the last rise to be first and the first humbly step back.

Christ hoped we would love one another by aspiring to uphold others' feeble knees and to strengthen the tired hands. He said, "By this shall all men know that ye are my disciples if ye have love one to another."[27] When I found myself discouraged and overcome by depression, Eric was by my side on the football field and at every bus stop, encouraging me to keep working toward every goal. Side-by-side we must all work together, seek together, and suffer together if we are to overcome the influences that overwhelm us in our circumstances.

The most significant rewards in this life and the next depend on our ability to become doers, starting with accepting the yoke of responsibility to build a more just society. Prospective servant-leaders understand the need to build a better society and continually ask, "How do we know where to start? How do we get the right things done?" The answer to these questions is whether our efforts help all people—privileged or impoverished, leader or follower—to grow healthier, stronger, more autonomous, and more disposed to serve others.

Every generation leaves behind historical imprints or influences, and those impressions become crucial in contouring the course toward change. Aspirations to turn our dreams into a powerful force for meaningful change must lie in embracing life's complexity and persistently working toward our goals. By seeking to live out our dreams and exemplifying the idea of serving one another, we can enhance our vision by transcending the circumstances that impede progress. What rewards await those who bring such dreams to realization?

We measure the rewards of living an abundant life in joyous moments rather than days or years. These are the treasures that return to the mind in the quiet hours. The moments graciously lived, challenges met, the truth spoken, the slur turned aside, the challenges conquered, the helping hand extended, and the simple expressions of gratitude, the burden endured. We fulfill our dreams by setting our course on a star and steering toward it, minding not the obstacles that impede progress.

---

27. John 13:35.

CHAPTER 4

Calloused Hands and Fusing of Servant-Leadership

A stone that slips from the fingers will fall to the ground, as will an ideal that drifts or plummets away from the grasp of those chosen to lead. If we put our ears to the ground at any hour of the day or night, we will hear the repetitive thud of broken dreams and hopes, as some opportunities are lost continually for those on the margins.

Why might leaders lose sight of their ideals? Some may feel that their knowledge has only a limited reach, that their personalities are immovable, and that there is no hope for systemic improvement or change, like a fixed star in the night sky. Yet even a fixed star shifts from different vantage points, like our life's trajectory can reposition us and help us grow in our aspirations. Others embrace their weaknesses as intrinsic, failing to recognize them as opportunities for growth. They, too, accept adverse circumstances as if divinely ordained, relinquishing the continuing pursuit of a more meaningful life. And, some leaders fall into the temptation to misuse their privilege or influence, turning their eyes away from those in need of help.

Leadership is an opportunity given or assumed that can be taken away or bestowed on the person who is, by nature, a servant first. Our abilities, circumstances, gender, or race do not dictate our limits. The only confines restricting our achievement are the ones we impose on ourselves. Leaders emerge in myriad personalities and appearances, but all leaders faithfully lead by example.

We will become leaders from what life has enabled us to learn and from challenges set before us, partly from self-knowledge that others have helped us achieve. Beyond that, time and events will teach us. Mistakes and failures will teach us. Despite our admiration for historical leaders, we do not fully understand—may never understand—the emergence of leadership especially in the bleakest of circumstances.

The most effective leaders, seek after risk-taking, leading subtly and inconspicuously by extending their open hands, conveying the good for all people. Their hands may be soft and pliable, but they become instruments of progress that continue the Lord's work forward. Outstretched toward our loved ones, these hands give a sincere welcome or greeting. Laid upon a friend's shoulder, these hands provide encouragement and hope. Upon the head of the sick, they manifest faith and confer God's blessings. Lifted firmly in salute, our hands signify loyalty and obedience. Raising one's right hand to the square and left hand anchored upon the Bible, great men and women accept the weight of responsibility, thereby demonstrating their integrity and devotion. And, when the path ahead is unclear and challenging, shaking hands binds us to purpose and imbue our words with meaning. Like the heart, the hand renders incredible services through symbolic labor to build a just society.

For our hands to be effective, however, their purpose must be clear. Greenleaf posed a simple yet profoundly important question: "What are [we] trying to do?"[1] Leaders must focus on a common goal, a shared vision, and then ensure that they and their followers navigate the journey together.

Greenleaf also reminded us that "a 'good' society is seen as one in which there is widespread faith as trust that encourages and sustains . . . the needy, the aged, and the disabled."[2] Rather than ignoring the characteristics of servant-leadership, *we* must accept them with full responsibility and use of our hands to help carry the weighty burdens of others despite the obstacles, knowing the direction we will go. Our hands may sometimes become heavy, but when we drop them from frustration or fatigue, the progress of building a better society will stall.

The book of Kings provides a fascinating account of the battle between the Amalekites and the hosts of ancient Israel, where we learn the importance of the uplifted hand as a spiritual trolley to help us do the work. Joshua led the Israelites, supported by Moses's uplifted hands.

1. Greenleaf, *Servant Leadership*, 29–30.
2. Greenleaf, *The Power of Servant-Leadership*, 115.

When Moses "held up his hands, Israel prevailed; when he let down his hands, Amalek prevailed."[3] However, Moses's hands were heavy. So, Aaron got on one side of Moses and Hur on the other, and together, they held his hands steady until the going down of the sun, when God placed victory in their hands.[4] When we hold up our hands with the characteristics of servant-leadership, humanity moves forward.

Nelson Mandela's Calloused Hands

The most significant challenge is transforming our inherent individual mindset of "I" into "we." Greenleaf envisioned a shift toward shared leadership with inclusivity at its core when he said:

> The servant-leader . . . wants to serve first; then one aspires to lead. This is sharply different from one who is leader first, perhaps because of the need to assuage an unusual power drive or to acquire material possessions. A servant-leader focuses primarily on the growth and [happiness] of people and the communities to which they belong. The servant-leader shares power.[5]

Imagine a pair of hands, once peaceful, now weathered and calloused from enduring years of injustice amid unfavorable circumstances. These hands have borne the weight of heavy hammers, relentlessly breaking rocks. Each strike represents a challenge faced, a prejudice endured, or a barrier broken. Motivations that once clung to "I," seeking personal gain and influence, are now on a path of metamorphosis, embracing the perspective of "we." Collective community growth emerges from a willingness to put the beloved other first. This "we" perspective can break down barriers, empower others, and create a society where the healing touch of servant-leadership soothes the calloused hands of injustice.

Nelson Mandela, a model of servant-leadership, demonstrated to us that prison walls cannot contain our aspirations, nor can a destructive influence of hateful resistance diminish them. He used his decades of imprisonment to sharpen his ideals of leadership. President Obama praised Mandela's vision and works, saying, "Mandela understood the ties that bind the human spirit. There is a word in South

---

3. Exodus 17:11.
4. Exodus 17:11–16.
5. Greenleaf, *The Servant as Leader*, 6.

Africa—Ubuntu—a word that captures Mandela's greatest gift: his recognition that we are all bound together in ways that are invisible to the eyes; that there is a oneness to humanity; that we achieve by sharing ourselves with others and caring for those around us."[6]

Mandela's story exemplifies the heart of a humble servant who transformed "I" to "we" out of the cauldron of oppression to become a pillar of refined strength for South Africa. His experiences in prison, marked by years of adversity, polished his character and fortified his determination to fight for fairness. That commitment to justice and service was epitomized by the pair of hands he raised during his trial in the 1960s:

> I have dedicated myself to the struggle of the African people. I have fought against white domination, and I have fought against Black domination. I have cherished the ideal of a democratic and free society where all people live together in harmony and with equal opportunities. It is an ideal that I hope to live for and to achieve. But if needs be, it is an ideal for which I am prepared to die.[7]

After his release from prison, as the country's first Black head of state, Mandela eloquently reiterated his role as servant during the Grand Parade in Cape Town, South Africa:

> I stand here before you not as a prophet but as a humble servant of you, the people. Your tireless and heroic sacrifices have made it possible for me to be here today. I therefore place the remaining years of my life in your hands.[8]

Life is the canvas upon which we paint our existence, showcasing the beauty and richness of our experiences. Calloused hands adorn Mandela's life canvas, symbols of his commitment to justice and equality.

During a speech on leadership, Dr. Myles Munroe recounted his encounter with Mandela, highlighting Mandela's strong commitment to justice that drew South Africans to him.

> When I first met Mr. Nelson Mandela, he changed my life. It was a private dinner, and I tell this story because it had such a profound

---

6. Obama, *Speeches*, 447.
7. Mandela, "I Am Prepared to Die."
8. Mandela, "I Therefore Place the Remaining Years of My Life in Your Hands," para. 1.

impact on me when I shook his hand. His hand was rock hard, only thirty days after his release from Robben Island. . . . When I walked into the room to meet the recently released Mr. Mandela, it was like history on two legs, standing before me. When I shook his hand, I distinctly recall the sensation of his unyielding grip, like steel or cement, leaving an indelible impression and said to myself,

"My God, this man's hard hand is hard like steel, like cement."

He looked at me and smiled, and then, as the meal was over, he leaned over to the table where I was sitting, and he said, "Young man, are you okay?" I said, "Yes, sir." He then told me that for the 27 years he had been in prison, they had given him a hammer and rocks, and told him his job was to break the rocks into smaller pieces. His hands had become calloused from all the work. And so, Mandela's hands became so callous, after 27 years of breaking rocks because of his conviction. Despite being offered numerous deals to secure his release from prison, Nelson Mandela declined, stating that he could not compromise his conviction. He told me that story, and I began to weep because I was listening to a man who was President of a country, but we forgot the rocks. [Mandela] said, That's why my hand is hard, my whole hand is callous. . . .

I left that dinner with a thought that I still carry with me: "Oh God, make my hand hard." Mandela taught me that, to be a leader, you must pay a price. If you want to be liked, do not try to be a leader; if you want to be famous, do not try to be a leader; if you want to be popular, don't try to be a leader. He said, True leaders do not seek followers; followers are attracted to true leaders. Leadership is a privilege given by the followers, and it is a trust that people give to those who are inspired by a willingness to die for their convictions. Followers embrace a leader because they believe that the leader is willing to sacrifice for what they believe in. This is the heart of leadership.[9]

In striving to fulfill a broader aim of pursuing social justice and equality, irrespective of race, gender, or identity, leaders must ask, "What are we trying to do?"[10] Mandela's storied journey demonstrates the indestructible influence of an individual identifying and then championing a cause that resonates for the collective good. Greenleaf reminds us that "people grow taller when their leaders empathize with

---

9. Munroe, *The Most Important Aspect of Leadership*.
10. Greenleaf, *The Servant-Leader Within: A Transformative Path*, 44.

them and accept them for who they are."[11] The people of South Africa stood taller in dignity and began to walk faithfully with the light of hope shining down upon them due to Mandela walking beside them.

Mandela offered the world a fundamentally good heart supported by the work completed by calloused hands. He became a ray of light in the darkness of generational struggles. As we encounter difficulties in our own lives, we draw strength from the lessons of perseverance and hope embodied in Mandela's calloused hands. His journey epitomizes the union of servant and leader.

The Fusing of Servant-Leader

Inspiration excites the imagination and challenges people to work simultaneously to encourage their faith in God's goodness and chip away at unjustness. Greenleaf wrote:

> A leader ventures to say, I will go; come with me! A leader initiates, provides the ideas and the structure, and takes the risk of failure along with the chance of success. A leader says, "I will go; follow me!" while knowing that the path is uncertain, even dangerous. . . . If one is leading, one always has a goal. . . . It is something presently out of reach; it is something to strive for, to move toward, to become.[12]

Dr. King expressed the essence of soul-stretching service—of living a sermon of Christlike service to others—when he said:

> I choose to identify with the underprivileged, I choose to identify with the poor, I choose to give my life for the hungry, I choose to give my life for those who have been left out of the sunlight of opportunity. . . . This is the way I'm going. If it means dying for them, I'm going that way because I heard a [prophetic] voice saying, Do something for others.[13]

Through such thoughtful reflection, we respond to the Savior's invitation to follow Him. Greenleaf explained:

> The leader, acting on inspiration, may simply say, "Let's go this way." But the leader always knows what it is and can articulate it for any who are unsure. By clearly stating and restating the goal the leader

---

11. Greenleaf, *Servant Leadership*, 35.
12. Greenleaf, *Servant Leadership*, 29.
13. Baldwin, *The Arch of Truth*, 261–265.

gives certainty to others who may have difficulty in achieving it for themselves.[14]

The discovery of how leaders know whether they are making a difference in the lives of others can prove challenging, but Greenleaf states that the best and yet most difficult test to administer is to ask:

> Do those served grow as persons? Do they, while being served, become healthier, wiser, freer, more autonomous, and more likely to become servants? And what is the effect on society's least privileged; will they benefit or, at least, not be further deprived?[15]

Greenleaf termed leadership as having a better-than-average sense of what needs to be done immediately and demonstrating the willingness to say, "Let's do this now."[16] Servant-leaders must strive to be genuinely unselfish and envision what will move humanity forward by considering the least privileged. They must possess scholarship, not in terms of college degrees but in the life lessons they have overcome, like the kind Dr. King had acquired during the civil rights movement. Servant-leaders hear the stories of the broken and then challenge pervasive injustice with great force to serve humanity and narrow the chasm between potential and opportunity.

The fusing of servant and leader is evident in the legacy of Dr. Martin Luther King Jr. The characteristics defining Dr. King as a leader was that, like Mandela, he was willing to uphold the mantle of leadership for human dignity and decency. King foresaw both our current and historical problem: too many of us who presume to lead do not see the unjustness of our society and strongly argue that we must preserve the system—which Greenleaf characterized as fatal.[17]

Greenleaf poses the question, What direction will the movement take? and he contends that the answer depends on whether those who lead stir the ferment and come to grips with the age-old problem of how to live in a humane society.

During the civil rights movement, Dr. King took a firm stance against injustice and hypocrisy, becoming what Greenleaf termed "an

---

14. Greenleaf, *Servant Leadership*, 29.
15. Greenleaf, *The Servant as Leader*, 6.
16. Greenleaf, *Servant Leadership*, 21–61.
17. Greenleaf, *The Servant as Leader*, 16.

affirmative builder of a better society."[18] The rigorous trials required to build a better society required the spirit of hope that Dr. King embodied. Many believe that he did not deliver his final speech as prepared but instead spoke from his heart and from a spirit of inspiration that touched his soul. Although "I've Been to the Mountaintop" was brief (slightly over forty minutes), Dr. King's remarks exhausted him to the point that he was sweating and breathing as if he had run a race, which in a sense, he had. In the race toward the promised land for all, something had changed for King. He had slipped the mantle of leadership responsibility onto his shoulders, with determination shown deeply in his eyes as he spoke. His words and his body both hinted at a sense of awareness of his impending death as he said:

> We've got some difficult days ahead. But it doesn't matter with me now. Because I've been to the mountaintop. And I don't mind. Like anybody, I would like to live a long life. Longevity has its place. But I'm not concerned about that now. I just want to do God's will. And He's allowed me to go up to the mountain. And I've looked over. And I've seen the Promised Land. And [we] may not get there [together]. But . . . we, as a people, will get to the Promised Land. I'm not worried about anything. I'm not fearing any man. Mine eyes have seen the glory of the coming of the Lord.[19]

Eerily and prophetically, Dr. King revealed to the audience that he knew he might be permanently silenced. The challenge of his time was that society would build with one hand and tear down with the other. As a servant of those living in poverty and experiencing oppression, King sought to dismantle the structures upholding systemic racism, prejudice, and inequality. He disrupted the established order of authority with his simple phrase "I've seen the Promised Land." King recognized that the road ahead of him and behind us in history was no longer a road that would guide humanity home.

Jesus foretold the significance of Dr. King's sacrifice, teaching His disciples, "Whosoever will lose his life *for my sake* shall find it."[20] That phrase implies that the world cannot conceivably remove a servant-leader from the fabric of history. Dr. King lost his life attempting

18. Greenleaf, *Servant Leadership*, 248–261.
19. King and Washington, *A Testament of Hope*, 279–286.
20. Luke 9:24; emphasis added.

to heal society, driven by the truth that we are all children of God, proclaiming that all people have access to the American dream. He preached the truth that race, ethnicity, gender, religion, or socioeconomic position cannot obscure our innate beauty as individuals created in God's image. But his truth continues to ring out through the voices of those who have followed in his path.

"Servant-leaders walk by faith and not by sight, remaining centered during times of trouble while listening and believing,"[21] proclaims author Lea Williams regarding African American leadership. Those leaders who do not embrace "servant" as part of their journey may have an exclusionary arrogance and passivity toward those who experience deprivation. While servant-leaders display quiet confidence among the least privileged, accepting that service is but one dimension of our testimony in the love of Christ. The Spirit has witnessed the latter when we serve, and we, as followers of Christ, stand as witnesses of Christ's light in all things as they are, as they were, and as they are to come.[22]

Like the proverbial treasure-seeker, a mariner without stars, or a traveler without a compass, a leader who moves through life without both purpose and a commitment to serve will become lost. Assurance of purpose and the certainty of shared success in the present and throughout eternity comes to those who live their lives in harmony with the gospel of Jesus Christ.

---

21. Williams, *Servants of People*, 144–145.
22. Doctrine and Covenants 93:24–25.

CHAPTER 5

Servant-Leadership: Bearing the Burden of the Cross

In C. J. Langenhoven's novel *Skaduwees van Nararet (Shadows of Nazareth)*, Pilate's inner turmoil and moral conflict while presiding over the trial of Jesus Christ is depicted. After Jesus's trial, Pilate writes a remarkable confession to a friend in Rome. Nelson Mandela recounted this story in first person in correspondence with Winnie Mandela from Pretoria Prison in January 1970.

> As governor of a Roman province, I [Pilate] tried many cases involving all types of rebels. But the trial of Christ I shall never forget! One day a huge crowd of priests and followers, shivering with rage and excitement, assembled outside my palace, and demanded that I crucify Christ for claiming to be the [Son of God], at the same time pointing to a man whose arms and feet were heavily chained. I looked at the prisoner and our eyes met. In the midst of all the excitement and noise, he remained perfectly calm, quiet, and confident as if he had millions of people on his side. . . . Christ had become a mighty force in the land and the masses of the people were fully behind him. . . . For the first time in my experience I faced a man whose eyes appeared to see right through me, whereas I was unable to fathom him. Written across his face was a gleam of love and hope; but at the same time, he bore the expression of one who was deeply pained by the folly and suffering of [humanity] as a whole. He gazed upwards and his eyes seemed to pierce through the roof and to see right beyond the stars.
>
> So it was, that even though I well knew that this man was innocent, my duty demanded that I give him the death sentence and so I did. The last time I saw him [Jesus Christ] he was struggling toward Calvary

amidst jeers, insults, and blows, under the crushing weight of the heavy cross on which he was to die. I [Pilate] have decided to write you this personal letter because I believe that this confession to a friend will at least salve my uneasy conscience.[1]

When the weight of discouragement becomes unbearable, we can have faith in a compassionate Heavenly Father and Savior, ever-present and confident in our ability to endure trials. Dr. King once said that "the cross is the eternal expression of the length to which God will go in order to restore community."[2] As we witness the radiant image of Christ, we are captivated by the irresistible allure of His love, offering us strength as we struggle to bear the weight of our own rugged crosses.

My experiences, too deep for anyone to comprehend, belong uniquely to me. Christ's heavenly principle of love expanded my heart, cultivating a deep empathy for young men who, like myself in the past, remain ensnared in the struggles of street life. My focus shifted toward the well-being of the underprivileged who traverse the inner avenues of Los Angeles and other marginalized communities.

Throughout my journey, I encountered people who selflessly helped me carry the burden of homelessness when I could no longer bear it alone. These mainstays of support steadily placed their faith in me. Amid lonely days and dreary nights, I heard an inner voice reassuring me, "Lo, I will be with you always."[3] When the chains of fear and the handcuffs of frustration threatened to hinder my progress, I felt God's love transforming weariness into the buoyancy of hope, helping me avoid the pitfalls of the city's unforgiving streets.

The Cross, the Yoke, and the Journey

The burden of carrying the cross is a test of devotion and faith that followers of Christ willingly endure. Jesus instructed His disciples to deny themselves, take up their crosses, and follow Him, embracing His name and ideals. Christ's command reveals that His teachings are not merely ideas; they are actions meant to reassure the fallen through love.

---

1. Mandela, *Conversations with Myself*, 223–226.
2. King and Washington, *A Testament of Hope*, 20.
3. Matthew 28:20.

Servant-Leadership: Bearing the Burden of the Cross

During His crucifixion, Christ struggled to carry His actual cross toward Golgotha, a place outside Jerusalem. Despite a dire need for assistance, not one person stepped forward to assume our Savior's burden, which He was willing to bear for the sake of humanity. As the crowds jeered and led Him away, finally Simon of Cyrene came forward and tried to help Christ bear the cross.

This act of service, as well as the honor borne by carrying Christ's cross, represents an opportunity for us to serve within our communities in His name. Christ's call to "take up your cross, follow me"[4] still stands as an invitation to lead in the Lord's way. As we walk with Christ, His invitation offers us the chance to bear others' burdens in the same manner as Simon did for Him.

As we witness Simon stepping forward to bear the weight of the cross, he exemplifies how we can follow Christ's example. When someone needed to carry on after the crucifixion, he essentially said: "Here I am. Send me." When Christ needed someone to preach the gospel to the people in their day, Saul of Tarsus said, "Lord, what wouldst thou have me do?"[5] Or, in other words, "Here I am. Send me." They did not respond to the call to lead in the Lord's way by saying, "I will try it out for a while and see how I like it." Joseph Smith was only fourteen years old when he declared in the spirit, "Here I am. Send me." The persistence to keep up with the call is as important as the initiative that starts it. What a thrilling attitude!

As followers of Christ, should our devotion be any less? God's most compelling question still stands as His most significant challenge. "Whom shall I send? And who shall go for us?" Let us enthusiastically answer His call with greatest of all replies, exemplified by the Redeemer Himself: "Father, here I am. Send me."[6]

As we reflect on the opportunities to bear one another's burdens, we should consider another of Jesus's profound teachings: His request to "take my yoke upon you."[7] As the son of a carpenter, Christ spent a considerable amount of time in a carpenter's shop, carefully crafting many yokes out of rough wood to be fit around the necks of oxen. A yoke enables oxen to increase the amount of weight they can bear by sharing a load more

---

4. Matthew 16:24–25.
5. Acts 9:6.
6. Moses 4:1.
7. Matthew 11:29–30.

evenly without hurting their necks. The idea that Christ offering to take up His yoke symbolizes His willingness to serve by sharing any burden. The yoke represents Christ's preparedness as a carpenter, carrying the cross toward Golgotha with little to no strength. "Come, follow me. Take my yoke upon you," Jesus beckoned, inviting us to tread His path, to live and lead as He did. He urged us to see the world through His eyes—a landscape rich with opportunities to fulfill His Father's will by uplifting the overlooked: the have-nots, the least among us, the downtrodden.

Like a yoke's potential to help oxen work together and share the load, the yoke of love allows us to join with others in uplifting the least privileged. It is a representation of love and compassion binding us together as a community, enabling us to work toward a common goal with shared purpose. Like the sturdy and dependable device used for oxen, the yoke of love brings reassurance to our lives, enabling us to progress together with confidence and strength, knowing we are not alone in the struggle. I am thankful for my beloved companion who became my yokemate, enabling me to endure the inward and outward journey with renewed vigor and faith.

When we willingly take upon ourselves the yoke of Christ, we find comfort in knowing He will never abandon us, even amid our most challenging struggles. The greatest rewards in both this life and the next depend on our willingness to accept the yoke of responsibility to build a more just society. As we learn to place others' needs before our own, we begin to empathize with those around us. Our Heavenly Father has placed loved ones, friends, family, and companions in our lives to help us bear the yokes we carry and sustain our strength.

Greenleaf contended that "the word strength, when used as a symbol for achieving ethical goals, poses a challenge because the term's contemporary connotations detract from the concept of leadership."[8] Pictures tend to portray strength as inherently powerful and typically masculine with grim determination, the head bloodied yet unbowed, denoting the stereotyped attributes of a person's strength. Greenleaf's idea of strength, instead, opposes authority and seeks cheerfulness of persuasion by way of a light touch. The word *strength* can have positive connotations, particularly when referring to the spiritual strength and discernment needed to make the right choices leading to accomplishment.

---

8.   Greenleaf, *Servant Leadership*, 25.

Strength conveys our ability to determine a range of potential aims, select the most appropriate one, and consistently pursue that aim responsibly over time. However, this strength necessitates spiritual reflection. For servant-leaders, the proper aim begins with asking, "What is right for this particular individual in this particular situation?" Rightness refers to an action or concept uniquely tailored to the current circumstances, whether it is a new, untested idea or one from the past adapted to current times and needs. In weighing the rightness of our decisions, we can remember that every circumstance changes with time, and our views enlarge, diversify, and become enriched by experience.

Traditional thinking may no longer suffice; we must approach our experiences with a fresh perspective that challenges prejudices and breaks down barriers. Pursuing justice and understanding what is right is a never-ending process, making it increasingly difficult to determine the correct aim. Choosing to ease the burdens of others by taking on the weight of their suffering is particularly relevant in today's world, where we face complex and pressing issues like the COVID-19 pandemic, climate change, political polarization, and social injustice. The righteous choice is to treat every beloved child of God with respect and to decide whether to speak out against systemic injustice. As we strive to create a fairer and more just society, we encounter these challenges daily.

Bearing the Burdens of Others

Christ's decree to take up our cross and follow Him implies that even when faced with opposition from others, we must be willing to share the burden with those who struggle regardless of deferring beliefs or circumstances. Despite being the Son of God, Jesus Christ had only one person step up and willingly shoulder the weight of His cross. Notwithstanding our own personal challenges, we must draw upon our strength to serve with love as we endeavor to support those who are weak.

Carrying others' burdens is a fundamental maxim of love. The act of intentionally bearing the load of others becomes an expression of love and a reflection of Christ's Atonement. Without love, benevolence becomes egotism, and martyrdom becomes spiritual pride, as Dr. King explained:

Calvary is a telescope through which we look into the long vista of eternity and see the love of God breaking into time. Out of the hugeness of His generosity God allowed His only begotten Son to die that we may live. By uniting [ourselves] with Christ and [humanity] through love [we] will be able to matriculate in the university of eternal life. In a world depending on force, coercive tyranny, and bloody violence, [we] are challenged to follow the way of love.[9]

Carrying the cross is no ordinary labor. It is a task that demands a more thoughtful commitment. While a yoke can make for more efficient work, carrying the cross is reserved for only the most devout of believers, disciples, friends, and servant-leaders. Those who assume the heft of Christ's cross are the ones who connect and identify with Him down to their very core or essence. Not only do they believe, but they are eager to dedicate their energy to the labor required of them. They prepare to endure the murkiest depths of suffering and to assist Christ's mission to bring redemption to humanity.

Whether through indifference or explicit refusal, when we neglect the opportunity to lend our strength in easing others' burdens, allowing Christ to carry His cross alone, our words and testimonies lose their luster and become ineffective. Following Christ's example, however, we become a wellspring of strength from which others may draw as we bear their burdens alongside them, encouraging them to persist through their trials. Through our acceptance of Christ's yoke, we discover a previously unknown source of might, with which we hoist our crosses and follow Him.

Simon from Cyrene bore the cross of Christ to the top of Golgotha. What if leaders with significant influence sought to bear the burdens of the least privileged and those without the fortitude or ability to carry them alone? They would inspire collective action among groups of people. In so doing, even one person could significantly transform an entire community's morale.

The mantle of leadership is akin to carrying the weight of the cross. Like Jesus taking on the burden of the cross, those who choose to pursue an aim responsibly must also bear the weight of their actions and influence on others. The march of time represents a journey of carrying the cross, which requires faith and perseverance.

---

9.   King, *The Strength to Love*, 155–156.

The cross, as a symbol of strength, is universal, conveying our willingness to follow the path of Christ. Strength is the ability to stay the course and fulfill one's responsibilities despite the difficulties that may arise. The cross represents the two essential commandments that allow all would-be leaders to lead with love. In its physical representation, the cross has vertical and horizontal dimensions that embody the gospel of Christ.

Pointing from earth toward the firmament of heaven, the vertical beam of the cross reminds us of the great commandment to love the Lord our God with all our heart, soul, mind, and strength. We open ourselves to abundant blessings when we infuse our lives with love for God. This love enables us to receive inspiration and direction, acting as a seed of hope amongst unfortunate circumstances. The second beam of the cross reaches outward like the hand of God symbolizing love toward humanity. When He carried the cross, Christ's unyielding devotion served as an inspiration to keep our standards upright even in the face of opposition and to see the world through God's love. Together, the beams of the cross form a complete picture of our responsibilities toward God and the beloved other. As we lead in the Lord's way, we can wholeheartedly distinguish our lives around these two great objectives symbolically embodied by the Redeemer's cross.

Who is the beloved other? It could be your eternal companion, partner, son, daughter, or friend. The other represents the kingdom of God. What is loving? Love recognizes the presence of the other with admiration. Whether it's the embodiment of love in your heart, physical body, or relationship with your son, daughter, or partner, the declaration of love is always the same: "Dear beloved, I am here for you." When we are truly present, the other is present too. To be loved is to be recognized as existing.

Dr. King's prolific words "I have a dream" symbolized transcendent love that admires the beloved other with respect, kindness, and friendship. His dream avowed the hope that "we cannot walk alone. . . . And as we walk, we must make the pledge that we shall always march ahead . . . not turning back."[10]

In life symbols carry great meaning; among them are the ring finger representing a husband's devoutness to his beloved, a light in the window conveying to us where home is, and the rainbow after the

---

10. King and Washington, *A Testament of Hope*, 218.

rain depicting God's promise to His children. Our Redeemer's cross and yoke stand alone, representing the tremendous ideals that unite our shared humanity to be loved and recognized.

With its outstretched arms, the cross is a constant reminder of Jesus's compassionate love. In the hands of the carpenter, the yoke and cross become an invitation to embrace love, to carry it with us in our daily lives, and to share it generously with one another.

This kind of love—one that led Christ to the cross and kept Paul unembittered amid torrents of persecution—is not soft, anemic, or sentimental. It confronts poverty, injustice, and hatred without hesitation, embodying an infinite capacity to endure all things through Christ. Such love overcomes the world, even from a rough-hewn cross against the skyline.[11]

The sweat, tears, and pain of Gethsemane engrave our names eternally upon the heart, hands, and feet of the Savior of the World, who beckons us to come unto Him and partake of His unconditional love. We move forward with faith like travelers who take one step at a time as they traverse the toils of the strait and narrow path. As we gaze toward the heavens, we shall see them open, and our hearts will overflow with joy. When we allow these beliefs to take hold and become established, we can fervently say, "I am not the person I once was."

---

11. King and Washington, *A Testament of Hope*, 513.

CHAPTER 6

A More Excellent Way

The injustice that people in marginalized communities face can erode faith in love. After my eighteenth birthday, during my senior year at Westchester High School, a younger student accused me of stealing his shoes. Unaware of the accusation, I left class only to find police officers waiting to arrest me. As I stood there, I could hear them laughing, saying, "He just turned eighteen. We can take him to county." They assumed I was a gang member and showed no remorse, judging me solely by my appearance. This incident highlights the harsh reality of how the justice system often fails to see past labels and divisions, particularly when it comes to Black men.

As they put me in the police car, I had to sit sideways because I was too tall to fit in the backseat. They laughed as they forced me in. My heart raced as we drove off to the county jail. I lay face-down in the police car, my wrists aching from the handcuffs. Sweat poured down my face, and fear trapped me in walls of apprehension. I had no idea how I would get out of this predicament.

It felt like a scene from a movie. The experience was dehumanizing, as the police officers ordered me to bend over and spread my butt. I thought, "Why would I sneak in drugs when I just came from school?" Standing there naked while they questioned me only fueled my hostility toward the justice system. To them, I was just another criminal—guilty of no crime but still deserving of their judgment.

I spent twenty-four hours in county jail before being released due to insufficient evidence. All I could recall that night was the officers' laughter as my fear grew with each toss and turn on the bunk. We watched TV from behind bars and had to use the bathroom in front of one another. I wanted to sleep the nightmare away. I saw the rejected faces of those beaten by gang violence, their faces swollen, and older men who had spent months in the county, warning me not to get caught up in the system. The harsh reality of life without freedom led me to pray to God for release. I didn't go to church, but praying to God from my bed was the only comfort I could find.

I was released the following day and handed my belongings in a plastic bag with no laces in my shoes. They didn't give me a phone call; they just sent me away as if I deserved the judgmental stares and unwarranted treatment. Sitting in front of the jail, miles away from Slauson Avenue, I felt lost and abandoned. I saw the adverse realities of poverty within a five-block radius: liquor stores, graffiti, and pornography outlets lined the streets, while bars on windows hinted at the lack of safety. Homeless individuals struggling with addiction occupied parks meant for children, seeking their next moment of euphoria.

With no money to get home, I desperately asked passersby for change to use the pay phone. Most people walked by, overlooking me without concern. Overcoming the harsh realities of poverty felt nearly impossible as I walked the streets outside of county jail, where dreams seemed to drift further out of reach with each passing moment.

The most significant challenge of our time is the need to follow a "more excellent way." The Apostle Paul coined this phrase when he said, "Covet earnestly the best gifts: and yet I show unto you a more excellent way."[1] We bravely embark on the less-traveled path, guided by our unwavering faith in a singular fixed star, despite the narrowness of the way forward.

Dr. King encouraged all people to use love to combat the evils of poverty, racism, and economic deprivation that harm marginalized communities, stating, "There is a more excellent way, of love and [nonviolence]." While our society's emphasis on individualism can weaken belief in the omnipotence of God's love, "through the gift of His son, Jesus Christ, God has provided a more excellent way," offering us renewed hope and directing us toward unimaginable opportunities.[2]

The possibilities for improving society are not in the ways of a scholar or theologian; rather, it is through sincere goodwill toward one another.

1.   1 Corinthians 12:30–31.
2.   Ether 12:4, 11.

In time, with Christ's teachings as our compass, our diligent effort can clear the seemingly unassailable obstacles hindering social progress.

At the age of eleven, I understood the injustice of discrimination when I encountered the harsh reality of police harassment on the streets of East Los Angeles. While waiting in the car for my dad outside an apartment complex, Eric and I entertained ourselves with a game of counting passing cars. Growing up in Los Angeles, my dad, known as Cheese, navigated the streets while involved in drug dealing. Sloppy Joes, drug use before my eyes, and the pervasive smell of cigarettes in the air are interwoven in my memories of him. The signs of his success were evident in the cars he drove and the stacks of cash prominently displayed in the center console.

While we waited inside our dad's run-down Cadillac, we gazed across the street at an apartment complex. Whenever a car passed, we'd duck down toward the floor to hide ourselves. After several minutes, we were horrified to realize that several policemen had surrounded the car, shouting over and over and over, "Get out of the car!" The officers shoved us to the ground, pointing shotguns and pistols at us as if we were hardened adult criminals. They initially hurled us onto the hood of their cars and proceeded to throw us on the ground, pushing our faces into the pavement. As we sobbed, we could see and hear nothing but the sirens atop their vehicles.

Growing up in LA, the piercing sirens of police cars could illuminate entire blocks, casting shadows on every corner. Those lights blinded me as I looked up at them, a backdrop to our nightmare of fear. At a young age, the sirens' red and blue colors symbolized injustice, instilling fear, and eroding trust in the LAPD. This incident is so prevalent in marginalized communities that nearly anyone can recall a time when apprehension or anger eclipsed their faith in justice. The blaring of sirens now serves as a reminder ingrained in my consciousness to shield my sons from unjust scrutiny, teaching them a more excellent way to live and move about in a world where they must be constantly aware of their surroundings.

Removing the lid of circumstance, we unlock the potential to surpass the constraints of our environments and reach for aspirations that elevate us. I have gradually recognized the difference between the pitfalls of street life and my aspirations to close the gap between occasionally seeing my father and becoming a better man for my own family.

Every day presents us with opportunities for growth; it is in the moments of doubt and struggle, when we feel the love of God, that we begin to change the trajectory of our lives. When striving for excellence, we learn that the outcome of our experiences, no matter how imperfect, encourages us to relentlessly exert every drop of effort—whether sweet or bitter—we can possibly give. Hard work does not guarantee an easy or tranquil road to excellence; it is the continuous pursuit of goals despite challenges, leading to countless blessings.

From a young age, I faced barriers that shaped my worldview. I likened myself to a boxer being knocked down, and I accepted the fact that the world might look down on me. Despite the weight of discouragement, we must all find the strength to rise from the pavement with resilience and discover a more excellent way.

Marching to the Beat of a More Excellent Way

Life may not unfold as smoothly as we wish, but the love of Christ offers water to the parched after relentless struggles within the circumstances of life's opposition. President Howard W. Hunter once said, "If our lives and faith are centered upon Jesus Christ and His gospel, nothing can ever go permanently wrong."[3] Amid challenging circumstances we occasionally witness our communities marching to diverse drums, where some follow the tempo of righteousness and others refuse to march or, when they do, perceive only a fading echo. We can choose between marching to the steady, familiar drumbeat of conformity, or instead, follow the beat of a more distant rhythm that directs us toward righteous pursuits.

Choosing to selectively follow only the comfortable and effortless aspects of Christ's teachings will not lead us toward lasting change. Instead, we must venture outside our comfort zones and embrace the teachings that challenge us. By stepping into the unknown, we embark on a transcendent journey that opens the doors to an enjoyable life. It was the pure love of Christ that compelled Dr. King to

---

3. Hunter, "The Great Commandment," 2.

inspire others, awakening them to their moral responsibility to upend injustice. King's leadership was costly and never comfortable, symbolic of that fabled walk through the shadowy valley of suffering.

To find that more excellent way, we must cast aside our old selves, including undesirable routines and archaic or toxic ways of thinking. In contemporary leadership, we often overlook the timeless values of love and consider the teachings of Christ as outdated. When we acknowledge Christ's teachings as a way of living and leading, we will begin to witness a change in ourselves and our communities. We will be less prone to hate by responding to unforeseen circumstances with love, moving beyond labels and divisions, thereby bridging the gaps in our differences.

Journeying toward change is often a winding path, a twisting road we cannot see ahead, but with each step, we move forward into a better tomorrow. Dr. King's vision of a world united becomes possible when we collectively build a bridge of hope, cross it together, and grow closer to an ideal society where all join hands—both figuratively and literally—as we walk together into a life made anew under the influence of God's love. The Apostle Paul taught the Corinthians, "If any child of God be in Christ, they are a new creature: old things are passed away; and behold, all things are to become new."[4]

The significance of the journey we all embark on, often unbeknown to us, is beautifully represented in a simple yet cryptic statement from Dr. King that seems oddly out of context: "I'm so happy I didn't sneeze."

In his final speech, Dr. King shared a touching story about a letter from a ninth-grade student at White Plains High School, referring to an incident several years prior to that evening when a woman in Harlem had assaulted him. While at a book signing, Dr. King had been stabbed with a letter opener, narrowly missing his aorta. He underwent emergency surgery to remove the blade and was told that, had he sneezed, he would have died. The young girl inspired by Dr. King's leadership wrote, "I'm so happy that you didn't sneeze."[5] A decade after receiving the young girl's letter in Pleasantville, New York, Dr. King anchored his final speech around the impression of that one line.

---

4. 2 Corinthians 5:17.
5. King and Washington, *A Testament of Hope*, 285–286.

Dr. King's testimony of nonviolence resonated with the phrase "I'm so happy I didn't sneeze." Had he sneezed, King would have missed out on monumental crossroads: the student lunch counter sit-ins of 1960, the citizen uprising in Albany, the impactful protests in Birmingham that led to the Civil Rights Bill, the awe-inspiring gathering in Washington in 1963, where he shared his dream born out of love, and the courageous journey from Selma to Montgomery. He led the underprivileged of America along the harsh roads of inequality, enabling their growth to become wiser, freer, more autonomous, healthier, and more likely to become servants themselves.

King foresaw a world "reimagined with love." He envisioned and embodied the essence of servant-leadership before we could fully grasp its underlying ideals. From the mountain of justice's highest summit, where his leadership journey culminated, he witnessed the promised land flowing with milk and honey, where the love for all people shone brilliantly. The difficulty of his journey was evident in the sweat upon his brow and the fleeting smile gracing his face. King declared that his eyes had beheld the glory, a glory only revealed along the path of servant-leadership, leaving him with tearful eyes as a testament to his determined pursuit of leadership imbued with love.

When we seek to light the lanterns of hope for pain-ridden communities, the gospel of Jesus Christ requires we bear the cross of opposition prior to donning the crown of glory. Dr. King affirmed that followers of Christ must take up their cross, with all of its unbearable difficulties and tragedy-laden burdens, carrying it until that tribulation leaves its marks upon us and reveals to us a more excellent way.[6]

From the Gridiron to a Life of Purpose

We often stand in amazement when someone from a disadvantaged background achieves remarkable success. Why, though, are we surprised? The story of humble, unlearned fishermen and tax collectors who became saints and apostles should remind us not to prejudge. Throughout history, diverse images of excellence emerge: Florence Nightingale nursing the wounded at Balaclava, Leonidas defending

---

6. King, *Strength to Love*, 19.

the pass at Thermopylae, Mozart composing his first oratorio at the age of eleven, Martin Luther King Jr. fearlessly championing civil rights and equality in the face of adversity, and Ruth declaring to Naomi, "Thy people shall be my people."[7]

Excellence and greatness differ significantly. Excellence demands persistent effort, like hitting the same spot on a tree until it falls. Greatness alters the trajectory of life and unveils previously inaccessible opportunities. I encountered excellence on the football field, but I discovered greatness following the path of Christ, changing the trajectory of my life. My kids will not experience the struggles I encountered traversing the streets of Los Angeles. Like Nephi from the Book of Mormon, I experienced "many afflictions in the course of my days, nevertheless, having been highly favored of the Lord"[8] I persevered through His "tender mercies."[9]

I attained excellence not by receiving high marks in school but by accelerating my graduation from Los Angeles Southwest Community College by a year and a half to improve my quality of life. If I graduated in a year, I could receive a scholarship, enabling me to leave behind the anxiety of every hotel room. I took eighteen credits (equivalent to six classes) during the spring and fall semesters, alongside a forty-hour work week. My effort was deliberate, mirroring my approach to motivation on the football field, clearing the path for my eventual achievements. I was not the most talented, but I relentlessly pursued my goals, leaving an indelible mark on the football field of LA Southwest.

We have the Light of Christ within us to disperse the clouds looming over us. Amidst the battle between happiness and sadness, we often find ourselves measuring our worth against others. Yet, I made another comparison—between my best self and my worst self. The latter comparison helped me clarify my goals, particularly on the football field, where I focused on conditioning my body and strengthening my muscles. In doing so, I also conditioned my mind to seek improvement and my heart to withstand discouragement. Instead of dwelling on our troubles, we can seek outlets for expression through words, art, sports, or any activity that allows frustration and hope

---

7. Ruth 1:16.
8. 1 Nephi 1:1.
9. 1 Nephi 1:20.

to surface. Through these channels, a clearer perspective on life will emerge, offering a more excellent and hopeful outlook.

No matter the challenge, true leadership aspires toward the never-ending pursuits of accomplishments beyond ourselves and toward leading others to do the same. Excellence can be relative, meaning different things to various people. For some, it could mean becoming a notable scholar or accomplished athlete. For others, it could mean a unique expression of their aspirations by faithfully discovering the ideals that make the heart smile and excite the imagination.

We must not settle for complacency or mediocrity; instead, we should seize opportunities when they arise. If there's an additional mountain to climb, climb it. If there's another degree you need to obtain, pursue it. Those who achieve excellence among us wake up every day striving for accomplishments that require effort—aiming to be better than they were the day before.

We often must walk up the muddy mountains of life, where we might stop moving, go backward, and lose our progress. During times of struggle, when we feel we have no more strength, our Savior speaks to us through His Spirit, saying, "I'm here to help you up this muddy hill, and I'll be here if you slip backward. Your strength is within you; don't give up."

We often become what we believe ourselves to be. If we repeatedly say to ourselves that we are children of God, then we shall surely acquire the capacity to be perfected by His hand, even if we fight to achieve it along the way.

Motivation is not a muscle we develop by exercise and flexing; it is not the result of a series of logical steps, nor does it emerge spontaneously by acknowledging a belief. Our aspirations cannot be found on a registry, nor are they capable of manipulation. In *Ego Is the Enemy*, Ryan Holiday explained how we can aspire for excellence:

> When we set out to do something. We have a goal, a calling, a new beginning. Every great journey begins there. . . . One might say that the ability to evaluate one's own ability is the most important skill of all. Without it, improvement is impossible. . . . We will learn that though we think big, we must act and live small in order to accomplish what we seek. . . . We will be action and education focused, [forgoing] validation and status, our ambition will not be grandiose but iterative—one

foot in front of the other, learning and growing [by] putting in the time. . . . Although we share with many others a vision for [excellence], we understand that our path toward it is very different from theirs.[10]

We occasionally marvel in wonder, grateful for achieving what we had never even dared to dream! Nevertheless, with God's blessing, success can be ours.

In the 1992 NFL draft, the San Diego Chargers selected my older brother, Chris Mims. From the outset, our family had found itself trapped within the social and economic hardships of South Central Los Angeles. Chris had come of age in the 1970s and 80s when pervasive gang violence in the area exposed him to the harsh realities of gangbanging. Fortunately, he recognized the opportunity to escape those realities on the football field.

Chris's friends joked about his worn-out football cleats at Dorsey High School. He'd lightheartedly say, "These are the only shoes I've got. What do you want me to do?" Despite people talking about how run-down Chris's shoes were, opposing teams could not stop him. Chris's passion for football burned so fiercely that he joined the team at Dorsey without telling our mom. He pursued his love for the game so intensely that he did not let anything stop him. One day, Chris fell on a sprinkler head hidden in the grass, cracking his rib and puncturing his lung, a painful reminder of the lengths he would go through to go after his dreams. Despite suffering a severe injury, Chris remained undeterred and continued to reach for his dreams, practicing regardless of his circumstances. He pursued a more excellent way.

Chris began to bridge the gap for himself through his remarkable talent in football and was known as Nasty Blade for his tenacious effort. His faithful search of excellence in football became a blueprint for accomplishment that Eric and I could emulate on the field. Chris not only saw the gap but also took action to narrow it.

In 2008, three years after I accepted the gospel of Jesus Christ, our family suffered a heartbreaking loss when Chris passed away unexpectedly at a young age. Still, he left behind the lessons he learned on the football field. We visit Chris's gravesite in the Hollywood Hills of Los Angeles each time we visit California. On one occasion, as I knelt and

---

10. Holiday, *Ego Is the Enemy*, 14–22.

began to wipe my brother's headstone, clearing away debris, our kids, Kingston, Titan, and Athena, began to wipe it down and lay down some flowers. Titan, who was four years old at the time, started to pull away at the dirt on the perimeter of the headstone out of curiosity. He looked up and said, "I can't seem to get this open!" He stopped, paused for a moment, and said, "Oh, I remember now. Only Jesus Christ will be the one to open it for Uncle Chris." We shared with Titan that Uncle Chris lived an incredible life serving others and inspiring youth to strive for excellence under the bright city lights of football.

Chris's loving spirit is woven into the story of my football journey, providing Eric and me with support that extended far beyond words. Within the tape interlaced around our wrists and cleats was the love of an older brother who showed us how to become men destined to serve and lead their families. Rather than succumbing to the brutality of gang activity, Chris empowered us to identify our weaknesses and hone our talents with demanding workout routines. His determination, evident in the sweat beneath his LA hat, invigorated our pursuit of opposing quarterbacks. With every move learned, our steps forward became more secure along the narrow path of evading South Central's avenues of lost dreams. He did for us what no one else was willing to do; he taught us not to give up on our dreams. When I teach my sons the same drills that Chris taught me, I tell them, "See what my brother did for me. See what your uncle did for you."

The line-of-scrimmage uniquely marked for me and my sons by Chris's teachings was evident on a sunlit day in Puyallup, Washington. Throughout Kingston's middle school football game, his face lit up with a grin that told of a more profound joy. His energy was contagious, and every step he took on the field that day carried the spirit of someone who wasn't physically there. Chris's moves, style, and love directed Kingston across the field. The crowd could not look away, their cheers growing with each brilliant play. It was as if Chris's spirit was dancing in every blade of grass. Kingston received end-of-the-game honors, but it was not a personal victory; it was a culmination of months of learning, a journey intertwined with memories of Chris. With each move Kingston executed, it was as if Chris moved beside him, his teachings echoing through every step.

When we got home, my mom smiled at Kingston and said, "Good job! You really look the part—just like Chris." At that moment, it felt like Chris had left behind a faint but guiding path for us to follow, pushing us to strive for excellence both on and off the field.

The Hammer of Diligence and Servant-Leadership

Similar to Chris's story, we all have different paths that we will travel as we seek achievement in a more excellent way. Greenleaf compared the pursuit of excellence to Herbert Spencer's engaged process of sheet metal rolling:

> Occasionally a sheet of metal will come through the mill with a bulge in it. The uninitiated might say, Run it through the mill again and straighten it out. But Spencer pointed out, this would buckle the sheet at the point of the bulge and ruin it. The traditional method of removing the bulge was to lay the sheet on a large steel table and, with a smooth-headed hammer, start tapping it gently a few inches from the edge of the bulge and striking away from the bulge while going around and around. In this way, the surrounding metal is gradually stretched away from the bulge. With each trip around the bulge, the hammer is brought closer to the center. If the job has been done carefully [with excellence], when the center is reached, the bulge has disappeared. The moral, applicable to many processes, says Spencer: avoid hammering on the bulge but hammer diligently around it! Against the background of all the negatives, all the ways that do not encourage strength, Spencer's analogy gives us a cue: hammer diligently around it.[11]

In life, the bulge represents our weaknesses, one of which may be anxiety coupled with a lack of preparedness and self-confidence. The hammer is a metaphor for our effort and commitment to discover strength. Unlike sheet metal, we cannot merely hammer our imperfections out of existence. However, by hammering persistently around them, we can eventually find a more excellent way to achieve strength, encouraging growth and learning. What does this suggest to the pursuer of excellence? What can one do and do diligently? Greenleaf concluded:

> Here we come to a parting of the ways. Those who know what they want, or think they do, and intend to go after it go one way. Those who cannot

---

11. Greenleaf, *On Becoming a Servant Leader*, 33.

make up their minds sit at the crossroads hoping that someone will pick them up and take them somewhere. Those looking for an answer that will guide them will turn to the [accomplishment] of people who presumably know. Some will respond to the idea that there are gifts around if we can dispose ourselves to receive them. They will choose the faint, slightly trodden path, which is nevertheless a path—but it is marked destination unknown.[12]

When we view determination as a gift, we understand that anyone receptive to diligent effort can receive God's endowments. Like the artisan working around the bulge in sheet metal, those seeking excellence approach weaknesses with persistence, resilience, and devotion. Instead of directly addressing flaws, they diligently work around them, gradually progressing until weaknesses become strengths. The destination becomes the goal, mirroring the artisan's patience in achieving pride-worthy results. The destination is a place, goal, or skill we aspire for, but the unknown represents the lessons we will learn while accomplishing our aspirations.

Through the uncomfortable, long, and arduous process, we realize that developing into a leader who seeks first to serve is not about hunting down and eliminating difficulty. Instead, it is important to recognize that imperfections are inevitable, and leadership entails transforming struggle into opportunity. We cannot eliminate weaknesses in ourselves or others, but we can utilize them to initiate progress by addressing their root causes. Progress focuses on the barriers that impede growth, reconciling with their causes and impacts, and finally, working around or removing them so that others can experience the progress necessary to move their lives forward.

RUN IT—Pursuing Excellence

Excellence requires embracing all that comes our way—enjoyable wins and frustrating defeats—before learning from each and using them to reach new heights. We must expect to fail some of the time if we are to be realistic in the pursuit of our goals. Excellence is never a given. We must earn it. Our success cannot be attained through shortcuts or settling for less. Success is for risk-takers and the doers,

---

12. Greenleaf, *On Becoming a Servant Leader*, 33.

for the celebrated and those hidden in their labors as they pursue their dreams on the rough path to achievement.

With Christ as our proverbial Sherpa, we are strong enough to keep our eyes and hearts focused on reaching the mountaintop. When those without privilege persevere their way to success, despite the barriers they encounter, their most precious asset is their determination, sense of purpose, and indomitability. Amid the challenging streets of Slauson Avenue, while I struggled for survival without material possessions, I found that my only path to excellence was through determination. When I was sitting at the number 42 bus stop, amid the busy Los Angeles streets with no money in my pocket, only bus tokens, and hunger gnawing at my stomach, I was frustrated and my faith was tested. But every day, I stepped up on those bus steps, surrounded by others aspiring to survive. We must constantly build up faith and develop enough ambition to carry us above every obstacle to live life at its best.

Discouragement can slip in secretly, hiding behind our clothes, makeup, and the mirror. Discouragement is so bold that it will hide behind a smile, and if we listen to discouragement, it will cause us to lose faith and give up on our goals. The thoughts of "it's too hard" in our minds oppose faithfulness.

I, too, repeatedly faced discouragement. One year before my career-ending knee surgery, I struggled to acclimate to college life and balance football responsibilities. Amidst the parched grass of our football ambitions on a scorching summer day, Eric and I stood shoulder to shoulder, our feet tracing the painted lines of the field. Our past struggles remained known only to a select few, successfully concealed beneath the veneer of our new life at the University of Idaho. Our grades were faltering, and hope was slipping through our fingers. Our coach had demanded extra running sessions after football practice in response to our academic underperformance. And so, we worked unrelentingly, the heat intensifying as we pounded the field without pause, our stomachs empty and our bodies growing lean. Without refuge, our desperation peaked, and out of frustration, I finally threw my helmet, with the ear-pieces, mouthpiece, and chin strap suspending momentarily in the air. The fear of expulsion and returning to the unforgiving streets of Los Angeles gripped us, threatening to snuff out our aspirations.

Within the turmoil, the clatter of my helmet against the ground became overshadowed by our coach's vehement shouts: "RUN IT." That command reverberated—it was a blinding reminder of our vulnerability and lack of options. The coach threatened to send us back home, but he was unaware that returning was not an option. It was then that a realization dawned: education was my only pathway out. There was no retreat, no fallback—only our unyielding determination to "RUN IT," to transcend our circumstances. Eric's words cut through the sweltering heat and my frustration: "Put your helmet back on." Together, we pressed forward, running side-by-side, leaving the imprint of our resilience on the practice field. When my spirit weakens and enthusiasm eludes me now, I turn back to those moments of silence and shout to myself, "RUN IT."

When striving for excellence, we must focus intently on building our perseverance. As parents, friends, or leaders, we can pass on our wealth, knowledge, and influence, but we cannot pass on the memory of hardships, the will to achieve, or the fierce determination born of struggle. "RUN IT" is not just a phrase or call to action; it is a mindset that conveys that I will grow despite my circumstances; obstacles will not get in my way or impede my progress; what others think or believe in me will not stop me from succeeding.

Life is a journey. We may stumble and fall along the way, but a more excellent way invites us to rise, shake off the sting of failure, learn from our mistakes, forgive, and resume such an expedition with renewed faith and vigor. There is something to the idea that surmounting hardships strengthens our character and reveals God's love while overcoming each challenge faithfully.

Directing our lives toward Christ helps us to keep going forward, overcoming our struggles, biases, and mistakes as we strive for excellence. Concerning our individual pursuits of excellence, President Gordon B. Hinckley said:

> Be excellent in every way. . . . Stand a little taller, rise a little higher, be a little better. Make the extra effort. You will be happier. You will know a new satisfaction, a new gladness in your heart. . . . We will not become perfect in a day or a month or a year. We will not accomplish it in a lifetime, but we can begin now, starting with our more obvious weaknesses and gradually converting them to strengths as we go forward

with our lives. . . . Do not sell yourselves short. . . . The excellence of which you dream may not be attainable in its entirety. But there will be progress as you try. There will be growth. There will be improvement. And there will be much added happiness. . . . Tremendous is your opportunity to reach beyond the hoped-for goal of wealth and worldly success . . . to build and strengthen others, to relieve suffering, to aid in making the world a better place.[13]

Without the aspirations that propel us toward excellence, our efforts land with a dull thud, relegated to the realm of meaninglessness, quickly forgotten, leaving no legacy, no impact, and, worst of all, no relief for the suffering within our communities.

Excellence is an elusive ideal. It is the vessel of treasure rewarding the seeker after reaching the end of a rainbow like the one Noah's eyes looked upon in awe, presented as God's promise to the world. As seekers looking for guidance and hope like Noah, if we strive to find the reward at the end, we may not be able to locate it alone. If we follow Christ's teachings closely and chart our course faithfully, the pursuit will not be necessary. The reward will emerge and persist as we seek to serve first, like how the poet Nathaniel Hawthorne described the serendipitous nature of happiness:

Happiness in this world, when it comes, comes incidentally. Make it the object of pursuit, and it leads us on a wild goose chase, and is never attained. Follow some other object, and very possibly we may find that we have caught happiness, without dreaming of it; but likely enough it is gone the moment we say to ourselves, Here it is! like the chest of gold that treasure-seekers find.[14]

In the search for excellence, we become so connected in the journey that we eventually pass the shadowed boundaries of time and stand redeemed, savoring and celebrating each other's joys. Nurturing and encouraging a more excellent way, we become privileged to abide by one another in blameless love that seeks to rid the world of impassible barriers that discourage human possibility.

---

13. Hinckley, "The Quest for Excellence," 4–5.
14. Hawthorne, *Passages from the American Notebooks of Nathaniel Hawthorne*, 254.

CHAPTER 7

Agape: How Unconditional Love Conquers All

Servant-leadership is not effective without the integration of selfless love, a type of love known as agape. Agape is unconditional, a love given without any expectation of return, conveying respect, adoration, and high esteem for the unique qualities within each of us. In expressing the nature of love for every child of God, President Russell M. Nelson said:

> The New Testament contains many references to the Lord's commandments that human beings love one another. Those verses become even more meaningful if considered in the New Testament's original Greek language. It is a very rich language, having three different words for love, in contrast to the one available to us in the English language. The . . . words for love apply at various levels of emotion . . . the highest level of love is agape, to describe the kind of love we feel for the Lord or for other highly esteemed individuals. It is a term of profound respect and adoration.
>
> The second level of love is expressed by the term phileo, to describe affection felt for a beloved associate or friend. It, too, is a term of great respect, but less formal.
>
> The third level of love is depicted by the term eros, to describe physical desire and intimacy.
>
> . . . Quoting the Lord: "A new commandment I give unto you, that ye love one another; as I have loved you, that ye also love one another." Right! The level of love cited in this verse is that of agape: with highest respect.[1]

---

1. *Teachings of Russell M. Nelson*, 188–189.

Years before, Dr. King echoed President Nelson's sentiments, affirming that agape is the most powerful force in every community. Drawing inspiration from Swedish theologian Anders Nygren, King declared, "Agape does not recognize value, but creates it. Agape loves and imparts value by loving. What gives us value is the truth that God loves us. Agape is not a weak and passive love. It is love in action. Agape is a willingness to go to any length to restore community. It doesn't stop at the first mile; it goes the second mile to restore community. Agape is a willingness to forgive, not seven times, but seventy times seven."[2] When we observe the life of Christ, we see Him restoring community with every life He touched, believing that we are all children of God, deserving of His agape love.

When our efforts go unnoticed and we do not feel seen, love provides the reassurance to continue in faith. The teachings of Christ work through us in the same way as when He proclaimed, "By this shall all [people] know that ye are my [friends] if ye have love one to another."[3] Like water, love can be soft and gentle, washing away hurt and pain, or it can be powerful, cutting through barriers of prejudice and hatred. Like a ripple moving across the water, servant-leadership's influence moves in all directions, bringing us closer to God.

Jesus imparted, "Greater love hath no man than this, that a man lay down his life for his friends."[4] This teaching is evident in the narrative of Josiah Henson. His journey from slavery to freedom is a story underscored by agape—the unconditional, selfless love that surpasses personal sacrifice—enduring the brutalities of slavery. As a conductor of the Underground Railroad, leading enslaved people to freedom in Canada, Henson chose service over revenge and community over isolation. His journeys traveled into New York, Connecticut, Massachusetts, and Maine, where he attributed much of his success to what he called friends—people who treated him kindly while earnestly gifting money and resources to aid in founding the Dawn Institute. Like ripples moving across water, the Dawn Institute offered formerly enslaved people trade education that allowed them to improve their lives and communities across Canadian territories.

---

2. King and Washington, *A Testament of Hope*, 16, 20.
3. John 13:35.
4. John 15:12–15.

In his autobiography *The Life of Josiah Henson*, Henson wrote that rather than focusing on the trials he had endured or the life he could have lived, he would focus on his gratitude:

> I will conclude my narrative by simply recording my gratitude, heartfelt and inexpressible, to God, and to many of my [friends], for the vast improvement in my condition, both physically and mental; for the great degree of comfort with which I am surrounded; for the good I have been enabled to effect; for the light which has risen upon me . . . and the religious hopes I am permitted to cherish; for the prospects opening to my children, so different from what they might have been; and finally for the cheering expectation of benefiting not only the present, but many future generations of my race.[5]

Henson's words resonate across generations, expressing the gratitude we feel or inspire in others when we serve selflessly as friends.

Dr. King reaffirmed that agape is inherent in human dignity and friendship:

> A friend is a friend whether [their] hair is brown, black, or blonde. What makes [them] your friend is how [they] feel about you and how you feel about [them]. This is not influenced by whether he is Spanish or East Indian, light, dark, brown, or black. Friendship does not come in colors of skin, hair, or nationality. It is the result of what happens when two personalities meet in harmony. . . . Whether [individuals] are short or tall, stout or thin, white or black does not reveal what is in [their] soul, mind, and heart. This can only be learned and understood by experience [with love]. . . . Among us are many things that differ: race, language, and culture. Underneath these differences is a similarity. We possess hearts, minds, and souls. By comparison with these the differences are of minor importance.[6]

People create many causes, but there is one cause of God: to love one another as we love Him. As we journey alongside Christ, we must emulate His walk on the dusty roads of Palestine by being more resolute and charitable. Christ, the embodiment of love, had no physical home to call His own, and He had no place to rest His head. He approached everyone with kindness, unhindered by societal barriers

---

5. Henson, *The Life of Josiah Henson*, 95–96.
6. Baldwin, *The Arc of Truth: The Thinking of Martin Luther King Jr.*, 254–255.

or personal biases. His love flowed freely and unconditionally, blessing all humanity. We should follow His example.

The Apostle Paul clarified the reason we must all love one another when he said, "Beloved, let us love one another: for love is of God . . . and the manifestation of God's love toward us is that He sent his only begotten Son into the world that we might live through him."[7]

Dr. King described agape as a testament of hope, suggesting that when we love on the agape level, we love because we choose to—not due to family ties or obligations but because we are called to love. Love is not only the starting point but also the center and destination of the journey of discipleship.

Surviving Hardship with Unconditional Love

As I traversed the Los Angeles streets, love helped me overcome my dismal circumstances by believing that God was constantly aware of my family and me. While I was at LA Southwest, my mom, Eric, and I were transitioning from hotel to hotel because we had run out of money to pay for our room the upcoming night. The hotel near the airport was too expensive, and we were at the bus stop moving to a more affordable hotel in Inglewood.

We had our belongings in bags as we waited for the bus stop when our mom looked at us and told us to leave her there. We told her we wouldn't leave her there at the bus station. We followed as she continued to walk, determined to overcome the challenges ahead of us. It was terrifying, and uncertainty clouded our future. We had scarcely any money, no car, and no shelter—only each other. With our eyes full of tears and hearts full of love, we hardened our weak spots. Despite the wretched circumstances that could have ruined our faith, the love shared between a mother and her sons allowed us to come up with the money each night. In those days, we were rotating between La Quinta Inn and Motel 6, with an unspoken love holding us together.

Eric and I faced constant financial struggles for nearly two years as we navigated the strip of hotels stretching from Sepulveda to Manchester in Los Angeles. We utilized every resource for hotel

---

7.   1 John 4:9–11.

rooms: Pell grants from financial aid, tokens to catch the bus, and our money from work. Elder Joseph B. Wirthlin once said, "The line between failure and success is so fine that we scarcely know where we pass it; so fine that we are often on the line and do not know it."[8] Unstoppable by adversity, Eric and I knew no one could help us if we failed. In those defining moments, I felt surges of determination course through me, revealing a strength I had not fully realized. It was not only a test; it was a personal revelation.

As I faced challenges head on, I discovered the resolve necessary for leading or solving problems within myself, a belief that I could conquer any obstacle and achieve any goal I set my mind on. Now, when solving problems, I decisively make my decisions, not faltering at difficulties but constantly adapting and staying determined. Like most notable leaders, I never gave up; I stayed the course.

Elder Joseph B. Wirthlin once asked, "How many of us have thrown up our hands at a time when a little more effort and a little more patience would have achieved success?"[9] Those specific challenges in LA became the first rung in my ladder of leadership development. I realized my potential to lead, beginning with following and sometimes leading my family as we maintained our lifeline from one hotel to another. Some days, I followed Eric as he spoke with hotel managers who allowed us to pay late. Other days, I took lead, determining the appropriate bus routes and workout routines. Our desperation developed our leadership skills. If we couldn't lead ourselves, how could we recognize the doors of opportunity opening ahead of us?

Reflecting on those experiences, I understood the importance of leadership that provides opportunities for those struggling with street life in every community. I adopted the mentality of a survivor, always prepared and never content with temporary success—a mindset initiated by the love shared among a family stranded outside the margins.

Amid the shifting sands of time, the uncertainties that darken our days, and the vicissitudes that cloud our nights, our altruistic and loving God keeps us traveling along the covenant path. His love is a roaring fire that consumes all doubt and fear, burning brightly and illuminating even the darkest corners of every community. One of our

8. Wirthlin, "Never Give Up," 8.
9. Wirthlin, "Never Give Up," 8.

most significant tasks in life is to kindle those embers that will keep our love bright and strong.

The infinite beauty of God's love can transform the fatigue of desperation into hope, as it did for me. Our dreams will sometimes be shattered. Challenging as it may be, we must keep walking ahead with courageous faith, even when our steps forward are lonely. With tear-drenched eyes, Eric and I stood firm in our love for each other and our mom. Agape encompasses living and witnessing the world through an imagination big enough to encompass all the pain and joys of life.

President Gordon B. Hinckley imparted his belief that "love conveys more than the words I love you. Instead, it is the very essence of life. It is the pot of gold at the end of a rainbow. But it is not at the end of a rainbow; it is at the beginning, and from it springs the beauty that arches across the sky on a stormy day."[10]

The Light of Love

Like light through a window, servant-leadership illuminates God's love. There is no fear in love, but perfect love casteth out fear. As Dr. King said, "Darkness cannot drive out darkness; only light can do that. Hate cannot drive out hate; only love can do that."[11] Love can soften the hardened hearts of those who have suffered the most, allowing them to heal and grow.

While history often repeats itself, it is time to bring a permanent end to embedded roots of racism, prejudice, and marginalization. Most of those issues are linked to hatred or ignorance, both of which lead us to a separation from God's love. We must show our love to rekindle the Light of Christ in those who have lost hope in humanity. As we allow Christ's atoning love to manifest in our lives, we become less influenced by enmity. We witness life in a new light, and the hatred that grows out of fear, pride, ignorance, or prejudice is lessened as Christ's image is ineffably etched in those who follow Him.

Throughout history, the oppressed and downtrodden have been forced to live in shameful conditions and, over time, have become bitter, responding to injustice with corresponding hate. Dr. King

10. Hinckley, "And the Greatest of These Is Love," 1.
11. King, *Strength to Love*, 47.

advocated that "we must in strength and humility meet hatred with love."[12] However, while we abhor the injustice, it is imperative that we love the doers of the injustice. Like walking into a dark room, where we can continue to stumble blindly in darkness or choose to light a candle and illuminate the path forward. Dr. King's message of love is the proverbial candle whose light guides us out of the darkness of enmity. Through the influence of that love, potential becomes reality, we extend love to all, and we replace animosity with serenity, doubt with trust, and hatred with unconditional love.

Substituting love for ingrained hostility takes great time and effort, but it is the only way to bring about lasting agreement. As an attribute, characteristic, or action, love is the only force capable of transforming an enemy into a friend—we will never transform an enemy by meeting hate with hate. Let us choose love over hate, kindness over meanness, and empathy over indifference. It is important to remember that love can always be more influential than hate.

How can anyone leave a lasting influence on their community without athletic prowess, wealth, or fame? Growing up in Los Angeles, I initially understood charity as solely material giving. However, agape revealed charity as selfless service that could "succor the weak, lift the hands which hang down, and strengthen the feeble knees."[13] Although I had never said "I love you" to anyone, I have felt agape's significance in the love Ruth and I share. Over time, the words "I love you" became a part of my testimony in Christ, shifting my perspective on influence. I realized that love could remake communities and ignite potential within those who, like me, are overlooked or undervalued to feel accepted and recognized as children of God.

The most significant charity comes when we are kind to each other and don't judge or categorize someone else, while giving each other the benefit of the doubt. As the Apostle Paul said, "If we have not charity, [we] become as sounding brass, or a tinkling cymbal. . . . Charity suffereth long and is kind; charity envies not; charity vaunteth not itself, is not puffed up . . . is not easily provoked . . . rejoices not in iniquity . . . beareth all things, believeth all things, hopes all things,

---

12. King, "Strength to Love," 50.
13. Doctrine and Covenants 81:5.

endureth all things. . . . Charity never faileth."[14] Agape is accepting someone's differences or imperfections, helping them overcome their disadvantages, and having patience with someone who has let us down—expecting the best of one another.

Climbing the Summit of Love

To succeed on the journey of a fulfilled life, one must have a faith-filled attitude toward failure and doubt. Realizing the will to love is akin to a climber reaching the peak of a summit after an arduous journey. Standing upon the summit, the climber gazes through tear-filled eyes, marveling in wonder at the breathtaking landscape below—a land filled with the promise of life and love. The climbers endured many challenges during the ascent; nonetheless, through focus, they attained their goals by refusing to give up, which is the very definition of true faith. Bolstered by the will to love and standing atop the summit to behold the beauty of the promised land, the climber is overcome at the realization of the journey's worth.

The will to love requires similar determination, endurance, and discernment, although it may not include the same physical difficulties. Still, love is no less challenging to realize than the highest mountaintop, as the obstacles we face when ascending those proverbial mountains of life present an even more demanding emotional, mental, and spiritual commitment. As we persevere and stay firm in our resolve to allow love to prevail, we eventually reach our own summit and, with tear-stained cheeks, behold the beauty of a world filled with the love of God and the radiant hues of the Light of Christ.

Agape confronts evil without flinching and reveals an infinite capacity "to take it" through our demeanor and attitudes. Despite the progress made during the civil rights movement, a lack of love is evident in broader societal structures perpetuating racism and inequality, demonstrating a failure to recognize the inherent worth of all individuals. If there is a will to love, we must also acknowledge a will to hate, as shown when we regard people as "less than" and disbelieve that God's image shines brightly upon their countenance.

---

14. 1 Corinthians 13:1–8.

Evil shapes history, evident in Caesar's living in a palace while Christ suffered a horrific, painful demise upon the cross. But Christ's atoning love was powerful enough to split history into AD and BC, making His name the mark that dates even the life of Caesar. Enveloped in Christ's loving embrace and emboldened by His love, we can now openly proclaim that "Black Lives Matter" and that they mattered then, now, and always, while realizing that there is still much progress to be made. We can use soul force to oppose social injustice. We can urge equality for women, uplift the impoverished, lend our voices to those who have been silenced, and boldly rise in place of those unable to stand for themselves, because all is made possible by knowing that God's love will lead all to the promised land. The resurrection of Christ symbolizes God's victory over hostile forces that sought to impede His perfect plan, facing hostility with empathy and unbiased love.

Dr. King famously said, "Never succumb to the temptation of becoming bitter. As we press forward, be sure to move with dignity and discipline, using love as our chief weapon. Let no person pull you so as to hate them. If [we] sow seeds of . . . struggle, unborn generations will reap whirlwind of social disintegration."[15] Agape personifies the truth that all life is interrelated and that the diverse masses worldwide can and should intermingle like the waters of the ocean, reflecting the heavens as a singular, unified expression of God's love.

When teaching His disciples, Jesus emphasized every aspect of love. Our responsibility as His followers is to rediscover the meaning of God's word by striving to live it out passionately in our daily lives. Hate and love are like two sides of the same coin, yet the effects of each can be worlds apart. Hate is a destructive fire that rages through our beloved communities, scorching everything in its path, while love is a gentle rain that descends on parched land, bringing life and restoration.

Herein is love, not that we loved God but that He loved us first.[16] In the Savior's ministry, Jesus calls us to do our part to balance the scales of injustice—not simply to talk about it, study it, or establish a planning committee, but instead to act. To truly minister and clothe the beloved other in the garment of God's righteousness, we must combine acts of generosity with uncompromising faith in the testament of Jesus Christ.

---

15. King, *Strength to Love*, 153.
16. 1 John 4:9, 19.

Anciently, a black siliceous stone tested gold purity using a touchstone that, as gold was rubbed on it, produced a streak with a color that indicated the percentage of gold and impurities such as copper. Like a touchstone, our ability to love one another serves as a measure of faithfulness, bestowed upon us to gauge our devotion to selfless service as we follow in the footsteps of Christ. Agape becomes the touchstone, representing the measure of love's purity.

The Lord's touchstone for us—our personal, heavenly touchstone—is how we love and serve Christ. The Savior said, "Inasmuch as ye have done it unto one of the least of these my brethren, ye have done it unto me."[17] President Howard W. Hunter explained, "The Lord has prepared a touchstone for you and me, an outward measurement of inward discipleship. What kind of mark are we leaving on the Lord's touchstone? Are we good neighbors?"[18] Our measure of servant-leadership is unmistakable in the parable of the Good Samaritan. Will we leave a mark of pure gold, or will we walk the other way, keep our distance, and avoid it completely like the priest and the Levite, failing to embody agape?

Agape on Jericho Road: Lessons from the Good Samaritan

The Good Samaritan who put himself into harm's way by helping the Jew on Jericho Road demonstrated his Agape as he responded to the needs of another, with no regard for his own safety. Christ's parable demonstrates that despite their positions, both the priest and the Levite failed to fulfill the opportunity afforded them.

As Elder James E. Talmage wrote, "Excuses are easy to find; they spring up as readily and plentifully as weeds by the wayside."[19] Love moves us to help those in need, especially when inconvenient, uncomfortable, or sacrificial. President Monson recounted the story of the Good Samaritan, emphasizing its importance and relevance:

> Each of us, along the journey through mortality, will travel his or her own Jericho Road. What will be your experience? What will be mine? Will [we] fail to notice him who has fallen among thieves and requires

17. Matthew 25:40.
18. Howard W. Hunter, "The Lord's Touchstone," 34.
19. Talmage, *Jesus the Christ*, 431.

[our] [service]? Will you? Will [we] be [the] ones who sees the injured and hears their plea, yet crosses to the other side? Will you? Or will [we] be [the] ones who sees, who hears, who pauses, and who helps? Will [we]?[20]

Christ's declaration of love opens our view to a vista of peace seldom equaled and never surpassed. With profound compassion, he rushed to the injured man's aid, tended his wounds, and escorted him to safety. The Samaritan's love manifested his recognition of our shared humanity through his care, financial assistance, and concern to ensure the man's well-being. In the end, this parable reveals the significance of being a good neighbor—regardless of differences. President Monson continued:

> Now the Jericho Road may not be clearly marked. Neither may the injured cry out that we may hear. But when we walk in the steps of that Good Samaritan, we walk the pathway that leads to perfection. . . . Can there actually occur in my own life, on my Jericho Road, such a treasured experience? . . . My answer is a resounding yes.[21]

When we become entirely focused on ourselves, our actions have little influence on others; however, love can magnify even the smallest gestures of kindness. The key to magnifying love is to strive to love those who are easy to love, as well as those who challenge us. We must remember that, while we may choose our friends, heavenly experiences choose our neighbors from all corners of the world. Love knows no boundaries and requires no narrow allegiances. If we only love those who love us back, what kind of reward is that? We can only fully expand our hearts and make a lasting impression on every community by embracing all people with love.

The boundless love of God remains ever-present, unchanging, and undeterred. President Monson defined love as an expression "in many recognizable ways: a smile, a wave, a kind comment, a compliment. Other expressions may be more subtle, such as showing interest in another's activities, teaching with patience, and visiting one who is ill or homebound." How can we, unlike the priest and the Levite, ensure that we are the Samaritan—and not the priest and Levite? How can we ensure that we ourselves do not pass by on the other side when

---

20. Monson, "Your Jericho Road," 2, 4.
21. Monson, "Your Jericho Road," 2, 4.

crossing the road will make a lasting impact comparable to streaks of pure gold? Dr. King eloquently encapsulated the concept of agape through his retelling of the parable of the Good Samaritan:

> A good man, whose example is a flashing light to [awaken] the dozing conscience of humanity. His goodness was not found in a passive commitment to a particular creed, but in his active participation in a life-saving deed; not in a moral pilgrimage that reached its destination point, but in the love ethic by which he journeyed life's highway. He was good because he was a good neighbor.
>
> The ethical concern of this man is expressed in a magnificent story, which begins with a theological discussion on the meaning of eternal life and concludes in a concrete expression of [agape] on a dangerous road. Jesus is asked a question by a man who had been trained in the details of Jewish law: Master, what shall I do to inherit eternal life? The retort is prompt: What is written in the law? How readest thou? After a moment, the lawyer recites articulately: Thou shalt love the Lord thy God with all thy heart, and with all thy soul, and with all thy strength, and with all thy mine; and thy neighbors as thyself. Then comes the decisive words from Jesus: Thou hast answered right: this do and thou shalt live.
>
> The lawyer was chagrined. Why, the people might ask, would an expert in law raise a question that even the novice can answer? Desiring to justify himself and to show that Jesus' reply was far from conclusive, the lawyer asks, And who is my neighbor? The lawyer was now taking up the cudgels of debate that might have turned the conversation into an abstract theological discussion. But Jesus, determined not to be caught in the paralysis of analysis, pulls the question from mid-air and places it on a dangerous curve between Jerusalem and Jericho. . . .
>
> [Christ] told the story of a certain man who went down from Jerusalem to Jericho and fell among robbers who stripped him, beat him, and, departing, left him half dead. By chance, a certain priest appeared, but he passed by on the other side, and later a Levite also passed by. Finally, a certain Samaritan, a half-breed from a people with whom the Jews had no dealings, appeared. When he saw the wounded man, he was moved with compassion, administered first aid, placed him on his beast, and brought him to an inn, ad took care of him.
>
> Who is my neighbor? I do not know his name, says Jesus. He is anyone toward whom you are neighborly. He is anyone who lies in need

at life's roadside. He is neither Jew nor Gentile; he is neither Russian nor American; he is neither [Black] nor White. He is 'a certain man'—any needy [child of God]—on one of the numerous Jericho roads of life. So, Jesus defines a neighbor, not in a theological definition, but in a life situation.

What constituted the goodness of the Good Samaritan? Why will he always be an inspiring paragon of neighborly virtue? One of the great tragedies of humanity's long trek along the highway of history had been the limiting of neighborly concern to tribe, race, class, or nationality.... We see people as Jews or Gentiles, Catholics, or Protestants, Chinese or American, Black people or whites. We fail to think of them as fellow human beings made from the same basic stuff as us, molded in the same divine image . . . The priest and the Levite saw only a bleeding body, not a human being like themselves. But the Good Samaritan will always remind us to remove the cataracts of provincialism from our spiritual eyes and people as [children of God]. If the Good Samaritan had considered the wounded man as a Jew first, he would not have stopped, for the Jew and the Samaritans had no dealings. Instead, he saw him as a human being first, who was a Jew only by [chance]. The good neighbor looks beyond the external [coincidences] and discerns those inner qualities that make all people human and, therefore, [children of God] . . . for it is not enough to aid a wounded person on the Jericho Road; it is also important to change the conditions which make robbery possible.[22]

The Samaritan's willingness to risk not only staining his clothing with blood but also an attack on his own life demonstrates the depth of his love, which went far beyond mere pity. His love was rooted in genuine concern for the well-being of a child of God in need, a human being dying upon the roadside of life. His shift in perspective from self to other demonstrates the influence of servant-leadership and highlights the importance of attending to that which might at first seem insignificant. When we focus on the needs of others, we cultivate a culture of service that benefits all members of every community. Eventually, we stand stronger in our ability to lead with love.

In the same way the Samaritan's hands were used for service, so too must a leader's hands serve those in need, applying their healing

---

22. King, *The Strength to Love*, 21–27.

hands after fearlessly rolling up their sleeves, getting their hands dirty, and taking on any necessary task to provide encouragement to those in dire circumstances.

The Good Samaritan was inwardly loving and expressed a Christlike love for the man he encountered through a twist of fate along life's highway. He possessed a mindful understanding of what transcended temporal distinctions of race, religion, and nationality. As we contemplate the systems that constrain humanity and impede equality, we must reflect upon Dr. King's statement, "What are the devastating repercussions of this narrow, group-centered attitude?"[23] This shallow mindset implies a lack of concern for the welfare of those beyond one's own group.

Dr. King concluded:

> It is possible that the priest and the Levite feared that if they stopped, they would be beaten. Perhaps the robbers were still nearby. Or maybe the wounded man on the ground was a faker, who wished to draw passing travelers to his side for a quick and easy [attack]. I imagine the first question the priest and Levite asked was: If I stop to help this man, what will happen to me? But by the very nature of [Agape], the Good Samaritan reversed the question: If I do not stop to help this man, what will happen to him? The good Samaritan engaged in a dangerous altruism. . . . The measure of a man is not where he stands in moments of comfort and convenience, but where he stands at times of challenge and controversy.[24]

During the George Floyd incident, bystanders who witnessed his tragic murder demonstrated the relevance of Dr. King's words. The officers involved in the incident appeared to have had a narrow, group-centric attitude that prioritized their authority over the well-being of a man pleading for his life. The bystanders who watched Floyd's murder unfold may have been part of a different group. However, their failure to intervene and stop the injustice indicated a lack of concern or disbelief for the suffering of someone outside their immediate circle. King's message serves as a reminder that we cannot allow loyalties to specific groups to create tribalism that closes our eyes to the suffering and mistreatment of others. We must stand up and speak out against

---

23. King, *The Strength to Love*, 23.
24. King, *The Strength to Love*, 25–26.

injustice everywhere and toward anyone, because our shared humanity transcends prejudice.

Driven by inspiration to positively influence change through Christlike love, Dr. King embarked on a tireless leadership journey, traversing 780,000 miles and delivering 280 speeches in 1957 alone, diligently countering hatred with love. Dr. King's "I've Been to the Mountaintop" is a testament to the unbreakable bond between humanity and God's love. Our connection with the spirit of Christ should compel us to live better lives and love those different from us as if they are brothers and sisters in Christ.

Disinherited people worldwide have been robbed of their humanity, deprived of dignity, and overlooked as they lay on the wayside. God's love is eternal and unyielding because we are uniquely special to Him. The most meaningful service we can give to others is to share the gospel of Jesus Christ with them by reaching out and serving, whether toward individuals or entire communities, and conveying a message of agape love.

CHAPTER 8

Cultivating Greatness

There is hope in the notion that difficulty is the harbinger of greatness. One of the best ways to discover greatness is to abandon our failures. Jesus implored, "Ask, and it shall be given you; seek, and ye shall find; knock, and it shall be opened unto you."[1] And we must ask loud enough, seek long enough, and knock hard enough to receive the right answer. Greatness will be built over time with the sort of patient, persistent effort described by President Howard W. Hunter:

> There is no such thing as instant greatness because achieving true greatness is a long-term process; it may involve occasional setbacks. The result may not always be clearly visible, but it always requires regular, consistent, small, and sometimes ordinary and mundane steps over a prolonged period of time. . . . True greatness is never a result of a chance occurrence or a one-time effort or achievement. . . . It requires a multitude of correct decisions for the everyday choices between good and evil. . . . Surely, we need not look far to see the unnoticed and forgotten heroes of daily life. . . . those . . . who quietly and consistently do the things they ought to do. . . . Those who are always there and always willing. . . . The uncommon valor of the mother who—hour after hour, day, and night—will stay with and care for a sick child, or the disabled person who struggles and suffers without complaint . . . those who always volunteer to give . . . those who may not be mothers but who nevertheless mother the children of the world . . . always there to love and nurture. . . . As we evaluate our lives, it is important that we look, not only at our accomplishments, but also at the conditions under which we have labored. . . . We have each had different starting points

---

1.   Matthew 7:7; Luke, 11:9.

in the race of life; we each have a unique mixture of talents and skills; we each have our own set of challenges and constraints to contend with. Therefore, our judgement of ourselves and our achievements. . .should also include the [circumstances] that have existed and the effect that our efforts have had on others.[2]

Life can be a joyous experience. The journey of leadership is not for the faint-hearted, those who prefer leisure over demanding work, or those who seek only the pleasures of affluence and fame. To accept the responsibilities of leadership, one must first understand that serving others is not beneath them, but rather, it is the foundation upon which we build leadership. Only by placing the needs of others on the mantle of leadership can we truly become great.

Greenleaf posed the question, "What does it mean to be great? What lifestyle, cultivated when one is young, augurs for greatness over a life span?"[3] A great life remakes the world and brings it more in accord with fairness and God's love. Life at its best demands that we always remain faithful to the most outstanding beauty we witness and the highest inspiration we have felt. We can condition our memories to appreciate the goodness of God, beauty, and devotion as we experience the height of meaningful moments in life. We experience greatness when a dream deferred is brought to life by beginning to live that dream—no matter how discouraging the circumstances may be, the dream deferred can be recalled and become a reality.

The exposures and experiences of our early lives shape our paradigm for greatness. We do not control the experiences that shape our lives; many are filled with great beauty, but others rock us to our core and threaten to break us. Although I thought I had been thrown into unfavorable circumstances and lacked control over the conditions of my existence, the gospel of Jesus Christ offered me meaning, and I began to grasp that all my experiences, both positive and negative, were for my benefit. A vision of greatness elevates people's sight beyond their immediate circumstances, unbound by limitations. Such a vision may demand the impossible, yet when led by a compelling vision, people can sometimes achieve the impossible.

---

2. Howard W. Hunter, *True Greatness.*
3. Greenleaf, *Servant Leadership*, 268.

Climbing the Summit with Determination

Greenleaf encourages us to choose the ground upon which we will stand. He stated:

> One of the qualities of a lifestyle of greatness is the ability to know with some certainty the solid ground one stands on at any one time. It gives one a toughness of mind with which one looks out upon a seething, troubled world with a quiet eye and asks the meaning of it all—not so much judge it as to enlarge the perspective from which to build even more solid ground for one's own two feet to stand on—and stands alone.[4]

In life, we endure periods of testing. Embedded within us is the spirit of Christ that enables us to stand faithfully without our foundation crumbling, withstanding the storms of life that will come upon us. The sun shines upon the firm ground beneath us while the rain washes away the day's troubles, preparing us for a new day.

Life can be like a climber earnestly attempting to reach an impassable summit. Leadership development is the mountain where personal struggles and challenges initially seem insurmountable. As the climber must use every ounce of strength and determination to reach the summit, leaders must seek to overcome challenges through experience. The climb's challenging grade builds character with each step, and leaders thereby fortify their ability to face additional challenges. Like the climber who cannot reach the summit without taking that perilous first step, prospective leaders will never reach their potential without facing the struggle of experience and confronting unforeseen problems.

The achievement of greatness often occurs when inspiration compels us, amidst unfavorable conditions, to hew out for ourselves a path toward success. In a peculiar sense, we become architects of our good fortunes in life, indebted to ourselves for every possibility and opportunity. If life requires that we travel far, we shall construct the road we will travel. If we must ascend the mountain, we can build our ladders to reach the summit. I define greatness not as a singular achievement but as a commitment to fulfilling our dreams and changing the trajectory of our lives.

---

4. Greenleaf, *The Power of Servant Leadership*, 100–101.

In the book of Proverbs, we read that "a friend loveth at all times, and a brother is born for adversity."[5] Eric and I have ascended the mountain of adversity, feeling indebted to one another to stay the course. It was the final game of our first year at LA Southwest, and we were ready to face off against Pierce College. That year had been a whirlwind of challenges as we grappled with homelessness, the transition from high school to college, and juggling full-time work alongside our studies. Despite the difficulties, we had managed to carve out a reputation for ourselves both on and off the football field.

The morning of the game arrived, and Eric and I were up bright and early, excited to leave our mark as we headed into our sophomore year. We went through our pre-game routines meticulously, ensuring we were fully prepared for the day ahead. However, as we sat at the bus stop, anticipation turned to frustration as the minutes ticked with no sign of the bus. What we thought would be a short wait stretched into over an hour, and we realized with growing dread that we were running dangerously close to game time.

With only ten dollars and a handful of bus tokens between us, panic set in as we watched precious minutes slip away. Eventually, we flagged down a taxi in desperation, pleading with the driver to rush us to the football game. As we hurried toward the stadium, the reality of our situation began to sink in. The game had already begun, and the meter's charges had rapidly surpassed the cash we had on hand. With no other choice, we made a difficult decision to ask the driver to drop us off a block away from LA Southwest, knowing we could not afford the full fare. Handing over what little money we had left, we hurried from the cab and sprinted toward the locker rooms, hearts pounding with embarrassment.

Arriving at the field, we were met with disappointed stares from Coach Washington as he directed us to the bench for the entire first half of the game. No one on the team knew the struggles we were facing—living out of hotels and constantly riding the bus. It was a sobering moment as we sat on the sidelines, watching our teammates play while we grappled with the weight of missed opportunities.

Eric and I were determined to make the most of the second half. We may have arrived late, but our resolve remained determined.

5. Proverbs 17:17.

Despite the odds stacked against us, we had overcome immense challenges throughout the year. As we stepped onto the field for the season's final game, we knew that while the end of our first season had begun with disappointment, we could still end it with achievement.

Despite the setback in how the day started, Eric and I were able and willing when Coach Washington let us play in the second half. Amid unfavorable circumstances, we seized the opportunity and delivered one of our best defensive performances of the year. With pads unbuckled and cleats barely laced, we took the field, silently shouldering the burden of disappointment that had plagued us that day. There were no excuses, no complaints. The embarrassment of our tardiness was a reality we could not escape. So, we buried the frustration beneath our feet, allowing disappointment to generate the force behind every hit. We did not discuss how we felt afterward; Eric and I had an unspoken understanding and commitment to one another.

In that moment, we embodied the essence of leadership. Like many influential leaders, we showed up and shouldered the responsibility; we were willing and able. We refused to let obstacles derail our aspirations. Instead, we focused intently on our goals to finish the game, overcome discouragement, and take the necessary steps to achieve them, even if our efforts went unnoticed or unacknowledged.

President Hunter asked, "With this definition of true greatness, how do we achieve it?"[6] The Lord has said, "Out of small things proceedeth that which is great."[7] As we evaluate our lives, we can look at our accomplishments and those who have helped us labor toward purposeful achievements and thank God for every opportunity.

If we understand what qualifies for a lifestyle of greatness, we shall lift every hand, accept every limitation, yet rise to every challenge ahead of us. At the end and the beginning of every challenge in life, each of us will declare, "This is the best of me." For every privilege we cherish, there is a duty we must fulfill; for every hope that we entertain, there is a task that we must perform; for every good that we seek, there is a loss of ease necessitated by our struggle toward reward. When striving for greatness, we recognize the risk when we accept the opportunity. Elder Sterling W. Sill shared a story that embodies

6. Howard W. Hunter, "True Greatness."
7. Doctrine & Covenants 64:33.

greatness: "Once, a man asked a young boy, 'Who gave you that black eye?' The boy responded, 'No one gave me that black eye; I had to fight for it.'"[8] In chasing greatness, we often find ourselves in a struggle that requires strong determination for victory, like the boy, while on the path toward accomplishment.

Chiseling Greatness

As parents, teachers, or leaders, our role is not to force greatness into existence or dictate its development because we cannot fully comprehend everyone's unique character and specific needs. Instead, our responsibility is to create an environment conducive to growth, recognizing that the emergence of greatness remains a natural and autonomous process beyond our control, guidance, or influence.

The renowned artist Michelangelo created images out of stone honing his brilliance before he became a renowned sculptor, painter, and architect. He learned to see the finished concept in the unrefined material. Michelangelo recounted:

> In every block of marble, I see a statue;
> See it as plainly as though it stood before me,
> I have only to hew away the rough walls
> Which imprison the lovely apparition
> To reveal it to other eyes, as mine already see it.[9]

Servant-leaders must first learn to see the possibilities and then to do the necessary things to bring about greatness. It is a common mistake to assume that only those already in leadership positions have the ability to lead. Jesus chose men like Peter and James, and then refined the leadership potential within them. Brilliant leaders and individuals destined for greatness all too often remain undiscovered, sometimes even to themselves. Like Michelangelo, we must perceive unrealized greatness as though it stands before us and hew away at the circumstances that prevent it from emerging.

Frederick Douglass's life began, like all of our lives, as a block of unrefined yet precious marble. He had a vision, however, as he

---

8. Sill, *Making the Most of Yourself,* 69.
9. Sill, *Leadership,* 174.

accepted the means of self-education and put it to the chisel of self-taught literacy. Douglass carved away the rough edges and imperfections to sculpt himself into God's intended vision. Once pliable and unsure, his hands, the rough-hewn tools of a former enslaved person, became powerful through his quest for knowledge, molding him into a leader. Douglass's determination to learn to read empowered him to overcome illiteracy, meticulously sculpting his own path toward self-realization. His legacy testifies to resilience but even more to the initiative and resourcefulness that gave Douglass the power to transform his own life and the history of a nation.

While it is true that we are all capable of achieving remarkable things, it is equally important to do so in a manner consistent with the values that God has set forth for us. We must be patient, consistently aspiring to be honest and genuine in all we do, recognizing that any success achieved through deceit and trickery is in the end meaningless. We can walk more uprightly and bear all things by being equally yoked and encouraging one another with sustained effort.

In his address "Self-Made Man" in March of 1893, Douglass declared:

> We have all met a class of [individuals], very remarkable for their activity, and yet make but little headway in life; [individuals] who, in their [boisterous] and impulsive pursuit of knowledge, never get beyond the outer bark of an idea, from a lack of patience and perseverance to dig to the core; [individuals] who began everything and complete nothing; who see, but do not perceive; who read, but forget what they read, and are as if they had not read; who travel, but go nowhere in particular, and have nothing of value to impart when they return. Such [individuals] may have greatness thrust upon them, but they never achieve greatness. . . . If it is lacking in the principles of honor, integrity, and affection, it will go down in the first storm. . . . All human experience proves repeatedly, that any success which comes through meanness, trickery, fraud, and dishonor, is but emptiness and will only be a [burden] to its possessor.[10]

In the same fashion that a sculptor carefully selects the best possible marble to skillfully craft into a work of art, overcoming obstacles can be likened to a sculptor chiseling away at a block of marble. Comparable to how a sculptor must first remove the rough and unrefined portions of

10. Douglass and Blight, *Frederick Douglass: Speeches & Writings*, LOA, 708–709.

the marble to reveal the beauty hidden within, we must also persevere through life's challenges to reveal the stunning achievements within ourselves. With each chisel strike, the sculptor is one step closer to bringing their vision to life. In the same way, each obstacle that we overcome is a step closer to realizing our dreams. Our hands must become the tools we use for sculpting the characteristics we strive to embody. Through our hands, we offer encouragement, instill hope, and demonstrate our faith in hard work that leads toward a goal. Each of us has a set of invisible tools with which we may fashion our own accomplishment. Should we feel lacking, weak, or in need of inspiration, we have no further to look than to the lives of great men and women who have gone before us and who have trod the path for us to follow.

I overcame homelessness with sheer determination. Every day, as I ended the day at football practice, my thoughts were racing with all the moving parts I needed to keep myself from falling further into deprivation. Yet, each morning, I woke up determined to focus on perseverance. I was burning the candle of hope on both ends. When we are consistent and keep working, we will eventually discover a path toward noticeable achievement. With each skill learned on the practice field, I developed hidden talents that helped me believe in myself. Failure became my only viable option, yet I persisted, giving each effort another go.

With every loss or missed target, we must learn to readjust our scope and master new skills, knowing that our progress will become evident in the still-unforeseeable future. Every dream we realize enables those who share in our struggles: I write about overcoming homelessness to resonate with those who have experienced scarcity; I share my testimony of Christ for those who have felt His redemptive love; I aspire for a future where silenced voices will be empowered to advocate for change with the optimism that we can use our voices for change.

While at LA Southwest, I began to study philosophy and write my thoughts on paper as an escape from my surroundings, which helped me feel that change was possible. In the process of learning how to write and articulate myself, life seemed like a flash of light on the football field, followed by long periods of darkness off the field. I began to understand how to craft my ideas into words. Writing reflected life; each moment or word can begin imperfectly, but with editing or correction, it becomes an expression of our faith to keep improving and become the change we aspire to see in life.

In their book *Lessons from Great Lives,* Sterling W. Sill and Dan McCormick said, "The act of writing an idea down improves both the idea and the mind. . . . You have to think an idea through before you can write it down. And to write the idea down gives it form, exactness, and makes it visible. When [our] ideas can be brought under the scrutiny of the eyes, the ideas can be more readily improved."[11] I have faithfully kept a journal throughout my life, writing down my thoughts, inspiring moments, helpful suggestions, and every achievement. Whenever I get discouraged, I revisit those ideas and impressions, revising them repeatedly to grow my spirit and character.

Today, I go into the world determined not to fall back into the strife, deprivation, and fear I experienced. The bigger the challenge, the more we stretch. We all live life with different temperaments and capabilities, but experience, discipline, and personal effort can take us the rest of the way. When cultivating greatness, we prepare with hard work, discover our talents, and wait for the right opportunity to arise. Luck has nothing to do with our achievements—we either succeed or don't. Therefore, we keep our dreams and aspirations alive by keeping them moving, and when things go wrong, we don't stop dreaming. Our belief in ourselves or the dreams toward which we aspire may seem insignificant, yet the weight of these accumulated feathers on the scale often tips the balance in favor of success. When God created us in His image, He endowed us with His characteristics so that every child of God possesses the possibilities they seek within themselves.

The artist James Whistler demonstrated this philosophy of greatness by painting a miniature portrait of a spray of roses. The artistry involved was brilliant. The portrait's imitation of nature was one-of-a-kind. Despite the popularity of the picture, Whistler refused to sell his exceptional work. He would say:

> Whenever I feel that my hand has lost its cunning, whenever I doubt my ability, I look at the little picture of the spray of roses and say to myself, "Whistler, you painted that. Your hand drew it. Your imagination conceived the colors. Your skill put the roses on the canvas." Then, I knew that I could do what I had done again.

---

11. Sill and McCormick, *Lessons from Great Lives,* 23–24.

Whistler then provided a great philosophy of success, saying:

> Hang on the walls of your mind the memory of your successes. Take counsel of your strength, not your weakness. Think of the good jobs you have done. Think of the times when you rose above your average level of performance and carried out an idea, a dream, or a desire for which you had deeply longed. Hang these pictures on the walls of your mind and look at them as you travel the roadway of life.[12]

The successes on the walls of my mind consist of my baptism into The Church of Jesus Christ of Latter-day Saints and knowing that families can be together forever. Overcoming homelessness and transforming my deprivation into achievement has become the backdrop to every success. As children of God, we can hang on the walls of our minds God's blessings and share our stories to help others see the beautiful landscape of His love in their lives.

Greenleaf concluded, "Personal greatness cannot be categorically defined, and because it is not synonymous with perfection . . . appreciation . . . will make more accessible that meaning about greatness that is beyond definition."[13] As we accumulate the experiences that capture God's love, we define our own greatness—those moments that change the trajectory of our lives.

Experience taught me to accept the challenging idea that in growth, there is likely a measure of failure, not so much as to overcome us but enough that we know failure well. Ralph Waldo Emerson once said, "That which we persist in doing becomes easier for us to do; not that the nature of the thing itself is changed, but that our power to do is increased."[14] To cultivate greatness, we must hold tightly onto a purpose that inspires us to cling tightly to our dreams. It is like cutting the distance toward any goal, one small victory at a time. Determination implies having an iron will to do whatever it takes to succeed and to steadily stick to our aspirations. When we approach every goal or task with this mindset, we achieve success and inspire others to do the same, celebrating successes collectively.

---

12. Sill, "Great Experiences," para. 6–8.
13. Greenleaf, *Servant Leadership*, 269.
14. Faust, "The Power of Self-Mastery," 45.

CHAPTER 9

Rising from the Margins:
The Talented Tenth as Servant-Leaders

Frederick Douglass once said, "The race is not to the swift nor the battle of the strong, but the prize is [begotten] within the reach of those who are neither swift nor strong. None need despair. There is room and work for all: for the weak as well as the strong."[1] The most valuable ideas are often conceived within a maze of doubt and apprehension, much like a mountain that conceals gold in its vastness and flinty rocks.

The *talented tenth* is a term coined by W. E. B. DuBois, referring to the ten percent of educated Black people capable of leading the African American community to social and economic progress. The premise of DuBois's idea was that talented groups of individuals should receive higher education and use their talents to invigorate their communities. He proposed that approximately one in ten Black individuals possessed the intellect, talents, and education necessary to become leaders in various fields, including politics, education, business, and liberal arts. DuBois envisioned the talented tenth serving as vanguards of progress, leading the fight against racial inequality and discrimination.

Servant-leadership, as exemplified by the concept of the talented tenth, seeks to elevate and empower all individuals, rather than a privileged few. In every community worldwide, some people live with purpose, despite their circumstances, and choose to develop themselves to reach for higher goals. It is difficult to quantify the qualities of patience, persistence, and fortitude, all necessary to generate the

---

1. Douglass and Blight, *Frederick Douglass: Speeches & Writings*, 710.

encouragement capable of pushing the boundaries of what is possible while inspiring others to shatter their own proverbial glass ceilings.

Leading the Talented Tenth

At LA Southwest Community College, Coach Henry Washington extended a helping hand to a select few, including me, Eric, Jesus Lopez, and Chris Phillips. Amidst the challenges of South Central's street culture, Coach Washington's commitment to success was palpable. While he couldn't assist every athlete, those of us he did aid were determined to seize the opportunity. Eric, CP, Jesus, and I were willing to invest sweat equity, both on and off the field in the classroom, while keeping the athletic facilities clean and participating in youth sporting events for the community. Hailing from marginalized communities, each of us embraced Coach Washington's vision of outperforming our circumstances.

I only recently learned of DuBois's concept of the talented tenth; however, it struck me that we, the four of us, embodied this concept. Our teammates jestingly dubbed us Coach Washington's kids, a testament to his tireless efforts in securing every available resource for each of us. Recognizing our challenging backgrounds, he poured love and support into us, leading us toward the possibilities that awaited beyond the streets of LA. In hindsight, Coach Washington wasn't just coaching us—he was servant-leading, helping us become the talented tenth of our community who would eventually earn athletic scholarships and graduate.

When measuring the impact of servant-leadership, Greenleaf proposed, "Do not ask . . . where is the great leader to come from to guide us from the present confusion? What system or way of approaching our problems will work best?"[2] Asking such questions shows a misguided understanding of leadership; instead, prospective leaders should ask themselves, "What is the great dream I would like to see brought to realization? What talents do I have, what talents might I prudently acquire to help move some part of the world toward that dream? Where can I make my effort count?"[3]

2. Greenleaf, *Becoming a Servant Leader*, 336.
3. Greenleaf, *Becoming a Servant Leader*, 336.

Our pliable hands can grasp hold of a problem, work it with all of our effort, and lift it where we stand. Greenleaf advocated that people of color, along with the deprived and alienated, will begin to assert their claims to the future's here-and-now opportunities for leadership.[4] He predicted that the privileged elite would not lead the least privileged of society in the future because of kaleidoscope times. Instead, exceptional people from their own background would lead those born without privilege.

Greenleaf concluded, "The tests of leadership are realistic and exacting. Whatever the goal is, does the undertaking move toward it? And what does the scorekeeper say?"[5] When the goal is both equality and the improvement of community well-being, leaders must demonstrate a commitment to solving the community's problems and uplifting its members. This leadership approach enables individuals to freely pursue their aspirations in a trusting, collaborative environment that respects everyone's potential. The scorekeepers in this context are the community members who can assess leadership effectiveness established on whether it is moving their community toward greater equality and improved living conditions.

Throughout the '80s, '90s, and early 2000s, Coach Washington was pivotal in leading young athletes toward athletic scholarships—and many of his mentees had successful careers in college and the NFL. Coach Washington offered disadvantaged youth in neighborhoods like Watts, Compton, and South Central an alternative to joining gangs. Over the years, he earned a reputation as a trusted servant of our community, with former players often choosing to send their kids to play LA Southwest. Coach Washington's impact extended beyond the football field. By instilling a sense of hope and providing invaluable opportunities, he provided student-athletes with the resources—tutoring, counseling, jobs, and government aid—to succeed academically and athletically.

Reflecting on his leadership in the community, Coach Washington said:

---

4.   Greenleaf, *Servant Leadership*, 48.
5.   Greenleaf, *Becoming a Servant Leader*, 337.

The main goal is to take some of these young people and change their attitudes. Make them respect their fellow man and get them prepared for the rest of their lives.

We ask them to be consistent, be on time, put in a full day's work and call if you can't make it. These aren't Henry Washington's rules; these are rules of life.[6]

After a winning season in 1989, during which Coach Washington sent thirteen student-athletes to four-year colleges, he said, "For me, winning doesn't just mean victories on the field. It also means getting kids in position to attend four-year schools."[7]

Turning Weakness into Strength

Regardless of background or circumstances, the leadership prize is within reach for those who may not consider themselves swift or strong. Booker T. Washington once said, "To do the most that lies within us, we must go with a heart and head full of hope and faith in the world. . . . The person who cultivates the habit of looking on the bright side of life, and who calls attention to the beautiful and encouraging things in life, in nine cases out of ten, is the strong individual." Success is to be measured not so much by the position that one has reached in life as by the obstacles which they have overcome while trying to succeed by focusing on brighter side of life."[8] Leadership emerges from those who have overcome challenges through determination, fortitude, and a commitment to higher ideals.

Just as homelessness challenged and stretched me, leadership aspirations often push us to pursue ideals that are challenging to attain and not readily embraced by our communities, organizations, and institutions. However, a select few persevere through the hardships of homelessness or physical constraints, and their exceptional talents shine brightly like a rare gem among the masses. They find joy in the journey, undeterred and steadfast in the face of obstacles that impede progress.

---

6. LAWT News Service, "Los Angeles Southwest College names new football coach," *LA Watts Times*, April 20, 2017.
7. Zepel, "Washington Can't Tell a Lie: Southwest Is Good."
8. Washington, *Character Building*, 23.

Chris coached me on the defensive line when I first began playing football at LA Southwest. He emphasized speed when getting off the ball—implying that I should move with the football in pursuit of the ball carrier once the play began. As the younger brother, I always wanted to mimic Chris's abilities in football and yearned to emulate his success. Yet, he often reminded Eric and me of the intricacies inherent in football that demanded more than raw talent. In South Central LA, where athleticism was abundant but discipline was scarce, Chris taught us excellence—combining talent with dedication. Education and hard work became levers that transformed athletes into student-athletes denoting our potential in the classroom and within the lines of football.

My success as a defensive lineman hinged on a lightning-fast first step in the gridiron trenches. My right-handed stance (hand on the ground before sprinting) granted me an initial advantage, leveraging my speed against opponents. However, I had limitations getting off the ball in a left-handed stance. Recognizing it as an opportunity to improve, Chris prescribed a solution: practice exclusively left-handed for the next few months.

Chris's coaching tested my confidence, sowing seeds of doubt about my potential for collegiate football. Daily practice from the left-handed stance transformed my weakness into a strength, presenting a unique skill that set me apart from other defensive linemen and afforded me confidence in my athletic potential. The determination to finish, the practice, and the faith that weaknesses do not necessarily have the authority to stop progress will reveal accomplishment. When I practiced my defensive stance, there were times when I wanted to give up because of its difficulty, but I resiliently kept practicing my routine until I became skilled at the left-handed stance. What God-given weaknesses do you have that will enable you to separate yourself from everyone else? It will only require faith to identify those opportunities to improve.

For those who follow the covenant path, there is no precise, single way, no list of defined goals, and no set of gauges. If there were, there would be no human dilemma and no need for faith; life would lack challenge. Whenever we find ourselves cornered and facing adversity, we must ask ourselves, Will I be the one who rises above adversity and becomes a pillar of encouragement for my family or community? Will

I be among the talented tenth achievers academically, earning a college degree? Can I, despite experiencing homelessness and lacking resources, become a doctor of philosophy? Will I allow life's disappointments to keep me down, or will I rise to a higher calling through the grace of Jesus Christ? These thoughts occupied my mind as I traversed the avenues of life, tirelessly working toward improving my circumstances.

Standing on the margins of what we call time, we are but single souls gazing upon the vastness of its range. Despite our finite limitations, we dream of infinite possibilities and eagerly seek to explore the never-ending contradictions of life by disproving them. Our fascination with the horrific past and mysterious future draws us in, providing endless opportunities for thought and study. The purposeful plan of God remains both an ever-present reality and tantalizing dream, temporally beyond our grasp yet endlessly captivating.

We do not view the talented tenth or influential leaders as essentially different from us but as individuals who identify with our highest aims, objectives, and possibilities as servants of their people. They become our best representatives, reflecting on a colossal scale the aspirations to which we would aspire. The negating of the big wave of oppression will require talented individuals with accumulated wisdom and unrelenting strength.

The unique talents and perspectives of the marginalized or disadvantaged are often overlooked or undervalued in society, due to prejudices toward race, ethnicity, gender, religious beliefs, or socioeconomic status. Prejudice and inequality stifle the opportunities of the marginalized, while the Talented Tenth await their well-deserved recognition and acceptance. The hope is that when the turbulence of the present time has passed, and those who were once marginalized have found their way into leadership positions, they will be able to draw upon their unique perspectives to create a more equitable society, one blind to judgments and limitations.

With time, there will also be far more opportunities for those with talents to step forward and lead themselves, allowing the Light of Christ to radiate over a greater distance. W. E. B. DuBois once said, "How then shall leaders of struggling people be trained and the hands of the risen few strengthened?"[9] There can be but one answer: the least privileged

9.   DuBois, *The Talented Tenth*, 10.

and most capable bearers of responsibility must be schooled in the colleges and universities of the land. Greenleaf used university athletic programs as a model to illustrate leadership opportunity, emphasizing that background should not limit possibility. He detailed:

> Usually in their college years, students are but dimly aware, if at all, of their potential in [leadership], nor do they always clearly see the significance of these talents . . . at a great cost to themselves and to the society they have the potential to serve well. . . . The growth of these students in their colleges years can be just as spectacular as growth in athletic prowess . . . using the athletic program as a model. I use it because it is the best way, I know to emphasize that potential bearers of responsibility need special help to mature their talents just as athletes do. . . . In the case of athletes, this is easy. . . . In the case of potential bearers of responsibility, it is difficult. The talent is usually latent, not clearly evident, and often not known by the student. . . . What I mean by a potential bearer of responsibility—a leader, if [we] want to use that term—is not a vocational category. . . . There is no surer way to guarantee the future than to have strong leaders in the making now.[10]

Education should excite and open our minds to the world of possibility, as opposed to just fulfilling an ardent thirst for information to enlarge the mind's capacity. The goal is to prepare talented individuals to serve, and be served by, the present society. In a good society, every person capable of being educated should be liberally educated first, without direct reference to any specific role.

The Talented Tenth: Illuminating Pathways

Booker T. Washington, in his book *Character Building*, asked, "What will we do to reach the people and bring them the light they so desperately need and yearn for?"[11] The least privileged of society are ready to follow that light upon witnessing it in their lives. Like a prism of light, the talented tenth shine brightly, refracting their gifts to elevate and empower those around them. Light still exists even when not visible and can illuminate any experience with hope. Washington continued, "[They] who accomplish the most, accomplish it in a humble

---

10. Greenleaf, *Servant Leadership*, 209–211.
11. Washington, *Character Building*, 142.

and straightforward way, by sticking to what [they] have undertaken. [Those] who do this find in the end that [they] have achieved tremendous success."[12] The influence of individuals who possess great enthusiasm to lead will be discernible over time and not always visible to the unaided eye. Yet, that influence can transcend missed opportunities and open doors that were once closed.

With each step we take on our educational journey, our understanding expands and deepens, allowing us to explore new horizons by unlocking more significant insights in life. If we study the most remarkable individuals in any occupation, we will notice that they are all educated, able to express themselves respectfully, studied proficiently, and have performed in their fields with unparalleled excellence. Dr. Martin Luther King Jr. earned his PhD at twenty-six. Not only could he articulate his ideas in a way that moved a nation to action, but he was so exceptional that we regard him as one of history's most visionary leaders and speakers. Leaders do not go where traditional paths may lead; instead, they go where there is no path and leave a impression of inspiration.

The poorest of our people, living in lower-income neighborhoods, towns, and cities, suffer from divestment and a lack of resources, resulting from not prioritizing education. There was a time in American history when it was illegal for a person of color to read or write. People of color could be thrown in jail, beaten, or lynched for becoming literate. When Frederick Douglass learned to read and write, he had to do it discreetly and humbly. He would practice reading and writing when nobody was looking. Douglass obtained his freedom when he took his education into his own hands. As an educated man, he was treated differently and had greater access to the American dream. Education unlocks the doors of opportunity to eventual progress and accomplishment.

The acquisition of knowledge is not the end goal, but rather the catalyst that propels us toward equality. Capable individuals who consider themselves as having already achieved their goals can become more devoted servants of their communities by working more astutely toward a more modest future. As we observe the emergence of the talented individuals from the margins, we become aware of the multitude of challenges they have overcome on the course of their journey.

12. Washington, *Character Building*, 140.

The prepositional phrase "to the end" has a special meaning to these enduring individuals, representing their commendable and unique achievements. The communities around them hold deep admiration and even awe for the ideals they embody, as these individuals demonstrate a remarkable commitment to the belief in themselves despite their unsupportive circumstances.

Servant-leaders have built bridges of purpose that have led marginalized communities out of the dark shadows of desperation into the light of self-realization, paving the way with pathways of hope. Although these bridges faced countless impeding blocks and challenges, these exceptional leaders' unyielding determination served as a source of inspiration for future generations. Through faithful devotion, servant-leadership can shatter barriers, creating opportunities for everyone to cross the bridge of equality, building with hewn stones of progress. As we strive to follow in the footsteps of Jesus Christ, we become magnets that draw people toward the hope and truth we seek to discover. In his autobiography, Frederick Douglass wrote:

> The mere circumstance of being born under the hatches, is not enough to disqualify a [child of God] from being captain of the ship of fate. One class of individual cannot, without insulting their nature, be content with any deprivation or degradation of their fellow human beings.[13]

Like others who have overcome repressive circumstances, Frederick Douglass's life exemplifies how an individual can become a leader for others despite living at a disadvantage. Douglass's life is a testament to the significance of grit, education, and moral conviction in overcoming adversity.

Douglass firmly held the view that any individual, irrespective of their background or circumstances, could ascend to positions of influence, inspiring others to do the same. He highlighted the idea that society should not disqualify an individual from being a leader or captain of their own fate simply because of their circumstances at birth.

The greatest evil today is in the deep-set attitudes of those who would minimize the dignity of others. We should feel the same about the monstrous rejection and demeaning of one person or group by the more privileged, a rejection that blankets the world. The greatest

---

13. Blight, *Frederick Douglass: Prophet of Freedom.*

depravity is in the hearts of those who deny their neighbor rather than in the wrong itself. Worldwide, we observe a pervasive rejection of humanity toward the least privileged, a phenomenon that consistently obstructs the path to unity and God's love.

In the sight of God there is no color line, and when we lead in His way, we cultivate a spirit that will make us forget that there is such a line anywhere on earth. As part of the talented tenth, we can become more influential and think more broadly than those who would oppress on account of color, gender, sexual orientation, social economic status, and religious belief. No one ever loses anything or fails to succeed by being loving toward others. No one has ever lost anything by being innovative or utilizing their talents to uplift someone else. The teachings of Jesus Christ remind us that if we are kind and advantageous, honest, and openly practice the characteristics of servant-leadership, no matter what others believe, they cannot pull us down.

Preface to Characteristics of Servant-Leadership

In his book *A time to Choose*, Elder Neal A. Maxwell said, "Jesus intended his disciples to be the 'salt,' the 'leaven,' the 'light' which could flavor, lift, and guide other people. It is not that his disciples are perfect, but that they are committed to a path."[1] Servant-leadership is not a destination; it's a continuous journey, a path we choose to walk, led by our devotion to follow Christ's steps.

As we begin to plan our journey toward servant-leadership, we "must know the difference between an action that points toward a benign result or activities toward progress"[2] so that a scaffolded plan will emerge to show the way forward. To surpass the limitations of our current circumstances, we need a clear and detailed vision of our ideals to visualize the path, paint a picture of where it begins, and then work toward achieving our end destination. Servant-leadership characteristics help us paint the picture of our shared journey and eventual accomplishments.

President Spencer W. Kimball once said, "One of the advantages of the gospel of Jesus Christ is that it gives us perspective about people . . . including ourselves so that we can see the things that truly matter and avoid getting caught up in the multiplicity of lesser causes that vie for the attention of humanity."[3]

President David O. McKay highlighted the significance of refining our character to reflect the teachings of Christ. Acquiring Christlike characteristics is a continuous and daily process requiring us to take responsibility in how we develop the characteristics to become more

---

1. Maxwell, *A Time to Choose*, 46.
2. Greenleaf, *Servant Leadership*, 143.
3. *Teachings of Presidents of the Church: Spencer W. Kimball*, 83.

like Christ. President McKay likened this process to an occasion when he visited a sculptor's yard in Florence, Italy:

> Scattered about were unbroken, irregular pieces of granite from which a sculptor was preparing to cut out a vision which he saw in his mind. . . . If you had stood in that yard, and a man had placed in your hands a chisel and a hammer, would you have dared to take one of the shapeless blocks of stone and carve a human image out of it? You could not do it. Or if someone had placed before you a canvas and given you paints and put in your hands a brush, would you have undertaken to paint on that canvas the picture of an ideal soul? You would have said to the first, "I am not a sculptor," and to the second, "I am not a painter. I cannot do it." . . . Nevertheless, each of us is carving a soul this very minute—our own. Is it going to be a [work in process], or is it going to be something admirable and beautiful?[4]

Perhaps some people might say that being what it is today, servant-leading is naive as a means to fulfilling life's achievements. We can remind the naysayers that humanity has gotten to where it is today by doing the unthinkable and believing in the impossible.

The words I compose on these pages are not merely text but lines of inspiration that seek to inspire hope. In crafting these words, I found myself growing into a better version of myself, not for my sake, but for the betterment of my family and those around me. From listening and empathy to foresight and awareness, the characteristics of servant-leadership reveal the steps necessary for us to go forward. In his study of Robert Greenleaf's writings, Larry Spears identified ten characteristics central to developing prospective servant-leaders who could, in time, build up communities with apsirations to serve first.

In his first epistle, Paul, a servant of Jesus Christ, greeted every child of God as "Beloved," bestowing upon them the grace and peace of God for their faithfulness in following Christ's teachings. The more we understand what happened in the life of Jesus, the more we, too, can live a life that reflects His teachings. The Apostle Paul served with love and gratitude, stating, "I press toward the mark for the prize of the high calling of God in Christ Jesus."[5]

---

4. *Teachings of Presidents of the Church: David O. McKay.*
5. Philippians 3:14.

Preface to Characteristics of Servant-Leadership

We love the stars for their characteristics. The sheer number of stars in the night sky—blue, white, yellow, and red—are at their best when we look upward beneath the freshness of a clear night. The Big Dipper rotates around the North Star, but no matter their position or location, stars point faithful travelers toward their various destinations. While watching the stars on a cloudless night in eastern Washington, I gazed at the brightness of each star, realizing that they shone brighter without the distraction of city lights always present in our lives.

Pursuing a higher calling feels like navigating the vast expanse of the sea, and like mariners, we set our course on the light of a distant star beckoning us to continue. This star illuminates our path with the ray of Christ's hope, calling us to sail on despite the tidal swells and stormy seas. As we follow that distant star, our course will remain faithful and steadfast, bolstered by our commitment to the path God has set before us. Like constellations directing the mariners of old, the points of light in God's plan present us with waypoints or reminders of the progress and challenges we have overcome. To navigate the metaphorical voyage, we can endeavor to recognize the signs and follow the course charted for us by Jesus Christ. Let us keep our eyes fixed on the horizon over the distant sea, with the Light of Christ, the brightest of all, drawing us ever closer to our destination.

Joseph Smith once recounted, "If [we] could gaze for five minutes into heaven, [we] would know more than by reading all of the books that have ever been written on the subject."[6] When we spot a star, the illuminating light leads us, inspires us, and uplifts our spirits. As we progress and look around, we become aware of the infinite expanse of stars in the night sky, each with unique brilliance. When we look up at the stars, the brilliance of the night sky reveals the path we have traveled. Like the stars, only the best and most faithful leaders give off light that allows people to witness the embodiment of God's love.

Like a researcher poring over the stars, like the stargazer's appreciation of the intricacies of each celestial body visible in the night sky, I have learned to appreciate the importance of each historical servant-leader's unique story. I remember that some heavenly bodies (stars) give off light that is a thousand times brighter than the sun, and servant-leaders strive to emit light far beyond their own individual capacity.

6. Still, *Leadership*, 365.

Like the stargazer's gaze toward the unique properties of the universe despite the incalculable enormity, servant-leaders devote themselves to marginalized communities, where the beauty of potentiality shines despite the most severe hardships and staggering disappointments.

President Gordon B. Hinckley once said, "None of us . . . knows enough. The learning process is an endless process. We must read, we must observe, we must assimilate, and we must ponder that to which we expose our minds, believing that improvement is possible."[7] As we journey together, we will recognize that while our learning experiences may seem profound, we will be given even more excellent opportunities and opposing challenges ahead.

Learning is a remarkable journey through which the vast knowledge accumulated over centuries gets distilled and refined. As we embark, we will gain insights that were once attainable only through extensive trial and error. Scholars, leaders, organizations, and institutions continue their research and freely share it with us as we attempt to comprehend the many benefits of servant-leadership. As I write about these characteristics, the spirit of Christ reminds me of the beauty of constellations in the night sky, where each is distinct yet interconnected. Similarly, servant-leadership's potential becomes effective when infused with love and modeled after the teachings of Jesus Christ. As we faithfully travel the path of Christ, every "word is a lamp unto [our] feet, and a light unto [our] path."[8]

The journey is of faith, led by trust rather than visual evidence. Great are the blessings to those who have not seen, and yet have believed, for we "walk by faith, not by sight."[9] My witness and testimony of leading in the Lord's way are reflected in the following chapters as I break down, explore, and apply Christ's teachings to each characteristic of a servant-leader from my vantage point.

We can memorize and practice these characteristics while heeding the advice of Paul: "Whatsoever things are true, whatsoever things are honest, whatsoever things are just, whatsoever things are pure, whatsoever things are lovely, whatsoever things are of good report . . . think

---

7. *Teachings of Presidents of the Church: Gordon B. Hinckley,* 30.
8. Psalm 119:105.
9. 2 Corinthians 5:7.

on these things."[10] We can use the teachings of Christ to deepen and broaden our spiritual grooves so that all future endeavors will follow the path of servant-leadership.

Sometimes leadership lacks spirit; sometimes, our faith and devotion lack enthusiasm. Servant-leadership grows the human spirit not through speeches or books but through connecting God's love with others so that it can change their lives.

When a people have a strong spirit pushing them to pursue their goals, they become less vulnerable to fatigue, less willing to yield to frustration or loss, and refuse to quit when behind. Shakespeare articulated the spirit of accomplishment when he wrote, "Care I for the limb, the physical strength, the stature, bulk, and big assemblance of a man! Give me the spirit!"[11] When we have a strong spirit about our aspirations, we learn to constantly push toward broader horizons and renewed levels of experience, while at the same time, the idea of "this one thing will I do" becomes our purpose. Despite the passage of time and its limitations, we can maintain a determined spirit to persevere and achieve every goal when we ask our Heavenly Father for support while seeking and knocking on earthly doors.

Navigating the Narrow Road

From time to time, as I navigated the bus stations near the airport, I found myself repeating in my mind, "I have my brother to help me through the challenges ahead of us," providing encouragement, winding up my faith, and fueling my ambition. Before I had the words to articulate myself, the spirit of Christ would whisper in my ear, "You've got this." These words, and others like them, wrapped me in psalms of faith and purpose directing my life when I sought to find a path forward.

Our Savior imparts to those who seek success, that "strait is the gate and narrow is the way, which leadeth unto life."[12] This road, however, is so narrow that most people cannot manage to stay within its bounds for long. The broad road may prove easier and provides more

---

10. Philippians 4:8.
11. Shakespeare, *King Henry IV*, 3.2.276–278.
12. 3 Nephi 14:14.

room to sidestep or meander, but it also limits the inward components of the journey and the discipline to make right decisions. Elder Neal A. Maxwell remarked that discipleship requires consistency, with constant roads ahead. He said, "It is a useful perception in the quietude of our own ponderings to remember that the straight and narrow is a heroic path to travel. It challenges us to love, to forgive, to render service, and to focus on basic things."[13]

We begin to fail when our aims become too broad and when we aim at everything but fail to hit specific targets. It is not a lack of effort or skills that causes failure but rather the lack of a clear goal. The prevailing ingredient of any endeavor for success in any vocation is to identify the precise aim of our aspirations, and then, as we progress along the road of personal growth, that road will not widen but will maintain its narrowness. When we set our minds on the proper aims and allow our feet to travel the narrow road marked by Jesus Christ, we strengthen ourselves for singular and collective achievement. With our aim to servant-lead, the characteristics of servant-leadership help us focus aspirations on the narrow road of hope.

Crossing the streets of inspiration, I found myself in West Los Angeles, where my peers garnered acclaim on the football field. Despite the allure of athletic stardom, I remained steadfast on the narrow road while steering clear of desperation. For me, desperation led to a lack of patience in achieving my goals and becoming distracted by alcohol consumption, gang banging, or the use of drugs.

While football showed the way to improve my life, it also revealed broader, less-defined paths that led to either success or failure without a distinct line discernible for me. Homelessness added another layer of complexity, necessitating a clearer, less-traveled path. While I was blessed with the ability to play football and receive some recognition in the community, it was easy to become distracted by the notoriety, miss class, and slack on the effort necessary to maintain my fleeting accomplishments. Complacency can be a companion of accomplishment, but with every achievement, I still ended the night in hotel rooms, studying to maintain my grades and keeping my body in shape by not smoking or drinking while at LA Southwest. I was not a member of the Church of Jesus Christ at that time, but I lived it by

13. Maxwell, *A Time to Choose*, 25.

Preface to Characteristics of Servant-Leadership

necessity, not choice; life forced me to have discipline and follow the path of Christ, even though I did not know it.

I noticed a common path my teammates chose: indulging in distractions like pursuing girls, smoking, and drinking before and after football games. They seemed drawn to the allure of being part of the popular crowd, celebrating rather than continuing to work hard, despite sharing some of the same struggles as me traversing the streets LA. However, upon graduating from LA Southwest, I could not help but notice a stark contrast. Those who had followed the broad road failed to set goals beyond the fleeting victories of football achievement. I realized that the difference between success and failure was incredibly subtle. It became clear that I needed to remain focused on my own goals of a scholarship amidst the distractions. While my teammates began to make more relevant goals, I had already achieved them out of necessity and determination.

With each stride forward, I have realized that my unaccompanied journey along the narrow road has prepared me for leadership. It has been a path where faith and grit were my steadfast companions. Grit grows as we realize our life philosophy, dust ourselves off after disappointment, and tell the difference between low-level goals that we can abandon quickly and higher-level goals that demand more tenacity. Navigating this road demands an intimate understanding of its contours, often without the support of others.

Though we aspire for companionship on life's journey, sometimes God requires that we occasionally travel alone to refine our resilience and deepen our faith in Him. Amidst moments of loneliness, I felt Christ's redeeming love urging me onward. Along the way, there have been valleys of hope and summits of challenge, yet through it all, our Savior has been my constant companion, even in the depths of discouragement.

Some days I caught the bus to school alone, gazing out beyond the strip clubs and liquor stores. Despite temptations to stray onto the broader path and live without concern, mirroring the lifestyles of those around me, I always had the prompting to keep focus. Concentration is not a six-lane highway. We travel this narrow road by limiting our scope and narrowing our vision by tuning out distractions to stay focused on our goals.

The mark of a leader places them in the position of showing others the way and pointing to the narrow road, accepting that some goals may be out of reach, not easily achieved, but individuals inspired to lead or achieve, still rise to the challenge. When we faithfully press forward, we discover inspiration and a sense of wholeness to be proud of.

No matter what you go through in life, despite the narrowness of the way, believe that you can achieve any goal, beginning with a dream that is uniquely your own. Behind every achievement is someone who overcame an obstacle or broke a barrier.

A Glimmer of Hope

Greenleaf saw a glimmer of hope that a servant-led society was possible. So, what would this society look like in terms of leadership? In my vision of a servant-led society, the prevailing privilege currently upholding inequality would be diminished, creating more opportunities for the underprivileged. In a servant-led society, the accurate measure of its quality is how the least privileged are uplifted and grow as individuals. Do those we serve grow as persons? The quality of a society is judged by what the least privileged in it achieve.

If we are to succeed—as we must—and eliminate biases related to gender, economic status, and race, many questions remain concerning the leadership needed to lessen barriers of inequality. Still, we must find people of color, women, the alienated, and the disadvantaged who can uphold the mantle of leadership. Leadership is more important than ever if we aspire to preserve our testament of hope. No flaming sword prevents us from acquiring the knowledge to become builders of communities, institutions, and families, where the goodness of our lives matches the assurance within our hearts to do the right thing.

The story of Job stands as a resounding testament to our capacity to stay resolute in our devotion to God, even amidst life's harshest trials, while still savoring the blessings bestowed upon us. At the beginning of the book, Job is a great man of wealth and power. Later, he is reduced to a life of poverty, subjecting him to seemingly insurmountable challenges and heartache. Then, in the third period of his life, Job's wealth is restored because of his faith. Through good and bad times, Job remains constant, not only in his devotion to God but also in his attitude toward life. After faithfully enduring his trials, Job finds joy in his later years: "So, the Lord blessed the latter end of Job more than his beginnings . . . for he had also seven sons and three daughters. . . . And in all the land were no women found so [beautiful] as the daughters of Job. . . . After this lived Job a hundred and forty years, and saw his sons, and his sons' sons, even four generations. . . . So, Job died, being old and full of days."[14]

We can liken our own determination to Job, enduring hardships with a sense of purpose. Some individuals grapple successfully with adversity, while others must endure tragic circumstances before experiencing success. For some, even minor changes can wield a profound impact. Despite his experiences, Job's testimony can invigorate us, as he proclaims, "While my breath is in me, and the spirit of God is in my nostrils: My lips shall not speak wickedness, nor my tongue utter deceit. . . . Till I die, I will not remove mine integrity from me."[15] Job's example teaches us that, even in the depths of opposition or when we cannot fathom the reasons behind our trials or the injustices evident in our communities, we can still anchor ourselves in uncompromising faith in God's love for us.

Leadership must enable people to believe in themselves and break free from the imprisoning circumstances that engender defeatism. The first task of servant-leaders is to keep hope alive and never deny difficulty, but instead to uphold their unimpaired belief in human possibility. Elder Maxwell observed that whenever individuals face their time to choose and respond to Jesus's entreaty to follow Him, they place their feet on the strait and narrow path where Jesus walked—a path that is always the same with only one gate at journey's end, and Jesus Himself is the gatekeeper, as "he employeth no servant there."[16] As followers of Christ, we approach that gate from afar on an ascending, experiential stairway—each step representing the characteristics of servant-leadership. Therefore, with eyes brimming with faith, we can examine the future and receive perspective through the retina of remembrance in the Light of Christ.

---

14. Job 42:12–17.
15. Job 27:3–5.
16. Maxwell, *A Time to Choose*, V.

CHAPTER 10

Empathy:
Illuminating a Path of Healing

When describing empathy, Greenleaf proposed weaving acceptance, concern, and consideration together as attributes of servant-leadership.[1] He explained that acceptance provides a path toward understanding, and leadership provides opportunity without judgment, requiring faith in the potential of others. Empathy is the ability, whether deliberately or not, to witness another person's experiences and to feel or understand their perspective during times of challenge or accomplishment. The opposite of both is rejection—refusing to hear or receive, throwing out an idea without true consideration, or rejecting the whole person, whether good or bad. Accepting one another without judgment requires patience, long-suffering, and recognizing the light of Christ in others, by supporting them in keeping it alive and bright.

Throughout His ministry, Jesus had a special relationship with those who found themselves outside the margins of society: the impoverished, the afflicted, the stranger, and others who were often overlooked or looked down upon—the least of these, as He referred to them in the Gospel of Matthew.[2] He not only ministered to these individuals, but He saw Himself in them, teaching His disciples that by doing good to such persons, ye have done it unto Him. From the day He was born to the day He died, Jesus was one of the least of these.[3]

---

1. Greenleaf, *The Power of Servant Leadership*, 35.
2. Matthew 25:40.
3. Becerra, "Following the Savior's Example of Empathy and Love."

Jesus spoke to His disciples in the Gospel of John, saying, "Feed my sheep."[4] As prospective leaders, we cannot feed them if we do not know where they are. We cannot feed them if we inadvertently give them reasons to resist change or to not follow the path of Christ. We cannot feed them if we do not lead with charity, the pure love of Christ, and we cannot love them if we are unwilling to demonstrate empathy. Embodying the characteristic of empathy aids us in our efforts to reach outward in imitation of the Savior, creating a feeling of belonging.

When we lead in the Lord's way, we gain the confidence of those in our charge by listening with our eyes, ears, and heart, trying to empathize with how the person feels and then letting them know by our actions that we understand. No one can lead or serve with sarcasm or ridicule. A dictatorial or "I'm right, you're wrong" approach will hinder progress in helping all people achieve a shared understanding of one another's aspirations. We lighten the burden of animosity as we construct a bridge imbued with understanding that transitions us from damaging relationships to relationships that heal. This bridge, though intangible, leads us away from the haunting corridors of historical atrocities and toward the restorative abodes of love. In conventional Western concepts of leadership, we often envision the leader as the individual leading the way in a parade, proudly holding the flag, or as a solitary figure positioned at the pinnacle of success, benefiting from the labor of the less fortunate.

That exclusionary nature of accomplishment is one where power structures remain intact and achievements are not collectively celebrated, although accomplishment is routinely shared. This lies in opposition to a servant-leadership model.

Accomplished individuals who exhibit gratitude attribute their achievements to the support they received from various people along the way—caring parents, encouraging teachers, passionate coaches, and insightful mentors who recognized their potential even before they did. A servant-leadership model prioritizes collective achievement over personal accolades. When we express gratitude for the support and belief others have shown us, our appreciation opposes the exclusionary nature of achievement. When I received my scholarship to the University of Idaho, I expressed that sentiment to

4. John 21:16.

Coach Washington for his support in helping me move forward in my dreams.

By experiencing homelessness, I knew firsthand the immense challenge of finding a stable place to call home, relying on garbage bags or the trunk of a car for storage, and using a car for shelter in addition to transportation. It may be challenging for someone from Beverly Hills to develop empathy for those who survived—or failed to survive—the streets of Los Angeles. When faced with such complex situations and varying experiences, genuine empathy demands a conscious effort to change our perspectives and remain open to understanding others. Empathy in leadership is an invaluable tool when used correctly; it goes beyond merely hearing someone and requires genuine, intentional listening.

Greenleaf acknowledged that aspiring servant-leaders accept, never reject.[5] The phrase "never rejects" is unorthodox, but to understand why people perform acts of hatred or goodness, we must never invalidate the dreams, hopes, hurt, and pain that causes them to move about life with a different perspective than our own. Hatred is complex, with nuances shaped by individual experiences, but, if we are to overcome it, we must begin with the understanding that we should never reject human dignity. Without judgment, we can build bridges of hope and love by recognizing that life is occasionally heartbreaking and beautiful.

We must humbly recognize that even the brute, the bigot, and the batterer are children of God, whether they know it or not, and we must treat them accordingly. If you can grasp even a portion of this truth, you will never be able to say that a criminal act is beyond human capacity, no matter how heinous. We must acknowledge that we share the same potential, although choosing to direct our energy toward constructive rather than destructive ends. If we can understand this about our own negative traits, imagine what we can achieve with our positive ones. If Dr. King or Nelson Mandela can dream noble dreams, dare to love, or strive to be courageous, then so can we aspire to reach beyond the limitations of our circumstances and strive for greater humanity.

People need to know the worst—about the evils to be remedied, injustices to be reconciled with, the calamities to be averted. Lasting change demands that we believe in ourselves and our future but still

5. Greenleaf, *Servant Leadership*, 33.

recognize that life is not easy. Life is painful, and rain falls on the unjust and just. Servant-leaders see failure and frustration not as a reason to doubt themselves or others but as a reason to strengthen resolve, keep hope alive, and never deny the difficulties ahead. When leading in the Lord's way, we aspire for hope in a world that often gives little reason for hope; we search for justice in a world where history depicts tragic injustice; we love in a world that is often unloving and unlovely. Still, the enthusiasm to understand ideas or perspectives that elude understanding becomes evident when we cease rejecting one another.

Leading with Empathy: Following Christ's Example

Jesus Christ is the expert on empathy—He never rejected. In ancient Judea and Galilee, He validated feelings, ministered, and helped those He met to feel heard and loved. An ideal example is when the Savior wept with Mary, Martha, and others after Lazarus's death.[6] His tears reflected love and empathy for His friends.

Daniel Becerra, BYU Assistant Professor of Ancient Scripture, recounted:

As the story goes, Jesus's friend Lazarus falls ill and dies while Jesus is away. After a few days, Jesus travels to Lazarus's home to raise him from the dead and is met by his grieving sisters, Martha and Mary. Mary falls at Jesus's feet and says, "Lord, if thou hadst been here, my brother had not died."[7] John then tells us, "When Jesus therefore saw her weeping, and the Jews also weeping which came with her, he groaned in the spirit, . . . was troubled, and wept."[8]

It doesn't seem like Jesus is weeping for the loss of Lazarus. He had known for days about Lazarus's death and was planning to raise him up shortly.[9] Rather, Jesus weeps for the pain that Mary, Martha, and others were experiencing, a pain that He knew would disappear within a matter of minutes but that was still real for them in that moment.

Jesus wept, at least in part, out of empathy.

---

6. John 11:1–35.
7. John 11:32.
8. John 11:33, 35.
9. John 11:4, 14–15, 17.

Empathy is the ability to understand and share the feelings of others, and because it is one of Christ's attributes, it is something we should all strive to better understand, cultivate, and express. . . . Jesus was in the business of building bridges, even when it wasn't popular.[10]

Servant-leadership, in the present and future, allows us to faithfully witness life through the eyes of the least privileged, helping us to decipher the intricate map of people's lives, a map woven with threads of hope, dreams, and fears. Empathy does not imply that we should compromise our goals or beliefs, but only that we should strive to understand diverging perspectives, helping remove or ease the barriers we experience physically and spiritually.

Aside from change, our only absolute or constant in life is that nothing exists as a simple binary or linear state. The intricacies and complexities of life defy simplistic reductions; with life's myriad challenges, an either-or proposition cannot exist. The notion that we can neatly divide perspectives into cleanly defined opposing sides is a fallacy. Leadership is interdisciplinary and requires diverse thought to transcend the challenges of our time.

Our emotions, for example, cannot be reduced to a binary choice of happy or sad. Every experience encompasses a spectrum of feelings, from joy and contentment to sorrow and longing, each intricately blending into the next. Knowledge and understanding, as well, are not static or fixed; they evolve and expand, weaving a tapestry of perspectives and interpretations. The pursuit of knowledge is a journey through an assortment of interconnected ideas, where the lines between right and wrong, fact and fiction, become blurred by a holistic empathy toward one another. As aspiring leaders, we all need to witness the world differently with a broader lens, and our leadership requires that individuals challenge us. At the same time, we can challenge the assumptions that lead to separation and uphold inequality in society. The more we become immersed and absorbed in something or someone other than ourselves, the more we become what we aspire to be.

There are no perfect people for us to lead, and leaders are far from perfect themselves. Jesus reminded us, "For I was hungry, and you provided me with food; I was thirsty, and you quenched my thirst; I

---

10. Becerra, "Following the Savior's Example of Empathy and Love."

was a stranger, and you welcomed me into your midst. You clothed me when I was naked and visited me when I was sick. Inasmuch as you have done it to one of the least of these my brethren, you have done it to me."[11] There have been situations that each of us can recall being a member of the least of these, needing the support of anyone willing to convey God's love for us. In those unique occurrences, we find the resolve to keep pressing forward with a brightness of hope by following the teachings of Christ.

Empathizing with the complexities of life choices becomes particularly challenging when we have little in common with the person or reside in different corners of the world. Realizing the other side of humanity's story can take time and effort. When we walk in the shoes of the beloved other, we can witness the challenging circumstances others must navigate in life, experiences that we have yet to encounter, even for those whom we consider close to us. Some may try to conceal their struggles under a "I am doing fine" banner, but doing so makes it difficult for others to empathize and offer support. Sometimes we need to be willing to take off our shoes and let others walk in them so that they can understand our unique experiences and help alleviate our burdens.

Recall the time when you struggled and were lifted out of the gutter of disappointment by our Savior's love through family or friends. As followers of Christ, we can reach out with love to those who find themselves lost in life's challenges and reassure them that the sadness of discouragement does not cloud their future. Love provides the strength to outlast the difficult seasons of life, to find the beauty of a rainbow at the end of the revolving seasons of circumstance. Elder Neal A. Maxwell observed:

> If we are constantly comparing ourselves to see if things are fair, we are not only being unrealistic, but we are also being unfair to ourselves. Therefore, true enduring represents not merely the passage of time, but the passage of the soul—and not merely from A to B, but sometimes all the way from A to Z. When, for the moment, we ourselves are not being stretched on a particular cross, we ought to be at the foot of someone else's—full of empathy and proffering spiritual refreshment.[12]

---

11. Matthew 25:36.
12. Maxwell, *Endure It Well*, 9–17.

We do not need identical life circumstances, but each encounter with fear, excitement, frustration, or anger is a lesson, helping us connect with the beloved other. By acknowledging and empathizing with shared experiences, leaders and followers recognize that these qualify us to lead when we follow Christ's path.

Walking in Empathy's Shoes

We will not find an account of our Savior condemning His followers for their struggles, the consequences of their circumstances, or the failures of the community. Whether Christ was healing the sick, teaching the people living in poverty, or ministering to those marginalized on the northern shores of the Sea of Galilee, He approached these situations with empathy, considering people's needs and exemplifying the potential of leadership. As Nephi imparted, "The Lord doeth not anything save it be for the benefit of the world; for he loveth the world."[13]

Daniel Becerra reminds us that "it is difficult not to love someone when you know their story." He advises us, like the Savior:

- We can listen to others with the intent to understand rather than to judge or reply.
- We can avoid the tendency to be dismissive, defensive, or critical of those we disagree with.
- We can patiently meet people where they are in their journey of progression rather than where we would like them to be.[14]

The complicated streets of Los Angeles reveal a backdrop of struggle and danger. Students from Los Angeles Southwest Community College make their daily journeys to school. Their morning routines commence long before the rest of the more privileged families have even awakened, as these students evade the clutches of street gangs' intent on stifling their ambitions, by braving the earliest available buses, which serve as their lifelines. The streets they traverse are a battleground where the aspirations of a select few become targets for others to destroy.

Upon reaching the campus, one can see that the desperation of a community is etched into every crevice of the worn concrete. The sun's

13. 2 Nephi 26:24.
14. Becerra, "Following the Savior's Example of Empathy and Love."

scorching rays intensify as they bounce off the dark pavement, further accentuating the harshness of the surrounding neighborhoods. Posted up at the nearby gas stations, the OGs, or original gangsters, embrace their fate and lay in wait, seeking eye contact from their next unfortunate victim. If there was no eye contact, you were given a pass for that day. Within the hallways of the school, members of the local Crip gangs take over, asserting their dominance by forcefully propelling a rival through the fragile window glass, demonstrating their power and shattering the dreams of those who witness it.

In another instance, a young man, brimming with the potential to become a statistician, slouches in his classroom, devoid of books, carrying the semblance of fading dreams while wearing a pair of loosely tied blue Chuck Taylors. His face bears the telltale bruised black eyes of hardship. The reason for his tattered appearance becomes evident as he navigates dangerous neighborhoods to catch a bus, his path fraught with danger and inescapable violence.

When we listen to the stories of the beloved others, we can identify our unearned privilege despite our own position within our communities, organizations, and places of worship. Privilege, whether based on race, social status, wealth, or gender, is frequently embraced as a rightful entitlement that people feel they ought to have. We can attribute such entitlement to our limited awareness derived from our belief that our own life experiences are the only realities of truth. It is human nature to accept the status quo, especially if we benefit from it. Those with privilege may not be able to discern how difficult it can be for some to distinguish between right and wrong or make choices that align with the teachings of Christ when daily struggles focus on mere survival. Imagine growing up in an environment where you see clouds of despair every time you look up. When those clouds eventually dissipate, it becomes difficult to readjust the eyes to the sunlight of opportunity and envision a different reality. The question then becomes, in the same circumstance, What would I do?

Some believe that individuals who fall victim to the injustices of street life have made a choice to succumb to the brutalities of urban violence and poverty. Consider, however, the student-athlete who courageously shows up to football practice days after being shot in the chest while on his way to school. In the face of such adversity, he consciously chooses to persevere, desperately clinging to a dream slipping away like a gust of wind.

The lives of the underprivileged at LA Southwest tell the story of a group of determined young men and women seeking to leave their street life behind. With every bus ride, holding tightly to a football or basketball while wearing a game jersey added further protection from the LA streets. Despite setbacks, these student-athletes remained hopeful, and some eventually transferred to universities, leaving behind the streets marred with broken dreams.

The greatest challenge for leaders and followers lies in determining their own paths and then supporting those who cannot find a path for themselves. It is essential to first break down barriers that obstruct the way before making a choice. Even when we find ourselves in environments devoid of viable solutions, we must recognize that there are alternatives, no matter how faint they appear. We must become the empathetic football coach who goes beyond mere words by extending an empathic hand, disregarding orders from the doctors, allowing those affected by gun violence to continue practicing. His motive is not personal gain or success for the team but rather keeping the flame of hope and dreams alive within the hearts of the student-athletes who navigate the scarred streets of Los Angeles.

Instead of merely acknowledging the experiences of people living in deprived circumstances and the choices they have, we should actively work toward improving the conditions that influence those choices. Rather than blaming individuals or groups for overlooking the barriers they face, we should focus on removing those barriers. When we make the conscious decision to place ourselves in the shoes of the young men and women navigating the gang-ridden neighborhoods of Los Angeles and other marginalized communities, we gain a deeper understanding of how challenging life can be for those who walk the line between failure and desperation, and how few choices may exist.

Servant-leaders can consciously choose to put themselves in the shoes of others and ask themselves, What caused them to behave in this way? Where do they live? Who do they live with? What are their life experiences? Are they loved? Considering the *why* and *how* behind others' choices, we may begin to feel differently about those whom we have judged and who often have risen from the underprivileged tier of society. Four plus eight equals twelve, but so does six plus six. One's perspective may differ, but it may not necessarily mean it is wrong.

When we begin to walk a mile in the shoes of the beloved other, we will witness the view of opportunities and broaden our perspective of what seems right or wrong when faced with difficulty. If you were to walk in my blue Chuck Taylors, you would witness the resilience developed during my life's challenges that eventually became instrumental to my success as a husband, father, and follower of Christ. Even the most horrific of experiences become opportunities to shape and refine our character, as genuine success lies in the ability to thrive and conquer challenges when failure looms.

When individuals from marginalized communities, particularly people of color, are unjustly labeled as criminals, when we wrongly perceive criminality as inherent to the nature of an individual or group of people, we must first examine their life circumstances. As we progress toward equality, we realize that the shoes worn by marginalized groups have been tattered and worn, traversing roads strewn with thorns and thistles, desperately needing someone to mend them. After a history of neglect, we can now empathize with marginalized groups, exemplified by movements like #MeToo and BLM. Whichever path we choose, the shoes we wear demand the presence of a humble servant with flexible feet, ready to undertake the arduous journey that lies ahead, united in the pursuit of shared success.

The Black Lives Matter and MeToo movements acknowledged that lived experiences go beyond marginalization based on race or gender. These challenges stem from our failure to empathize with groups of people bearing labels, particularly when we are attempting to create a sense of belonging. We cannot overlook that poverty, inequality, and ignorance give rise to crime, regardless of the specific racial group involved. It is a flawed line of reasoning to imply that every person has a choice between right and wrong as a justification for not changing the conditions in which people live their lives, perpetuating ignorance.

The sense of being alone or unloved is one of the most devastating human emotions, and our empathy can save others from the pain of isolation. Emerson once said, "There is a great deal more kindness than is ever spoken. The whole human family is bathed in an element of love like a fine ether. How many people do we meet whom we scarcely speak to, whom yet we honor, and who honor us? How many people do we meet in the street or sit with in church whom, though silently, we warmly rejoice to be with?"[15] Our expression of love must not be silent; it must also be actionable, and we must be willing to shoulder the burdens of one another. Sidney Smith said, "To love and be loved is the greatest happiness of existence."[16] People deserve happiness in life, and we can help to build an outpouring of love when we have empathy for others' life experiences.

---

15. Sill, *Leadership*, 314.
16. Sill, *Leadership*, 314.

CHAPTER 11

Navigating Leadership with Listening

Through the challenge of developing the characteristic of listening, the servant-leader learns to intuitively respond to any problem by listening first and constantly asking, How can I use myself to serve best? On that topic, Greenleaf said, "True listening builds strength in other people"[1] and does not leave disruption in its imprint.

When faced with difficulty, most leaders react by pinning their problems on others rather than taking accountability for their role in creating the problem. Servant-leaders react differently, wondering, What can I do about our problem? In seeking multiple perspectives on any situation, leaders can gain intuitive insight and begin to resolve problems through listening. Paraphrasing the famous prayer of Saint Francis, Greenleaf remarked, "Lord, may I not seek so much to be understood as to understand."[2]

As we seek to lead with purpose, there will often be an emphasis placed on strength and mastery, encouraging us to strive for success, be the best we can be, and achieve greatness in all we do. To be masterful in this way requires attention to the here-and-now possibilities inherent within any given moment. However, it is equally important to recognize that weakness, folly, and failure are important parts of the journey. Failure may be the greatest teacher of all, but we tend to avoid it because it is the one teacher who provides the test before the lesson.

When we learn to embody the characteristic of listening, we cultivate a safe space where failure is not stigmatized but embraced as a catalyst for growth. Leaders can then connect their own experiences

1. Greenleaf, *Servant Leadership*, 31.
2. Greenleaf, *Servant Leadership*, 31.

with the narratives of those they lead by understanding their challenges, strengths, and vulnerabilities, rather than relying solely on their personal journey.

The healing power of listening can profoundly impact both the speaker and the listener who learns and diligently practices this characteristic of leading. Listening isn't just about staying quiet or making responses to show you're awake and attentive. It's an attitude of faith that those being listened to will rise to the challenge of grappling with their issues and finding their own wholeness. When we listen, it is not to offer our opinions or judgements but to allow a person to navigate their circumstances, capabilities, and opportunities by asking the right questions. This enables them to see their own value and understand their potential as children of God. Everyone has a story that deserves to be heard, and when we listen in stillness, we allow their story to emerge as significant.

Listening in Stillness

The first step in listening is silence—not merely refraining from speaking but actively engaging in profound stillness. In this open-minded silence, we open ourselves to a deeper understanding. Silence is not a mere absence of action or inaction; instead, it immerses our entire being—body, mind, feelings, and spirit—in stillness. The visitation of stillness arrives quietly, as Ryan Holiday articulated in his book *Stillness Is the Key*:

> [Stillness]—to hear only what needs to be heard. To possess quietude—exterior and interior—on command. . . . It is an attainable path of enlightenment and excellence, greatness and happiness, performance as well as presence, for every kind of person. Stillness is what aims the archer's arrow. It inspires new ideas. It sharpens perspective and illuminates connections. It slows the ball down so that we might hit it. It generates vision . . . makes space for gratitude and wonder. Stillness allows us to persevere. To succeed.[3]

Stillness radiates outwardly like a star—like the sun—for circumstances that require light amid indiscernible challenges. Our thoughts

---

3. Holiday, *Stillness Is the Key*, 1–8.

become quiet, and our focus is fully rooted in the present moment. We start to discern visible expressions and unspoken emotions as sentiments beneath the surface. Listening in silence allows us to gain perspective into the individual stories, and these narratives become doorways into the vastness of shared experiences. When we hear the stories of communities, families, colleagues, and friends, we step into a world woven by the threads of human experience, accomplishments, and failures that reveal the less-traveled road toward change. It is as though God is touching our minds with His strength and keeping us in peace. In those moments when we feel the endowments of God, a spirit of understanding immerses the tensions and fears we sometimes experience.

Jesus's prominent teaching method was the parable—a comparison arranged to lead thinking from the known to the unknown. Mark said, "Without a parable spake he not unto them."[4] Drawing inspiration from Jesus's parables, we realize that listening transcends time and context. Listening enables the memory to hold the threads of narratives and emotions without prematurely weaving judgments; Jesus's parables beckoned His audience to grapple with the depths of meaning beneath the surface. His parables provided pathways to deeper understanding and appreciation, asking the listeners to navigate their own experiences by connecting with the truths He taught. Jesus was such a skilled storyteller that He navigated the hearts of His audience and cultivated relationships that transcended the words spoken. We witness Jesus revealing Himself openly and candidly, talking about the ideals that matter most in life, urging his followers to listen intently.

In *The Ten Most Wanted Men*, Elder Paul H. Dunn said, "Experience shows that the more successful leaders are willing to acknowledge their weaknesses and fears to those who work close to them. In this way, leaders can leverage the strengths of others to compensate for their own weaknesses."[5] Elder Neal A. Maxwell suggested this may be what "the Apostle Paul intended to convey when he wrote in his epistle to Timothy that leaders must be willing to communicate."[6] Communication requires openness and willingness to share one's failings, to listen with an open heart to criticism, to

---

4. Mark 4:34.
5. Maxwell, *A More Excellent Way*, 78.
6. 1 Timothy 6:18.

accept reproof or candid feedback. Reciprocally, when we aim to help others overcome challenges in their lives, we, too, must be forthright. Openness involves presenting the person with the realities they must confront while approaching the situation with a spirit of love, enabling feedback for personal growth.[7]

Two fishers were on a boat and lost in the oceans of life; a storm began to impact their journey. As the tempest began to rage, one of the fishers asked, "We have two choices, we can pray or row, which one should we do?" and the other replied, "Let's do both." The most dangerous place to be is remaining static in the middle of a storm. The reciprocity between leader and follower must be the same. When we understand the mutuality of the journey ahead, leaders and followers keep paddling together amid the tempest of life, embracing failure and imperfection. "Let's do both" conveys agreement without control or finger-pointing, lessening the chasm between opportunity and actualizing the shared journey.

Greenleaf affirms that anyone who aspires for strength or the ability to lead should consciously and regularly practice listening:

> Every week, set aside an hour to listen to somebody who might have something to say that will be of interest. It should be conscious practice in which all of the impulses to argue, inform, judge, and straighten out the other person are denied. Every response should be calculated to reflect interest, understanding, seeking for more knowledge. Practice listening for brief periods, too . . . thirty seconds of concentrated listening [can] make the difference between understanding and not understanding something important.[8]

Imagine Jesus traversing the hills of Galilee, not merely as a teacher but as a compassionate listener. He sat with the Galilean people, dedicating weekly time to hear their stories, struggles, and aspirations. He immersed himself in their narratives, uncovering barriers that kept them from healing, connecting, and finding hope. Jesus became a source of solace to the lonely and a beacon of hope to people experiencing discouragement. He offered the spiritually impoverished a path toward greater faith and God's love.

---

7. Maxwell, *A More Excellent Way*, 79–80.
8. Greenleaf, *On Becoming a Servant Leader*, 70–71.

Beyond Words: Listening with Humility

Listening should be the initial reaction to any problem, conveyed by simply asking, How can I help? Greenleaf affirms that:

> One must not be afraid of a little silence. Some find silence awkward or oppressive, but a relaxed approach to dialogue will include the welcoming of some silence. It is often a devastating question to ask oneself—but it is sometimes important to ask it—In saying what I have in mind, will I really improve on the silence?[9]

The purpose of dialogue is to go beyond individual understanding toward a shared reality of mutual respect. We are not trying to win in a dialogue. Through dialogue, we lay the foundation to build a beloved community where individuals gain insights through exchanging ideas that we cannot achieve individually. This willingness to engage in meaningful conversation by being receptive to others and embracing both the risk and possibilities of listening allows leaders and followers to experience wholeness.

Dialogue enables us to go beyond our own personal viewpoints and biases to reveal a path toward the lessening of prejudice, helping to bridge the chasm between discrimination and respect. Once a person begins to accept a stereotype of a particular group, that thought acts as an active go-between and shapes how they interact with another person who falls into that stereotype. The individual who upholds their own prejudice because of life experiences does not realize how prejudgment contours their view of the world and their interactions within it. Hidden biases characterized by narrow-mindedness often go unnoticed by those clinging to their past beliefs.

When leading in the Lord's way, we should not confuse humility with weakness; it takes great strength of character to put the needs of others before one's own. Humble leadership implies admitting our mistakes and being vulnerable, transparent, and fallible in front of our communities or people. President Gordon B. Hinckley once stated, "Humility means recognizing that we are not on earth to see how important we can become, but to see how much difference we can make in the lives of others."[10] Servant-leaders understand that their

---

9. Greenleaf, *Servant Leadership*, 31.
10. Hinckley, Goodreads Quotes.

significance lies not in self-importance, but in their ability to humbly listen.

President Spencer W. Kimball once said, "Let us not forget to be humble, to remember where our blessings, gifts, and accomplishments really come from. Humility will bring us closer to Christ."[11] What can be more unpretentious than a leader who patiently listens and, when moved by the promptings of the Holy Ghost, meekly follows as a servant of the Lord?

The journey can sometimes be lonely. As we climb the steep and challenging mountains of life, we might find ourselves yearning for a companion, much like when Jesus walked alongside His disciples on the road to Emmaus. We long for someone who can help us interpret the scriptures and guide us in applying God's word to our everyday lives. But at times that person is not readily available, leaving us to navigate alone. During these times, we must not shy away from the world's disapproval and the isolation that can accompany our commitment to leading in the Lord's way. Instead, we should find comfort in this adversity, knowing that it can bring us closer to an understanding of God's will.

The story of Cleopas and his companion on the road to Emmaus, as described in the Gospel of Luke, demonstrates the importance of following spiritual promptings. As the two men walked and discussed the crucifixion of Christ, the resurrected Savior joined them, though they did not initially recognize Him. They invited Him to stay with them, and as they shared a meal, Jesus revealed Himself to them. Afterward, they reflected on how their hearts had burned within them as He spoke. This story reminds us to pay attention to spiritual promptings, drawing us closer to God and leading us through life's journey.

The Apostle Paul, in his Second Epistle to the Corinthians, identified specific feelings the Holy Ghost places upon our hearts when we listen with the intent to serve: love, joy, peace, long-suffering, gentleness, goodness, faith, meekness, and temperance. These virtues help us understand our callings to minister and serve.

When we humbly submit ourselves, we can truly ascend the mountains of life with direction. Our acceptance of silence allows us to withstand thoughts of discouragement, being vigilant in faith and humbly accepting the promptings that follow. By recognizing our

11. Kimball, "Humility."

own limitations and turning to Christ for help, we will find that every burden becomes lighter and that our paths become more evident as we ascend to new heights of spiritual growth. As we humbly follow in the steps of Christ while listening to His spirit, we have the promise:

> As many as will hearken to my voice, humble themselves before me, and call upon me in mighty prayer . . . you are chosen out of the world to declare my gospel with the sound of rejoicing, as with the voice of a trumpet.
>
> Lift up your hearts and be glad, for I am in your midst and your advocate with the Father; it is his good will to give you the kingdom.
>
> And, as it is written—Whatsoever ye shall ask in faith, being united in prayer according to my command, ye shall receive.[12]

The hidden opportunities for leadership arise from our humble commitment to seeking guidance through prayer. We are chosen leaders through circumstance—prepared by life to improve the conditions of God's chosen to someday lead.

When aiming to achieve the highest level of humility, we can visualize our aspirations as ascending the lofty peaks of a mountain by embodying meekness in our lives. The Greek translation of *meek* conveys gentleness and humbleness, and Paul adored the meekness and gentleness of Christ.[13] We can set up the ladder ascending toward humility through meekness, like the one Jacob saw in his dream, with angels descending and ascending. Jacob's dream signifies the descent and ascent in leadership, ascending through humble service, seeking further ways serve as they ascend.

Humility helps us learn to wait in silence for extended periods, sometimes days, until ideas come to us like a gentle dove with the spirit of Christ directing every thought like a beam of light. We can view moments of spiritual silence as valuable opportunities for learning. While it may seem like we are only sitting and waiting, we are witnessing beautiful moments of spiritual inspiration.

---

12. Doctrine and Covenants 29:4–7.
13. 2 Corinthians 10:1.

Listening to the Spirit

Spiritual promptings are not always easy to follow, but they lead us to the answers of important experiences or complex problems. Usually, answers come piece by piece without the end in sight, but the more we act upon our promptings, the more we will receive discernment between good and bad choices. In this way, listening involves following the promptings of the spirit that prepare us for decisions we must make later in life. The Spirit's promptings will help us make wise choices, rather than remaining motionless and letting life unfold.

Witnessing firsthand the adverse effects of alcohol consumption, especially among men in the Slauson Avenue area, reinforced my resolve to avoid it. Despite facing challenges and discrimination, I never saw drinking as a solution to my circumstances or a remedy to my depression as I moved from hotel room to hotel room. However, upon entering college, the prevalence of alcohol at parties made it appealing, particularly amidst the atmosphere of accomplishment that surrounded me.

Countless nights of consuming Hennessey ended in blackout episodes, leaving me with no recollection of those evenings. I distinctly remember one night waking up to find myself vomiting on the side of the bed. Reflecting on that moment, I wonder how different things might be now if I had not detoured from the path I was on. Alcohol often fueled conflicts with fellow students over trivial matters that held no personal value for me, and instead of dissipating tensions, drinking seemed to heighten my anger and bring out my worst tendencies.

I fell into a pattern of weekly drinking and still remember the sound of trash bags filled with forty-ounce Old English and 211 Steel Reserve beer bottles clinking together as we disposed of them. Whether it was during the week or on weekends, my excessive drinking took its toll on my athletic and academic performance. Like sinking into quicksand, I fell back into desperation, unable to perform on the football field, maintain academic focus, and keep that determined effort as I had at LA Southwest. Despite attaining an athletic scholarship, I lost my grit and misplaced my determination to stay on the strait and narrow road that had previously helped me discover a path surpassing the streets of LA.

During practice, the coach often taunted me with sarcastic remarks like, "Davis, what's wrong with you? What's your poison today? Were you up all night drinking forties with the homies?" His words seemed to confine my potential to a limited box. However, I realized that I had imposed limitations on myself by straying from the routine that had helped me succeed while I was homeless, which had involved abstaining from drinking.

On the verge of academic probation, I realized that drinking provided no solutions to my problems. I chose to listen to and follow the promptings of the Spirit. I stopped going to parties and surrounding myself with alcohol, instead encircling myself with people who helped me accomplish my dreams. While some may perceive Christ's teachings as limiting, I have a strong witness and testimony that following the teachings of Christ allows us to grow into our best selves, not restricting us but freeing us from circumstances that limit our progress. The Spirit leads us to recognize our potential, and by heeding its promptings, we can more effectively discern the paths that lead to eventual success.

Our leadership pursuits, like a mariner embarking on a journey among the stars, should seek to remedy inequality, strengthen the weak, and recapture the desire to bring all into the light of love. Progress may likewise demand years, even generations, to become evident. Nevertheless, with vigor and hope, we can let out our sails, gather our resolve, and set the course toward eternal glory. Along the journey, we can gather every child of God to join us aboard a definitive voyage of faith where together we will navigate glassy seas under the warmth of the midday sun and endure the raging swells of an evening tempest. As we faithfully listen, the spirit of Christ will guide us on a path illuminated by God's love.

CHAPTER 12

Change with Healing, Love, and Wholeness

As we travel along life's journey, we will all carry and bear the scars of emotional wounds while having our spirits broken by the burdens of unfortunate circumstance. Elder James E. Faust remarked, "The psalmist stated, 'He healeth the broken in heart, and bindeth up their wounds.' The healing is a divine miracle; the wounds are a common lot of all [people]. . . . Somehow, we must find the healing influence that brings solace to the soul."[1] In *The Servant as Leader*, Greenleaf articulates this concept: "There is a subtle message conveyed to those being served and led when the implicit understanding between leader and follower includes a mutual pursuit of wholeness."[2] As a skilled healer gently mends a wound and makes it whole once again, servant-leaders strive to provide spiritual healing while repairing broken relationships and communities. Their gentle touch is characterized by the love, tenderness, and universal goodwill necessary for complete healing.

Servant-leaders submit to the subtle forces of life that lead us away from self-embeddedness and toward faith capable of healing. Ministering directly to the hurt and needy is the crux for churches or individuals who look up to Christ as their exemplar. Oppression and inequality relentlessly eclipse people's dreams far more quickly than even the most valiant rescue efforts to restore them, and, meanwhile, the marginalized inflict violence upon their communities, worsening their circumstances. Amid the harsh realities of every community,

1. Faust, "Spiritual Healing."
2. Greenleaf, *Servant Leadership*, 50.

the teachings of Jesus Christ afford us hope for the future through servant-leaders who become constructive healing influences on the lives they touch.

Dr. King's non-violent approach during the Montgomery bus boycott challenged racial segregation laws and lessened the division caused by race. The boycott, which lasted over a year, eventually led to a Supreme Court ruling that declared segregated buses unconstitutional. King's advocacy for love that transcended race continues to influence people today, despite backlash from some within the Black community who advocated for more militant approaches. His message of love, forgiveness, and understanding built lasting bridges between communities that have stood the test of time by providing paths toward collective healing. Progress is still needed in approaching the ever-moving mark of equality and societal healing. But because of the civil rights movement, my kids, your kids, and others from diverse backgrounds can attend school and celebrate the liberties of education, potentiality, and possibility, healing the scars of racism.

The cause of Christ requires not our doubts but rather our dedication of strength, time, and talents. As we actively serve, faith will flourish, and our doubts will diminish. Each act of service and love contributes to this path of improvement. A man asked Jesus, "What shall I do to inherit eternal life . . . what is written?" Jesus answered, "Thou shalt love thy God with all thy heart, and with all thy soul, and with all thy mind; and thy neighbor as thyself."[3] We must strive without guile and hypocrisy to fill the world with unconditional love that transcends bitterness and hatred, and to facilitate healing in relationships where love has been damaged. President Thomas S. Monson affirmed that "love is the catalyst that causes change. Love is the balm that brings healing to the soul."[4] Love that heals is a personal, face-to-face dialogue where we willingly take on the responsibility of caring for others, extending a boundless admiration that knows no limits— or at least strives to come as close to limitlessness as humanly possible.

Greenleaf recounted a thought-provoking experience concerning psychiatrists, ministers, and theologians from diverse backgrounds. After meeting together with a shared goal in mind, they identified a

---

3. Matthew 22:37–39.
4. *Teachings of Presidents of the Church: Thomas S. Monson,* 179.

single word that could bring comfort and renewal to struggling communities: *healing*. As leaders in the Lord's work, the pivotal question before this group of individuals is as follows: "Why are we in this business? What is our motivation? The answer was unanimous, replying. . . . *Healing*."[5]

Whether our primary goal is the healing of others or the healing of ourselves, we are all healers when we seek to uplift one another. When we strive to help others, we heal ourselves of selfishness, the myopic view of the world, and the power that binds our brokenness to the ability to see the best in all people. Healing is a process of helping others toward recovery, whether professionally, individually, or collectively, and the motive for serving and healing is the same—for our collective healing.

Forgiveness: Path to Healing

Dr. King once articulated, "Forgiveness is not a matter of quantity, but of quality. [We] cannot forgive up to four hundred and ninety times without forgiveness becoming part of the habit structure of [our] being. Forgiveness is not an occasional act; it is a permanent attitude. . . . They who are devoid of the power to forgive is devoid of the power to love. . . . Forgiveness means reconciliation, a coming together again."[6] As we seek healing in our relationships, communities, and society, we must first acknowledge the miracle of forgiveness. Too often we fall into the traps of addiction, hatred, or discontent, and we seem to think that those moments in time define who we are. Negative thoughts about ourselves and others cause our minds to remain motionless as we feel encompassed and trapped by walls of opposition. Walls of enmity block the Light of Christ from us, not allowing us to overcome the stumbling blocks immediately before us. Jesus Christ's Atonement transcends beyond mistakes and pain caused by others and enables us to find renewal through forgiveness and experience the tender mercies of the Lord.

Forgiveness does not mean ignoring what has happened or pretending a hurtful experience didn't affect us. Instead, it allows us to move beyond the pain, anger, or sadness, removing barriers to future

---

5. Greenleaf, *Servant Leadership*, 49.
6. King, *Strength to Love*, 33, 44–45.

relationships and successes that enable us to witness the blessings of life. Forgiveness acts as a catalyst, creating the atmosphere for a fresh start and a new beginning, a coming together that conquers the mental blocks that prevent us from experiencing God's love. Life is what we make of it by how we handle misfortune. When malice or trouble finds us, do we hold it so close to our eyes that we cannot see anything else? When someone judges you cruelly, do you use profanity toward them and fight? Do you quit on your dreams and goals? As we follow the path of Christ, we can learn to handle life's difficulties with forgiveness and faith. Do all these things, proving that life is what you make it, and you will enter the spirit of Christ.

While I was homeless, I felt like merely a paving stone in a concrete jungle, riddled with self-doubt. This impeded my progress. I never looked toward a future day because insecurity, poverty, and negative images marred my present and repressed my perspective. In my darkest moments, while sitting at the bus stop, the road seemed narrow and bleak, with no one to help me when I was displaced and lost. I would sit and witness my entire environment without turning my head from side-to-side, lost in the haze of uncertainty. I believed that God had abandoned me, and I was convinced that life was undeniably unfair. I had a myopic view of the world around me, surrounded by gangs, substance abuse, and temporary rooms for the marginalized. I spent too much time complaining, unable to appreciate life's gifts. "Why me . . ." and "Why I got to. . ." were loud grievances in my heart. It wasn't until I stopped bemoaning my past and saw it as a path toward growth that I could actually begin to grow.

Forgiveness was giving up the hope that the past could have been different to achieve the same result. It took time, but I had to reconcile with life for harboring negativity and resentment toward the challenges that shaped me. I started grasping the depth of God's love and forgiveness, realizing that His love empowered me to endure and discover my journey toward the gospel of Jesus Christ.

President Spencer W. Kimball once said that forgiveness makes a brilliant day of the darkest night of challenging experiences:

Great miracles will never cease so long as there is one person who applies the redeeming power of the Savior and his own good works to bring about [change]. . . . The essence of the miracle of forgiveness is that it brings peace to the previously anxious, restless, frustrated, and perhaps tormented [spirit]. In a world of turmoil and contention this is indeed a priceless gift. . . .

To every forgiveness there is a condition. The plaster must be as wide as the sore. The fasting, the prayers, the humility must be equal to or greater than the [transgression]. There must be a broken heart and a contrite spirit. There must be sackcloth and ashes. There must be tears and genuine change of heart.[7]

Forgiveness brightens the path for confronting the injustices of history and acts as a starting point for transforming our lives from the inside out.

The redemptive love of Christ's Atonement can bury our fears, anger, and resentment in God's grace as we reorient our focus toward the beloved other. The experience of healing amid brokenness allows us to rise from the depths of anguish everyone shares. When we leave behind our self-justification or denial, seek healing, and humbly say, "I am sorry, forgive me," we see light ahead of us.

During an October 1985 general conference address, President Ezra Taft Benson taught that we all receive inspiration from Christ:

The Lord works from the inside out. The world works from the outside in. The world would take people out of the slums. Christ takes the slums out of people, and then they take themselves out of the slums. The world would mold men by changing their environment. Christ changes men, who then change their environment. The world would shape human behavior, but Christ can change human nature.[8]

The beauty of overcoming the obstacles seemingly embedded into our life stories will bring us closer to our Heavenly Father and Savior Jesus Christ. We are both the slab of marble *and* the sculptor's hand, and God knows our potential.

We are all imperfect, making mistakes along the way as we live life. Our struggles will cause us to lose focus and our faith that life is a blessing. Like the Apostles, we sometimes question how we can endure this life. We travel on our tandem bikes and often must cycle

---

7. *Teachings of Presidents of the Church: Spencer W. Kimball, 38–39.*
8. *Teachings of Presidents of the Church: Ezra Taft Benson, 77–78.*

up the muddy mountains of life, where we might stop moving, go backward, and lose our progress. During times of struggle when we have no more strength to pedal, our Savior says through His spirit, "I'm here to help you up this muddy hill, and I will be here when you go backward. Your strength is inside of you. Listen to me and don't give up." If we repeatedly say to ourselves that we are children of God, then we shall surely acquire the capacity to be perfected by His hand, even if we fight to achieve it along the way.

Ubuntu: Shared Humanity and God's Love

Ubuntu highlights the extraordinary strength that arises from embracing our shared humanity. We can build community through an ethic of ubuntu, an African philosophy translating to "I am because we are," denoting inclusivity within every community and lessening notions of individualism. Ubuntu is expressed by caring for and serving others, encouraging us to drop judgment by empathizing with one another. Desmond Tutu described ubuntu as a philosophy of community:

> Ubuntu [is] the essence of being human. It is part of the gift that Africans will give the world. It embraces hospitality, caring about others, being willing to go the extra mile for the sake of others. We believe that a person is a person through another person, that my humanity is caught up, bound up and inextricable in yours. . . . The solitary individual is the common good because your humanity comes into its own in community, in belonging.[9]

The combined ideals of servant-leadership and Ubuntu seek to create communities that are a place of inspiration, inclusivity, solidarity, and mutual respect for people. With each act of kindness and each word of encouragement, ubuntu highlights the extraordinary strength that arises from our shared humanity and supporting one another on life's journey.

History vividly illustrates the extent of brokenness resulting from the prevalence of civil wars, genocide, dictatorships, and autocratic rule. Ubuntu is a process of being and a state of becoming, of openness and acceptance. It is also an ideal that opposes *-isms* like racism

---

9. Tutu, *No Future without Forgiveness*, 22.

and sexism, which are defined through conditions of finality, closedness, or absolutes, and incapable of forward movement. Ubuntu, therefore, is not, in its implementation, a noun; rather, it serves as a verb, a continuous process of becoming a beloved community.

When describing the atrocities of South Africa apartheid, Desmond Tutu asserted that "harrowing tales fill history with awful events that seem to defy description and call into question our right to be considered fit to be human at all."[10] It is understandable to view those responsible for atrocities as monsters and therefore not deserving of God's love. However, in addition to implementing Ubuntu into our daily life journeys, we must also realize that it is through the Atonement of Christ that enemies can become friends, with forgiveness bridging the chasm of injustice, leading to the healing embrace of God's love.

The barriers of sexism, racism, gangsterism, and classism can destroy unity within our communities. That darkness of hate can be dispelled only by the light of forgiveness, and the only way to create a beloved community is by not relinquishing both the privilege and the obligation to love. Love is the most durable influence in the world, and its creative strength so beautifully exemplifies servant-leadership as instrumental in humanity's journey toward shared healing.

One of the great tragedies of humanity's long trek along the highway of history is our failure to recognize the humanity in others, irrelevant of race or class. Marginalized groups often fulfill their need for community and acceptance through neighborhood gang membership, frequently creating animosity toward one another through urban violence. Leading in the Lord's way means that we look outside the myopic view and discern those inner qualities that make all people human and, therefore, our brothers or sisters. Recognizing the inherent value of all people undermines the significance of assigned race, gender, prejudice, gang affiliation, and socioeconomic status.

Answering Greenleaf's question, "Will she or he benefit, or at least not be further deprived?"[11] broadens our perspective, reminding us to build communities with love, so as to provide the appropriate light toward healing. Tutu remarked that "God binds humanity together," fulfilling King's premonition that "unless we learn to live together

---

10. Tutu, *No Future without Forgiveness*, 22.
11. Greenleaf, *The Power of Servant Leadership*, 6.

as brothers [and sisters] . . . we will die together as fools."[12] By learning to live together, South Africans epitomized servant-leadership by responding together to the question, If I do not forgive, how will the least privileged benefit?

Kintsugi of the Soul

Every wound will gradually close, our bruises will fade, and the pain of broken hearts will eventually subside through God's tender mercies. Our wounds do not leave just mere scars, but valuable experiences that contour our journeys and provide invaluable lessons. They give us insights that we cannot learn on our own, and become catalysts for seeking healing from the Savior, humbling ourselves, and relying entirely on Him.

We can learn from the ancient Japanese art of kintsugi. The Japanese *kin* embodies gold, while *tsugi* signifies connection. The historical tale of kintsugi is one of servitude that began with tea master Yusai Hosokawa of the Rikyu era. When Hosokawa was preparing tea for the warlord Hideyoshi, a young attendant dropped an invaluable piece of teaware, one of Hideyoshi's favorites, breaking it into five pieces. Hideyoshi began to punish the servant, but Hosokawa intervened, singing a poem advocating mercy toward the young servant who atoned for the broken teaware. As a servant, Hosokawa sought healing, saying, "I will be the one to be blamed for this mistake." The artistry of Hosokawa made whole the pieces of pottery, reconnecting them using the Urushi Japan lacquer technique with gold gliding. The exquisite art of kintsugi deeply touched Hideyoshi, and the story gained renowned distinction for its profound portrayal of restoring brokenness with empathy, love, and selflessness.

Imagine if we apply this same principle to our own lives. What if we embrace and celebrate the person we have become, not despite our struggles but because of them? We are sometimes inadequate, broken fragments of beauty created in the image of God, but American artist Makoto Fujimura said that "brokenness is the most significant proof of Christ's Atonement, that despite our imperfections and failings

---

12. Tutu, *No Future without Forgiveness*, 8.

over and over, we still have the gift of God's grace, which conveys His love for us."[13] Makoto encouraged us to remember that:

> Through the [cracks] of our broken journeys, with pieces of our own hearts shattered on the ground, we journey by God's grace into . . . New Creation. God sees beyond our shattered remains. He picks up and sings a song over us. . . . Kintsugi . . . creates anew . . . more beautiful and more valuable than the original, unbroken vessel.[14]

The Japanese *kin* embodies gold, while *tsugi* signifies the connection that mends broken vessels with Japanese lacquer before covering it with gold. Like the gold in kintsugi enhances the beauty of a repaired vessel, our healing journey will bring forth a radiant transformation that shines brightly even in the darkness of disappointment.

Just as the process of kintsugi delicately restores the shattered pieces and restores them into a visually more beautiful whole, restoration and healing are made possible through the atoning love of the Savior. Through His selfless sacrifice, we can leave behind our scars and the lingering pain of defeat.

The gospel of Jesus Christ begins with the awareness of our brokenness. Christ's Atonement exemplifies the process of kintsugi, as He fills in the cracks of our brokenness as we seek renewal. Japanese American artist and author Makoto Fujimura advocated that "Christ did not come only to restore us but also to create a new beginning for us. He did not come to fix us but to take our place and receive the fall we deserve."[15] On the cross, He bore our engraved names on His hands with unfeigned love. Christ arises in our lives with healing in His wings, reconciling all that is broken for those who believe in His name.[16] Most importantly, He reconciles our relationship with God.

To be or not to be, as Hamlet said, conveys a message of choice: We choose to be healed by Christ's redeeming love, made possible through His Atonement. We can recognize the enduring mark set by the Savior when serving His Apostles, washing their feet, and healing those broken throughout Galilee. We, too, can transcend our brokenness. Fujimura stated, "Even fixing what is broken is an opportunity

---

13. Fujimura, *Art + Faith*, 42.
14. Fujimura, *Art + Faith*, 43.
15. Fujimura, *Art + Faith*, 46.
16. 3 Nephi 25:2–5.

to transcend the original useful purpose." We can become better than we are, stronger than we knew, and more servant-like than what we dreamed possible.

What if we embraced every trial by appreciating the difficulty of experiences? What if we were to appreciate struggle as a refining process that makes us more valuable in the Lord's service? During the difficult moments in our lives, when life feels uncertain and broken, we can still seek the gentle blessings of God shining through, like the radiant gold that fills the cracks in kintsugi pottery. As light slowly emerges on our journey, we can search for the value of differing cultures, of diversity, and inclusion for all. Movements such as #BlackLivesMatter and #MeToo aim not merely to fix inequality but to guide us toward new perspectives where we can appreciate the inherent beauty, or *fairness*, in all people, illuminating a sunlit path toward oneness.

When we break free from the haze of hatred, we will witness the radiant miracle of forgiveness. Dr. King proclaimed, "When a people are mired in oppression, they realize deliverance only when they have accumulated the [influence] to enforce change. The powerful never lose opportunities--they remain. . . . The powerful never lose opportunities—they remain available to them. The powerless, on the other hand, never experience opportunity—it is always arriving later."[17] Healing our own brokenness can bridge the gap between the powerful and the powerless, eventually offering previously inaccessible opportunities to all.

When we find healing, we see the world differently and approach life with renewed vigor to dream new dreams. This healing opens doors to personal growth and self-empowerment, revealing God's love. Leading in the Lord's way offers a path where the disenfranchised can find their voices, reclaim their agency, and seize the once-elusive opportunity for wholeness.

---

17. King, *A Testament of Hope*, 303.

CHAPTER 13

A Journey of Awareness: From the Streets to Servant-Leadership

After football practice at Los Angeles Southwest College, Coach Henry Washington overheard a phone conversation in his office between two students. He heard them pleading with a hotel manager, desperately trying to secure one more night's stay before facing the burden of payment. Clearly, Eric and I had exhausted all viable options in their pursuit of funds. Coach Washington, embodying the spirit of a servant, stepped in to assist, guiding us toward the resources we needed. Before that day, he only knew us as Chris's little brothers.

We managed to find a hotel room nearby, relying heavily on LA Southwest as our lifeline. Coach Washington provided bus tokens and helped us secure jobs while offering a clear road map toward athletic scholarships and graduation, liberating us from the hopelessness of street life. He later shared that overhearing that conversation had broken his heart to the point of tears.

Coach Washington saw beyond the immediate circumstances of every student-athlete at LA Southwest. Instead of labeling us as gang members, he recognized our potential, leading us through the opportunity-laden doors of Southwest Community College, a bastion of safety in the heart of South Central. Coach Washington's profound awareness of each athlete was intertwined with the football field's concrete and blades of grass. As many of his players grappled with life's challenges on and off the field, Washington provided stepping stones that leveled the playing field, directing them toward a sense of determined purpose.

When we seek to change the conditions of a community, we must begin by withholding judgment toward the community or the people within it, as we cannot understand what we judge. When we slap a label on someone that says "He's a thug or a criminal," understanding will stop at that moment. Labels carry undertones of approval or disapproval that obscure leadership discernment. Coach Washington may not have changed the world, but his influence changed my world within the streets of Los Angeles.

Leaders must practice introspection and ask themselves, How can I approve or disapprove if I have failed to invest the time and effort to gain deep understanding? Our approach must be refined observation, studying the situation or conditions at hand. Taking time to comprehend does not mean that we are spinning our wheels. Greenleaf acknowledged, "Awareness is not a giver of solace. It is the opposite. It is a disturber and an awakener. Able leaders are usually sharply awake and reasonably disturbed. They are not seekers after solace."[1]

When we genuinely practice awareness, we become students of experience and say to ourselves in every situation: What good am I supposed to get from this experience? What is God trying to teach me? How can I use this idea or experience, good or bad, to improve my situation and make myself better? With faith, we can be confident that every circumstance or interaction has something to teach us if we only distill the good from every experience, while still learning what to avoid in the future. Along these lines, author Ryan Holliday, known for his work on stoicism, recounted:

> We cannot work with other people if we've put up walls. We cannot improve the world if we don't understand it or ourselves. We cannot take or receive feedback if we are incapable of or uninterested in hearing from outside sources. We cannot recognize opportunities—or create them—if instead of seeing what is in front of us, we live inside our own fantasy. Without [awareness] of our own abilities compared to others, what we have is not confidence but delusion. How are we supposed to reach, motivate, or lead other people if we cannot relate to their needs—because we have lost touch with our own? . . . A true student is like a sponge. Absorbing what goes on around [them], filtering it, latching

---

1. Greenleaf, *Servant Leadership*, 41.

on to what [they] can hold. A student is self-critical and self-motivated, always trying to improve [their] understanding so that [they] can move on to the next topic, the next challenge. . . .

Take fighting as an example, where self-awareness is particularly crucial because opponents are constantly looking to match strength against weakness. If a fighter is not capable of learning and practicing every day, if [they] are not relentlessly looking for areas of improvement, examining [their] own shortcomings, and finding new techniques to [learn] from peers and opponents, [they] will [cease to improve].[2]

Writing down your goals on paper will not make them happen by osmosis. I cannot wake up one day and expect to have a PhD. Success rarely happens that way. We will need heightened awareness, especially if we make repeated mistakes. Some of us become stuck in a cycle of making the same errors constantly. Having a heightened sense of awareness implies that, before making a move, we must take the time to study. When I make mistakes, I don't complain; I look at my life and recognize the need for change. This realization only happens with a heightened sense of awareness. Commit at least an hour daily to reflect on what you are doing well and where you need improvement. You can break it into smaller chunks—twenty minutes in the morning, twenty at lunch, twenty at night, or whatever suits you. Life is about adjusting and your ability to edit, correct, and adapt to life experiences.

When pursuing my aspirations, my chances of success seemed slim, perhaps even nonexistent. Instead of aiming solely for perfection, I aimed for consistency and progress toward my goals. Motivation wasn't always readily available, but I believed I could achieve my goals by having a few standout days each week. Some days, I excelled as a student but faltered in my roles as a husband and father—unable to help out with dinner or help the kids with their schoolwork. Other days, I fell short in my academic or leadership endeavors, yet I strived to excel in my family life. Recognizing that we won't always make the best choices or perform at our best is integral to the journey toward success. Sometimes, simply not giving up is better than some grand endeavor. When faced with opposition, finishing each day and not throwing in the towel is enough.

---

2.   Holiday, *Ego Is the Enemy*, 40–41.

Introspection and Discovery

In a heartfelt letter addressed to Winnie Mandela, Nelson Mandela shared the profound realization that his time in prison was an invaluable opportunity for self-discovery. Within those confines, he embarked on a journey of introspection, delving deep into the intricacies of his own mind and emotions. Similarly, I found myself on the streets of Los Angeles engulfed by metaphorical walls, accompanied by poverty and depression—which initially overshadowed for me the Light of Christ. However, I became gradually aware of my weaknesses and strengths. Unlike my peers who succumbed to the allure of the false authority offered by our neighborhood gangs, I chose a different path guided by personal growth and genuine aspirations to uplift myself, the community, and those young men in the hood who would traverse Slauson Avenue after me.

While my teammates reveled in the fleeting victories on the football field, I contemplated the next steps while riding the bus home. Peering through the window, I sought answers to a series of questions that burned within me: How can I propel myself toward sustained success? What skills could I enhance? What educational opportunities should I pursue? In those solitary moments, I implored God to guide me out of the desolate tunnel of homelessness.

As prospective leaders, it is crucial to chart our own course, establish our unique terms, and actively pursue every dream with unwavering awareness. Mandela continued:

> Honesty, sincerity, simplicity, humility, pure generosity, absence of vanity, readiness to serve others—[characteristics] which are within easy reach of every soul—are the foundation of one's spiritual life. Development in matters of this nature is inconceivable without serious introspection, without knowing yourself, your weaknesses, and mistakes. . . . Regular meditation, say about 15 minutes a day before you turn in, can be very fruitful. . . . [We] may find it difficult at first to pinpoint the negative features in [our] lives, but the 10th attempt may yield rich rewards. Never forget that a saint is a sinner who keeps trying.[3]

In prison Mandela seized the opportunity to reflect upon his actions and witness the transformation within himself, symbolized by broken

---

3.   Mandela, *Conversations with Myself*, 211–212.

rocks and calloused hands. Despite his confinement, Mandela chose to overlook the negative aspects of life by cultivating within himself the qualities of a leader, eventually becoming the future president of his nation. During my own struggles with self-doubt, I embarked on the journey of self-reflection daily on the bus, getting my advice from the lives that I witnessed as I peered out the windows of each bus. With each ride, I understood which bus route led to potential conflict. While waiting for every bus, I sat next to the homeless who stuffed their clothes with newspaper, and I witnessed the hard lessons of life from the hard-lived experiences of others etched upon the countenances of the faces upon the corners of poverty. I learned resilience from overcoming life's challenges and grew from what seemed to be unlikely leadership attributes that have allowed me to lead within my family, church, organization, and community.

As we navigate the complexities of our own journeys, we may encounter external forces that attempt to define us and limit our potential. Jesus was aware of these external forces, and before teaching His followers, He would in essence ask, "Who told you?" Similarly, Jesus asked questions like "Who do you say I am?"[4] or "Why do you call me good?"[5] to provoke thought and self-reflection among His followers, encouraging them to examine the sources of their beliefs and motivations. His words still challenge us today to question the origins of negativity and the acceptance of our supposed limitations. By asking these questions, Jesus invites us to reflect on the sources of the discouragement and doubt that may hinder our personal growth and fulfillment. The opinions of others or society's prejudices do not define our worth.

Our own leadership introspection is an attempt to follow in the footsteps of leaders before us, those who fought for justice and equality by analyzing the underlying motives or ideals that propelled them forward. We achieve such aspirations by internalizing our past leaders' spirit, resilience, and resolute commitment to freedom and human dignity. We must move beyond surface-level imitation, however, toward seeking the essence of what drove the influential leaders of our history. Servant-leadership ideals encourage us to study and to imbue within ourselves the principles and aspirations of our historical leaders, thereby

4. Matthew 16:15.
5. Mark 10:18.

enabling them to forge a path toward the sunlit path of equality. We, like Mandela, must immerse ourselves in pursuit of what past leaders sought, rather than simply replicating their external actions.

Awakening the Leader Within

One day, as I walked into the store with my son Titan, wearing my fitted blue LA Dodgers hat, I could not help but notice a man around my age and with a similar background. His gaze acknowledged my presence, and I could tell he was sizing me up, similar to my days on Imperial Highway. As chance (or God's plan?) would have it, our paths crossed, and he initiated a conversation, curiosity lighting up his eyes.

He asked, "Where are you from, bro? Which part of California?"

I smiled and responded, "I'm from Los Angeles, near Slauson Avenue."

He nodded, a grin spreading across his face, and said, "Yeah, you look the part, bruh. Lions recognize Lions."

We shared a laugh, a mutual sign of respect between survivors of the concrete jungle.

Titan asked, "Dad, what did that guy want? I thought you knew him."

I laughed, explaining to Titan that he knew I was from the hood!

Despite our differences in outlook toward life and life circumstances, the man recognized me as a brother, demonstrating the connection we all share as children of God. As we strive to be like Jesus, incorporating His lessons into our lives, we must first seek to enumerate and express gratitude for our many blessings. Too many of us move through months, years, or even a lifetime without fully appreciating life's blessings. Awareness becomes the measure of our aliveness; anyone who reverently looks into the starry skies will feel to shout with the psalmist, "The heavens declare the glory of God; the sky shows His handwork."[6]

As we internalize God's love and revel in the beauty around us, we will be more thankful for life's challenges, which teach us and eventually reward us. Like rivers changing course due to natural forces, we

---

6. Psalm 19:1.

can adapt and triumph over unforeseen circumstances. Like a lion roaring victoriously in the wilderness, we, too, can conquer challenging circumstances. Embracing God's love and appreciating our journey empower us to emerge victorious.

In his book *Awareness*, Anthony De Mello asked, "Do you want to change the world? How about beginning with yourself? How about transforming yourself first?"[7] He defined awareness as the recognition of possibilities that we overlook or suppress. De Mello recounted the story of a lion; as we explore these possibilities and tap into our potential, our perspectives change, "illusions drop away, delusions peel away, and we begin to get in touch with realities of life."[8] The story of the sheepish lion serves as a compelling reminder that we can transcend life's simplicity and take the lead in accomplishing Christ's work:

> One day, a lion came upon a flock of sheep and, to his amazement, found another lion among them. The sheep had been raising this cub as one of their own, and it would bleat like a sheep and run around like they did. The sheep lion trembled in every limb when the real lion went straight for him and stood in front of him. The lion asked, What are you doing here among these sheep? To which the cub replied, I am a sheep. The knowing lion took this cub to a pool and said, Look! When the cub saw his reflection in the water, he let out a mighty roar and was forever changed. In this moment, he recognized his true identity and embraced the character of a lion.[9]

Each of us has leadership potential, but it takes introspection coupled with faith in the unseen to awaken that spirit. Like the cub, we might feel lost and confined within the flock, until we are led to see our own reflection and potential.

Like the lion's confident leadership, we can use Christ's light to embrace our roles as servant-leaders. At times, we might allow our inner lion to lay dormant in slumber while our opportunities fade away, not by conscious choice but indirectly, by way of neglect. For our best future to be possible, we cannot cast our lot in the meadow, grazing among the sheep; we must ascend the mountaintop and join

---

7. De Mello and Stroud, *Awareness*, 36–37.
8. De Mello and Stroud, *Awareness*, 57.
9. De Mello and Stroud, *Awareness*, 57–58.

the pride. As we learn to lead in the Lord's way, we learn to roar, protecting those we lead and serving those who follow.

Dr. King warned us that although human nature's weaknesses are fundamental and inescapable, they should never lead individuals to define their value based solely on their imperfections. Instead, we must envelop a deep sense of self-worth, self-love, and self-acceptance—all essential for living a purposeful life. The story of the sheepish lion reminds us that despite our flaws and insecurities, we can and should strive to be our most authentic selves. We can never be anything other than what God created us to be, and that is enough.

I have yet to understand the meaning of all things or the reason for turbulent experiences. Still, through the gospel of Jesus Christ, I have known of God's love for me. Despite my imperfections, He encircles me in the arms of His love. When trials and affliction arise, and they will, we can remain faithful in our inherent potential and the truth that we are children of God and He loves each of us. The confidence that God is mindful of us is valuable when overcoming the malady of fear, for He gives us a sense of worth, belonging, and *at-homeness* in the universe. Dr. King affirmed, "The refusal to be stopped, the 'courage to be,' the determination to go on 'in spite of,' reveal the divine image within us."[10]

The Strength of Leadership

Greenleaf once asked, "What is it like to be strong? While he did not claim a definitive answer, he embraced the role of a seeker on the path of servant-leadership. He acknowledged that strength would manifest itself in different persons in different ways."[11] The strength we accumulate over our lifespan is a byproduct of purposeful awareness. Through conscious awareness, we discover an inner reservoir of strength, which we cannot compress or extract unless we hold a deep conviction of its righteousness.

On the great days, we can be great; on the bad days, we can be greater. Therefore, I urge you to be open to influences and actively seek opportunities that will expand your awareness of life's blessings

10. King and Washington, *A Testament of Hope*, 384.
11. Greenleaf, *On Becoming a Servant Leader*, 96.

and opportunities—problems and weaknesses are opportunities that allow for growth. Greenleaf acknowledged that these opportunities come in unexpected ways, and we can expect benign results except in the following outcomes:

- We will be free—on the inside. The most significant freedom the world cannot imprison, and we will have a better chance of helping build a community where outward freedom accompanies our sense of freedom—on the inside. The search for strength will help us feel free.
- As we cultivate the patience to let our achievements unfold naturally, we will be able to hone our decision-making through self-reflection in all circumstances.
- Active listening will become our forte, enabling us to understand the aspirations and obstacles of those we lead.
- We will learn to critique actions without condemning individuals.
- Offering silent support and unwavering faith will be our way of comforting others in distress.
- Through our mere presence, we will make a meaningful impact wherever we go.[12]

Moments of distinction, where individuals stand out despite their circumstances, mark the emergence of visionary leaders. Dr. King once articulated that as a leader, he understood and knew the problems of the people he was leading. He said, "On the one hand [we] must attempt to change the soul of the individuals so that their societies may be changed. On the other hand, [we] must attempt to change society so that the individual soul will have a change."[13] Dr. King coined the term "double consciousness," or an ability to look at oneself through the eyes of another, as a leadership capacity that develops as leaders become more aware. In his writings from prison, Nelson Mandela vividly portrays the trait of double consciousness through his friendships with fellow inmates Walter Sisulu and Ahmed Kathrada, who fearlessly critiqued his leadership journey:

---

12. Greenleaf, *On Becoming a Servant Leader*, 96–97.
13. Eig, *King: A Life*, 77.

They [Sisulu and Kathrada] never hesitate to criticize me for my mistakes and throughout my political career have served as a mirror through which I can see myself. I wish I could tell . . . more about the courageous band of colleagues with whom I suffered humiliation daily and who nevertheless deport themselves with dignity and determination. I wish I could relate their conversation and banter, their readiness to help in any personal problem suffered by their fellow prisoners so that [we] could judge for [ourselves] the caliber of the men whose loves are being sacrificed on the fiendish altar of color hatred.[14]

Leadership, like history, is guided by spirit and requires a constant awareness of a greater cause—a cause that only the spirit of Christ can help us see. We must constantly ask: What is going on here? What is likely to happen? Greenleaf advocated that *constant* is an important word when developing the characteristic of awareness. Unless leaders consistently ask such questions, they will be unable to respond sharply to the impeding actions of leadership.

Dr. King eloquently declared that overcoming imperfections begins with self-acceptance, and he encouraged every individual to pray this prayer:

Lord, help me accept myself. Every [child of God] should somehow say, I, [Person Doe], accept myself with all my inherited abilities and [imperfections]. I accept those conditions within my environment which cannot be altered or which I cannot control . . . this is a [vigorous] attitude of life. . . . There is within every [child of God] a bit of latent creativity seeking to break forth, and it is often blocked because we are busy trying to be somebody else. [The] first way to overcome [self-doubt]: accept yourself. That means accept your looks. It means accepting your limitations in every area. It means what it says: accept your actual self. And the thing that every individual should pray to the Almighty God for is to give them that sense of acceptance of the actual self with all limitations and with all the endowments that come as the results of being born into this world.[15]

We will never completely fill in the picture we see in our eternal mirror; rather, it will be an ongoing process built upon our testimony. Each day through scripture study, I receive inspiring impressions:

---

14. Mandela, *Conversations with Myself,* 211.
15. Baldwin, *The Arc of Truth,* 112–113.

energizing me to keep working and to edit my self-picture to make it resemble as closely as possible the image of our Savior. As children of God, we can envision our future and strive to shape it, rather than passively allowing our world to shape us. We cannot change our self-image unless we have a deep commitment not to be content with being average. Like grooves in the cement of a road well-traveled, our Father in Heaven provides pathways of light into our lives. Those pathways of light provide impressions and confirmation that we are beautiful, full of potential, and made in the image of God. We must keep our eyes open to that light.

The trap that sometimes brings failure to otherwise successful people is to substitute routine for awareness. Like the complacency of leadership, I encountered similar circumstances on the streets of Los Angeles when catching the bus through different neighborhoods. Occasionally riding the bus to school, I would fall asleep and upon waking, would discover myself in the wrong neighborhood, heightening the likelihood of trouble. I had to be constantly aware of who was around me and which neighborhoods were represented by red or blue flags. Growing up on inner-city streets required constant vigilance for one's conduct and environment. For me, the phrase most intricately connected to complacency in Los Angeles was "to be caught slipping." Without a sense of awareness on streets marred with violence, young people could get caught slipping solely by entering the wrong neighborhood or failing to recognize signs that gang members could be looking for bystanders to rob or to prove their toughness.

In high school, Eric and I often made ourselves aware of our surroundings as we strolled down Slauson Ave near Overhill Park in Los Angeles. We developed a habit of constantly glancing over our shoulders, a common practice for kids navigating the streets of LA, trying not to get caught slipping while traveling to school. One day, as we were crossing the street, a car pulled up directly in front of us. We locked eyes with the passenger reaching under his seat, presumably for a weapon. As he reached for his gun, memories of our school days together flashed before us. He was now a member of the Piru Blood gang. In that brief moment of recognition, our shared past bridged the gap of uncertainty, enabling us to respond without hesitation. Eric and I immediately ran for the nearby alley, weaving between apartment complexes in a frantic attempt to escape.

In a moment of panic, we hit a dead end and were forced to hop a gate leading back to the street. As I leaped over the fence, I watched in slow motion as Eric struggled to climb, his foot slipping on the gate. With adrenaline pumping, I yelled at him to hurry up, every second feeling like a scene out of a movie. We finally made it across the street to the Church's Chicken and waited for our sister Shay to pick us up. Like many other instances, we navigated the thin line of hope and survived another day in a community marked by the violence.

We constantly knew it was important to be aware of our surroundings while considering what situations might arise without notice. Walking into a room, I can still recognize unique circumstances and quickly discern any signs of trouble or suspicion among the people present. Street awareness became second nature to me—noticing individuals who might be carrying firearms, whether it's a visible bulge on their hip or tucked into the small of their back. These are the lessons I pass on to my children, instilling in them the importance of streetwise awareness, always being alert, and never being caught slipping.

Awareness encompasses appreciating the beauty of a sunset, listening to the captivating sounds of the street, and immersing ourselves in the efforts to live life purposely. Far from boring, awareness is the very essence of life itself. We can seek to discern the intricate interplay of situational, historical, religious, and societal influences within the complexities of every experience. As I traversed the streets of Los Angeles I often stumbled along the way, but I gradually accumulated the necessary experience to realize that I was a lion and that I could walk with confidence in the Light of Christ.

CHAPTER 14

Persuasive Leadership and the Illumination of Ideals

Elder Sterling W. Sill said, "The highest form of leadership is the leadership of persuasion, not the leadership of command."[1] Modern paradigms often labeled as "leading" would more accurately be described as simply managing, administering, or, in some instances, manipulating. We must remember that leadership is not defined as dominating or controlling others, but rather as persuading through a spirit of rightness and unyielding faith in people, community, and the realization of an ideal that has yet to occur. The characteristic of persuasion allowed the civil rights movement to transcend traditional barriers of race, class, and prejudiced ideology, thereby broadening its impact and igniting widespread progress that changed the course of humanity's history.

As I studied the various facets of successful change, I was fascinated to see that persuasive leadership is the key to every community or group of people moving forward collectively. If a successful movement is to take place in our current society, we will achieve it through persuasion and by following an unmarked path based on the rightness of a belief or action that may take time to reach.

"The vigor of the action depends upon the power of the motive,"[2] said Frederick Douglass, using the metaphor of idle wheels on a locomotive, which require the impelling force of steam to set the train in motion.[3] Like the wheels needing steam to move forward, leaders

1. Sill, *Leadership*, 91–92.
2. Douglass and Blight, *Frederick Douglass: Speeches & Writings*, 711.
3. Douglass and Blight, *Frederick Douglass: Speeches & Writings*, 358, 711.

require a driving force to propel them toward their vision. Without weakness, there can be no growth; without exertion, no improvement; without refining, no polish; without diligence, no knowledge; without action, no progress; and without opposition, no victory. Douglass encouraged that nothing great comes without effort: "Whether we look to the bright stars in the peaceful blue dome above us, or to the long shore line of the ocean, where land and water maintain their eternal conflict; the lesson taught is the same; that of endless action and reaction. Those beautifully rounded pebbles which [we] gather on the sand and which [we] hold in our hand and marvel at their exceeding smoothness, were chiseled into their varied and graceful forms by the ceaseless action of countless waves."[4]

Aiming at nothing results in hitting everything and wasting valuable energy misuses life's opportunities. However, when goals and ideals flow smoothly between follower and leader, everyone participates by sharing honest work, minimizing the temptation to misuse their power. Douglass proposed that we engage in work for its own sake while advocating that labor is a conscious expression of our ideals, worthy of every effort and dedication.[5] Servant-leaders must place a steady hand on the shoulders of those needing reassurance, working side-by-side to communicate what mere words cannot express.

Douglass also regarded order and systematic effort as critical components of success. He advocated structuring our efforts with a clear plan of action and being disciplined in our approach increase our chances for success. Douglass wrote:

> We succeed, not alone by the laborious exertion of our faculties, be they small or great, but by the regular, thoughtful, and systematic exercise of them. Order, the first law of heaven, is itself power. The battle is nearly lost when [our] lines are in disorder. Regular, orderly, and systematic effort which moves without friction and needless loss of time or power; which has a place for everything and everything in its place; which knows where to begin, how to proceed and where to end, though marked by extraordinary outlay of energy or activity, will work wonders, not only in the matter of accomplishment, but also in the increase of the individual. [Order] will make the weak strong and the

4. Douglass and Blight, *Frederick Douglass: Speeches & Writings*, 704.
5. Douglass and Blight, *Frederick Douglass: Speeches & Writings*, 710–712.

strong [person] stronger; the simple wise and the wise [person], wiser, and will ensure success by the power and influence that belong to habit.[6]

Failure begins when people fail to work together effectively and agreeably, and, as a result, cannot remain unified. If any person or group expects to attain the highest accomplishments, those working together must feel a sense of enjoyment, which will also lead to more agreeable relationships. Even when our backgrounds and the importance of each responsibility differ, our efforts to uplift one another will enable us to become one in Christ.

When individuals from diverse backgrounds gather and learn more about one another, the social constructs that once created division will diminish and give way to a more unified community. During the Montgomery bus boycott, Dr. King emerged as an exemplar of persuasion. For 381 days, the community rallied together, choosing to wield their collective power peacefully yet formidably in a nonviolent protest. Their tireless work and collective footsteps echoed with a resounding message aimed at stirring a dormant sense of moral responsibility within the hearts of all people. As a token of appreciation for the mutual support between their communities, women from the white neighborhoods extended gestures of kindness to Black women by offering them rides to work. King later said of the bus boycott, "We came to see that, in the long run, it is more honorable to walk in dignity than ride in humiliation. So . . . we decided to substitute tired feet for tired souls and walk the streets of Montgomery."[7] Day by day, their boycott revealed a path through the maze of prejudice, culminating in society treating and accepting everyone equally.

Lessons from Grimm's Fairy Tales

Storytelling can inspire our ideals to walk a path not traveled previously. Jacob Grimm, an author, linguist, and folklorist, crafted a collection of enchanting fairy tales in which he skillfully employed imaginary characters to convey valuable lessons to his readers. In one of these captivating tales, Grimm recounts the harrowing story of a stepmother who devised a plan to abandon her two children by

6. Douglass and Blight, *Frederick Douglass: Speeches & Writings*, 710–711.
7. King, *Strength to Love*. 161–162.

intentionally losing them in the vast woods. Unbeknownst to her, the children became aware of her mischievous plan. Guided by the gentle glow of the moonlight, they ventured into the wilderness, collecting a handful of peculiar pebbles that shimmered and radiated the ethereal light surrounding them. As they made their way through the dense forest, they discreetly dropped these pebbles behind them, marking the trail. When they found themselves lost and disoriented along an uncertain path, surrounded by towering trees, they patiently awaited the moon's illuminating light, which revealed the trail of radiant pebbles, leading them safely toward their redemption.

Servant-leadership characteristics symbolize pebbles illuminating a path of hope amidst opposing barriers that prevent progress. Servant-leaders use each characteristic at the appropriate time, revealing the way for those who faithfully embark on the journey of service marked clearly by the teachings of Jesus Christ.

As a society, we think highly of characteristics that teach, train, supervise, and motivate ideals that fall under leadership. There is a companion quality of equal or even greater importance that I dub fellowship. This entire manuscript is a journey mapped out by the teachings of Jesus Christ. How can we avoid costly errors for those who have never traveled on the path? When we journey toward the love of God, we can avoid costly trial and error by not following the delusion that we only learn through first-hand experience. A life misled can occasionally come to its finish pitted and pocketed with unnecessary blemishes.

Our Father in Heaven does not show favoritism; He loves each of us equally. Every soul deserves the opportunity to grow and receive His blessings through faithful service and by walking the path of Christ. Fellowship, in this context, is more than a word; it symbolizes a shared journey where we reach out with open hands and hearts—extending love to family, friends, church members, and those within our community. As we extend the hand of fellowship faithfully leading and following the illuminated pebbles ahead of us we can remember that "the worth of souls is great in the sight of God."[8]

Like the shining pebbles in Grimm's story, a well-lit and inviting path requires the persuasion of faith, where leaders inspire others through a deep conviction in their purpose. Like the moon illuminating

8.   Doctrine and Covenants 18:10.

Persuasive Leadership and the Illumination of Ideals

the pebbles at night, our faith illuminates the path we traverse amidst the darkness of uncertainty. If persuasion is ever to rise over coercive and manipulative leadership, the first initiative is to illuminate our ideals and the path ahead with faith.

Our lives can become so occupied with material gain, fame, power, and contentious living that there is little acclaim for choosing to do right in our communities. That is why it is crucial for anyone embarking on a significant journey to have reliable road maps in their possession. However, what about those who possess these road maps but are incapable or unwilling to follow them? Enlarging the idea of Mr. Grimm's pebbles shining in the moonlight, Jesus Christ clearly marks the highway of life with fluorescent signs that light up as we shine our lights upon them so that we can go through the densest forests or navigate the sharpest turns without danger.

Our Heavenly Father has established signboards with red, amber, and green lights. We have detailed travel specifications conveyed in the scriptures that provide us great opportunities to solve problems as they arise and maintain our course along the covenant path. When we wholeheartedly answer Christ's call, "Come follow me," we can travel along a path that was divinely constructed and proven, where the map reveals our destination before the journey begins.

From the Doctrine and Covenants we learn, "No power or influence can or ought to be maintained . . . only by persuasion, by long-suffering, by gentleness and meekness, and by love unfeigned."[9] Our Savior directs us on the covenant path, leaving behind pebbles that mark the path, representing timeless principles leading us back into His awe-inspiring presence across the vast ocean of thoughts and dreams. The light of Jesus Christ is shining upon the pebbles so we do not lose the way. We can devote our time more fully to developing our fellowship. Only then will we enjoy the benefits made possible by exemplifying the characteristics of servant-leadership. President Howard W. Hunter once said, "God will . . . stand by us forever to help us see the right path, find the right choice, respond to [His] voice, and feel the influence of His undeniable spirit. His gentle, peaceful

---

9. Doctrine and Covenants 121.

persuasion to do right and find joy will be with us so long as time shall last or the earth shall stand."[10]

This Is Where I Stand

Despite the mantle of leadership placed on the shoulders of those who already carry more than their share of responsibility, there is only one choice to lift where we stand. With a resounding yes, this is where I stand: Those who think of themselves as good must become better; they must become strong, confronting, choosing, pursuing, and becoming more aware of the possibilities to choose righteousness.

The phrase "this is where I stand" conveys that there is inherent strength within each beloved child of God to choose where they will stand. A leader's persuasive ability recognizes and respects the integrity of the person or people they seek to lead and the place where they have chosen to make their stand. Along every journey, however, there will be moments when a leader must demonstrate courage by carefully selecting the ideal time and best opportunity to persuade. Nelson Mandela believed that if leaders possessed eloquence and had strong intuition about the correctness of an idea, they would be driven to confront the situation, firmly declaring, "This is where I stand."[11]

In a letter dated April 27, 1980, Mandela beautifully articulated the internal struggle we face when contemplating the importance of standing firm in our ideals, and the delicate balance of knowing when to push forward or step back, to realize an ideal at an opportune moment in history. He wrote, "As I scribble these hurried lines, the heart and the head, the blood and the brain are fighting each other, the one [yearning] idealistically for all the good things we miss in life, the head resisting and guided by the realities in which we live out our lives."[12]

Mandela's poignant reflection while in prison highlights the inherent conflict within us as we grapple with our convictions and the need to navigate the practical realities of our experiences, while still striving to bring about positive change. His words illustrate the struggle between the heart's idealistic aspirations and the mind's pragmatic

---

10. Howard W. Hunter, "The Golden Thread of Choice," 18.
11. Mandela, *Conversation with Myself,* 74.
12. Mandela, *Conversation with Myself,* 222.

considerations as we strive for better families, communities, and improved conditions for the underprivileged.

When we find ourselves and a purpose for which to stand, we shall have the opportunity to drink the waters of wholeness. Like Mandela, we can seek the light in the rightness of our choices, accept responsibility for the inward journey, and convey courage in the face of opposition. In those brief moments of clarity, we will delight as we inwardly acclaim, "This is where I stand."

One of the most significant testing grounds in decision-making is satisfying opposing beliefs. Effective persuasion eases conflict when we try to state our understanding of the other person's position to their satisfaction, and then understand as much of their position as we agree with. Then, and not until then, we can state our own viewpoint. In leadership, persuading others to adopt a shared understanding requires finesse and a deep understanding, while also accepting differing perspectives.

Nelson Mandela remarked how we can keep ourselves on the path by not floundering in self-doubt, keeping our vision pointed toward the sun and our feet moving toward the brightness of hope. He stated:

> As a leader, one must sometimes take actions that are unpopular, or whose results will not be known for years to come. There are victories whose glory lies only in the fact that they are known to those who within them . . . where [we] must find consolation in being true to [our] ideal, even if no one else knows of it.[13]

Greenleaf said, "People who require tested or proven models in order to act rarely originate anything."[14] The imaginative person who takes risks by acting on a belief in new or untested ideas are the people who move the world along. Consider Jesus Christ, who moved along the shores of Galilee, serving and leading on the belief that the chiefest among them was a servant, and that loving one another would bring all persons closer to God's redeeming love, changing the trajectory of history, serving as the Redeemer of our imperfect world.

---

13. Mandela, *Long Walk to Freedom*, 356.
14. Greenleaf, *On Becoming a Servant Leader*, 127.

The Gradual Path to Change

Change emerges out of the blending of both actions and resistance to actions, moving our society forward or backward as we seek to change society through a gradual process of persuasion. Elder David A. Bednar eloquently described the harmonious interplay between action and resistance, using the metaphor of watching night turn into morning. He detailed:

> Recall the slow and almost imperceptible increase in light on the horizon. In contrast to turning on light in a dark room, the light from the rising sun [does] not immediately burst forth. Rather, gradually, and steadily the intensity of the light [increases], and the darkness of night [is] replaced by the radiance of morning. Eventually, the sun [does] dawn over the skyline. But the visual evidence of the sun's impending arrival [is] apparent hours before the sun actually [appears] over the horizon.[15]

Elder Bednar characterized the experience of witnessing night transform into day as a gradual discernment of subtle light. Transformation also gradually unfolds over time. We can start to perceive the radiant essence of Christ's light as we steadfastly serve and lead, giving faith to our ideas that arrive as softly as whispers amidst the clamor of discord.

Greenleaf defined this gradualism as more of a disposition than a method: "One is comfortable with a slow pace and accepts taking opportunities when they come, rather than trying to batter down offending walls that are not ready to give way."[16] The gradual increase of light emanating from the rising sun is like receiving a message from God "line upon line, precept upon precept," until our ideals lead toward change.[17]

It is easy to accept that we cannot quickly do away with the invasive effects of hatred. Still, we can give heed to the words of John Milton: "They also serve who only stand and wait."[18] As I traversed the streets of Los Angeles, I waited for the rising of the sun upon the dark corners of Slauson Avenue to reveal rays of opportunity for my brother Eric and me. Change for us was gradual, from days to months, and months to years.

15. Bednar, "The Spirit of Revelation," 1.
16. Greenleaf, *Seeker and Servant*, 68.
17. 2 Nephi 28:30.
18. Greenleaf, *Seeker and Servant*, 68.

Like gradual change, our persistent effort and influence will eventually illuminate the path of transformation by swaying hearts toward a new dawn of understanding. Greenleaf advocated that "the gradualists, because they are slow and willing to wait, run the risk [faithfully] of being mistaken for do-nothingers. But the difference is profound. The do-nothinger does not ever intend to push the wall over."[19] A gradualist like Dr. King fully intended to push over the wall of injustice when it was prudent to do so nonviolently, which took a long time. Sometimes our efforts, like Dr. King's, become tiresome as we lose strength in trying to batter down walls that do not want to give, but we must remind ourselves that change is gradual and that we may not witness the cracks in the wall of injustice for years or even decades. Like Dr. King, we passionately fight injustice, knowing that we are fighting for the future generations who come after us with their own dreams to fulfill.

Greenleaf posed the question, "How can we discern the skill of influence related to gradualism?" He concluded that "the gradualists stand tall in history as great achievers, with little or no negative consequences attached to their efforts."[20] True strength lies not in physical prowess but in the influence of actions. When we successfully persuade others to share our dreams and plans of action, we cause no harm to human dignity, physical coercion is nonexistent, and trust grows through agreement. We receive the blessings of change gradually, spontaneously, like the breath of the morning wind gently moving us forward.

The lives of Dr. King and Booker T. Washington exemplified the gradualism as they saw the power in human potential and sought to improve the human condition. King would not have had the place in history he now occupies, and the civil rights movement would not have had the influence on our current day if he had not pounded on the walls of injustice with the light touch of persuasion. Washington would not have helped the Tuskegee students realize their potential if they had given up on the gradual brick-baking experiment that served white and Black communities. Washington understood that actual change emerges through consistent effort by educating ourselves over time, throughout generations. King's dream was not for his present day; it was a belief in human dignity, a vision he aspired for future

19. Greenleaf, *Seeker and Servant*, 67–87.
20. Greenleaf, *Seeker and Servant*, 109–154.

generations. The invisible chains of oppression may persist across generations, but the eternal principles of love and service will endure forever. Both men will be remembered in the annals of history as servant-leaders from different eras, laboring to undo the chains of oppression.

Prospective servant-leaders wait in their fields of shared accomplishment, with a concentration apt to witness small miracles that the casual observer might fail to see. Rather than committing to the quick fix to solve problems, they will at least reflect on the slow, but sometimes more effective, gradual approach to upend injustice, allowing the least privileged to become wiser, freer, more autonomous, taller in spirit, and more likely to become servants themselves. With love as a compass, servant-leadership illuminate the path for those committed to service and charity inspired by Jesus Christ's teachings. Leadership, rooted in persuasion rather than coercion, empowers individuals to embark on their journey with a strong sense of purpose and commitment.

Let us demonstrate the faith of Abraham, who was one hundred years old and believed in the hope that he might become the father of many nations according to the promise given to him by God. "And not being weak in faith, he considered his body to be strong. He staggered not at the promise of God but was strong in faith, giving glory to God."[21] Abraham was fully persuaded of the promise given to him by our Heavenly Father because of faith. We become fully persuaded through faith in Jesus Christ. Although God's promises may seem impossible, belief in the power of God through Jesus Christ will allow us to overcome the impossible with a desire for our posterity and future generations to achieve their heart's aspirations.

---

21. Romans 4:18–21.

CHAPTER 15

Envisioning the Promised Land: A Journey toward Servant-Leadership and Conceptualization

Servant-leaders emerge from history motivated by their unwillingness to tolerate hate, inequality, and racial or religious bigotry. Two months before the 1963 March on Washington, Dr. Martin Luther King Jr. delivered an early rendition of his historic Detroit speech, incorporating the refrain "I have a dream" to catapult his message toward his visionary conclusion:

> I have a dream this afternoon that the [peoplehood] of [humanity] will become a reality in this day. And with this faith I will go out and carve a tunnel of hope through the mountain of despair. . . . With this faith, we will be able to achieve this new day when all of God's children . . . join hands and sing with the Negroes in the spiritual of old: Free at last, free at last, thank God almighty we are free at last.[1]

The crowd roared their praise, affirming their dreams for a future marked by freedom and optimism, illuminated by the Light of Christ.

Throughout history, inspired leaders have understood that an equitable society requires bridging the gap between hope and achievement. When Dr. Martin Luther King Jr. gave his famous "I Have a Dream" speech, he declared, "I have a dream that my four little children will one day live in a nation where they will not be judged by the color of their skin but by the content of their character."[2] Dr.

---

1. Eig, *King: A Life*, 322.
2. King and Washington, *A Testament of Hope*, 219.

King's words not only conceptualized his vision for the 250,000 in attendance at the Lincoln Memorial—all imagining a glorious image of a future based in love and equality—but also for the multitudes who continue to hear his words.

King exemplified the ideals of servant-leadership and clearly modeled the journey we must make in order to create change. Servant-leaders, with their clear sense of purpose, can define leadership challenges and bring vision to organizations and communities threatened by the myopia of inequality. Their vision contours a specific path for future generations to follow along the sunlit path toward God's love.

Five years later, however, in Dr. King's final speech, "I Have Been to the Mountaintop," he tempered his earlier predictions with a poignant recognition of his own mortality, where he himself would not see that future.

> We have some difficult days ahead. But it really does not matter with me now because I've been to the mountaintop. And I do not mind. Like anybody, I would like to live a long life. Longevity has its place. But I'm not concerned about that now. I just want to do God's will. And He's allowed me to go up to the mountain. And I have looked over. And I have seen the Promised Land. I may not get there with you. But I want you to know tonight that we, as a people, will get to the Promised Land![3]

Dr. King's words intended to conceptualize a brighter future filled with hope, yet interwoven with a sense of realism. He acknowledged his limitations and the inevitability of his death, allowing his listeners to witness the dream he had envisioned. Similar to Dr. King's approach, in leadership, vision is a picture of where we will end up—like a sketch of an idea we have imagined.

When I was down-and-out on the streets of Los Angeles, every morning, I encountered an obscure path, navigating the seldom treaded avenues of West Imperial Highway, where numerous side roads led to various dead ends. I had an invisible belief, a faithful dream of attending a university on the wings of scholarship. With football's possibilities and my perseverance and practice, my destination reachable.

Whenever we aspire to succeed, we take a motive, and by its enthusiasm, we can propel ourselves toward accomplishment. Sports became

---

3. King and Washington, *A Testament of Hope*, 286

my armor, shielding me from gang retaliation by focusing me on the dreams I held in my hands. As I honed my skills on the field, traversing every inch of turf, I realized that I could visualize and practice each day without faltering, fulfilling my vision of accomplishment. Every night, I imagined every move or goal I wanted to achieve. The next day, I would recall the moves and steps toward each specific goal I imagined the night before. Our imagination can combine individual experiences with those of others, adding hope and painting distant objectives so vividly in our consciousness that they seem even more significant than our immediate goals, illuminating the way forward.

We must learn to look ahead, think about the future, and hold fast against the illusions that make distant objects look unimportant. As we eventually stand on the horizon and cast our gaze behind, we will realize that what once lay ahead has now assumed paramount importance. Elder Sterling W. Sill once said, "The imagination is capable of running ahead and focusing the spotlight on the future so that it stands out like a beacon to light our way. . . . We need vision; we need understanding; we need appreciation. We do not see far enough, clearly enough, or soon enough. . . . Vision says, 'I see it.' Faith says, 'I believe it.' [Diligence] says, 'I will achieve it.'"[4]

When we see ourselves through the lens of Christ's light, we begin to look beyond the limitations of circumstance and see ourselves resurrected, perfected, and glorified by the hands of God. Once our minds expand and our understanding of what is possible broadens, we will never return to the limited thinking that restrained us. I never thought I would become a member of The Church of Jesus Christ of Latter-day Saints. Now my steps all go forward, and my weaknesses are now strengths—never looking back.

John C. Maxwell recounted that a great vision begins with a clear picture witnessed in people's minds that mobilizes them to join a leader's cause:

> A leader's vision of the distant horizon allows people to see the heights of their possibilities. While it is true that the individuals, [we] connect with will determine how far they want to go, it is [our] responsibility as [leaders] to put plenty of sky into the picture . . . A blind man's world is bounded by the limits of his touch; an ignorant man's world by the

---

4. Sill, *Laws of Success*, 206.

limits of his knowledge . . . As visionary [leaders] paint a picture of the future for people, [they] can expand their horizons.[5]

Every vision has challenges, especially as we seek to help others see their own horizon of possibility. A leader's purpose is to keep hope alive in the hearts and minds of those they serve. A leader must "study it out in [their] mind; then they must ask if it be right, and if it is right, God will cause that their bosom shall burn within them; [and] they shall feel that it is right."[6]

Colonel Ingersoll, a renowned orator from the late nineteenth century, shared valuable insights on becoming a visionary speaker, highlighting the influence of persuasive and inspirational speech:

> Behind the art of speaking must be the power to think [conceptualize]. Without thoughts, words are empty purses. Most people imagine that almost any words uttered in a loud voice and accompanied by appropriate gestures, constitute an oration. I would advise young [leaders] to study their subject, to find what others had thought, to look at it from all sides. Then I would tell [them] to write out [their] thoughts or to arrange them in their mind, so that they would know exactly what [they] wanted to say. Waste no time on the 'how' until you are satisfied with the 'what'. . . . Then you can think about the tone, emphasis, and gestures. But if you really understand and believe what you say, emphasis, tone, and gesture will more or less take care of themselves. All of these should come from inside that the thought will be in perfect harmony with the feelings.[7]

Dr. King's speeches articulately blended harmony and feelings. His iconic "I've Been to the Mountaintop" speech exemplifies the effective and innate use of gestures, voice, and body language to convey authority. Throughout the speech, King used gestures to emphasize his ideals and the unity of civil rights, using sweeping arm movements and raising his hands to symbolize ascending the mountaintop. His body language played a significant role as well; he leaned forward to implore the audience, leaned back as if considering the weight of his words, and occasionally closed his eyes as if lost in thought or prayer.

---

5. Maxwell, *Developing the Leader within You 2.0*, 181–185.
6. Doctrine and Covenants 9:8.
7. Sill and McCormick, *Lessons from Great Lives,* 89–90.

King's voice ranged from soft and introspective to booming and enthusiastic, employing dramatic pauses and repetition, reiterating phrases such as "I just want to do God's will" to convey his message. His emotional, determined voice resounded, building the intensity of his words, "And I have looked over. And I have s-e-e-e-e-n, the Promised Land." His voice ascended with a searching intensity as he reached the pinnacle of the word "seen," lingering momentarily before descending with a sense of hesitation. Then, with a sudden overflow of conviction, it landed firmly on the "Promised Land," as though discovering a friend in the vast expanse of possibilities, leaving a lasting impact on listeners past and present.[8]

Ingersoll's oratory advice also included the effectiveness of language, like the ideals put into words in Dr. King's speeches:

> The [individual] who aspires to become an orator should study language. [They] should know the deeper meaning of words. [They] should understand the vigor and velocity of verbs and the color of adjectives. [They] should know how to sketch a scene and so paint a picture with words and feelings that it is given life and action. [Rightness] requires lights and shadows, and now and then a flash of lightning may illuminate the intellectual sky. [A visionary] should be a poet and a dramatist, a painter, and an actor. [They] should become familiar with the great poetry and fiction that is so rich in heroic deeds . . . a student of Shakespeare. . . . [And finally] they should read and devour the great plays and should learn the art of expression and comprehension with all of the secrets of the head and the heart.[9]

The gestures and voice in Dr. King's speeches exuded a fervent dedication to the civil rights movement, derived from an all-abounding faith that all people are children of God, swathed in a single garment of destiny.

In her book *My Life with Martin Luther King Jr.*, Coretta Scott King beautifully captured King's enthusiastic spirit as she recounted his final speech delivered at Mason Temple in Memphis, Tennessee, on April 3, 1968:

> So intense was the audience's emotional response to Martin's words, so high was his own exaltation responding to their excitement, the action

8. Branch, *At Canaan's Edge*, 758.
9. Sill and McCormick, *Lessons from Great Lives*, 90.

and reaction of one to the other, that he was overcome; he broke off there. He intended to finish the quotation—His truth is marching on. But he could not.[10]

Having envisioned his ascent to the mountaintop, Dr. King sat, his body drenched in perspiration. The Mason temple was pulsating with faith, with hope surging through the corridors. His fellow preachers huddled around him to sustain his courage, their presence serving as a collective source of strength, fortifying his dreams. Tears flowed as they congratulated him on his thunderous conclusion, a mere hundred words emanating the power and witness of a vision beyond their dreams. Those who witnessed King's countenance declared that he surpassed mortality, encapsulating the essence of freedom as he gazed simultaneously forward and backward, transcending the boundaries of time.

Recounting the details of his speech, King drew parallels between his leadership and the biblical story of Moses. Like Moses, who stood upon Mount Nebo and caught a glimpse of the promised land beyond the Jordan River. Dr. King witnessed the same promised land, passing away before he could see his people begin to enter it. He climbed to the heights of justice and left all hateful prejudice below while orating and envisioning the golden dawn of a grander day.

When we reflect on historical successes, we remember the words or ideas leaders use to vividly capture their aspirations. Servant-leaders like King are deeply moved by collective accomplishments, advocating for the marginalized. Like sculptors, they stand by the block of stone. Every chisel is for a purpose, and shape soon begins to appear.

Conceptualizing an Ideal

The conceptualizer is neither Knower nor Doer, but Sayer, painting a picture of significance with the mind instead of the hands. A leader who can conceptualize is like a poet, one who traverses the whole scale of experience with an ideal that transcends the barriers of humanity and time. Dr. King's ideals soared higher than other leaders of his time, to a softer tenderness, a holier ardor, a grander daring to climb the peak of the mountain tops toward the promised land. His

---

10. Coretta Scott King, *My Life with Martin Luther King, Jr.*, 292.

"I Have a Dream" speech granted equality to all of humanity in the sight of God, and his words can still make the heart race and the eyes glisten with hope, filling the air with great dreams of possibility.

Greenleaf asked us to evaluate our ideas through a broader lens: "Does the idea have a healing or civilizing influence? Does it nurture the servant motive in people, favor their growth as persons, and help them distinguish those who serve from those who destroy?"[11] Conceptualization enables a leader to view today's events in the context of long sweeps of time and then creatively project them into the indefinite future. Our day-to-day movement toward change requires seeing the whole from the perspective of history—past and future—to articulate and adjust goals by foreseeing possibilities a long way ahead.

Dr. King dynamically conceptualized ideas, using symbolic words as mediators between opposing beliefs. His oft-repeated mantra, "I have been to the mountaintop," merges faith and action, embodying faith in a brighter future. Like a poet, King's words resonated as an attainable ideal that, for a moment, felt real, "distilling upon our spirits as the dews of heaven" inaccessible to hate.[12] Servant-leaders who can conceptualize the steps toward a goal impart ideals that become real, and the impressions of their vision fall like summer rain, blossoming the human spirit. Even if the goal is a long-range, generational one, King's words still carry us toward the realization of the promised land conceptualizing the nuance, inclusivity and diversity of God's love.

Our lives are not fully realized and cannot be until we achieve the dreams given to us by a spirit of hope. When one is surrounded by the darkness of poverty, words of hope can become rays of light. The poet's life is not poetic, and a leader's life is not a journey of leading, but a life of serving. When leading in the Lord's way, our reward is not self-empowerment; instead, it is a magic flare of imagination, an alluring glimpse of an unbelievable ideal only recognized in the radiance of God's love. King conceptualized the promised land in the following way:

> We have been forced to a point where we are going to have to grapple with the problems that [humanity] has been trying to grapple with through history. . . . Survival demands that we grapple with them. . . . We are

11. Greenleaf, *The Power of Servant Leadership*, 114–115.
12. Doctrine and Covenants 121:45.

determined to be people. We are saying that we are God's children. And if we are God's children, we do not have to live like we are forced to live. . . . It means that we've got to stay together. We've got to stay together and maintain unity. . . . Either we go up together, or we go down together. . . . Let us rise up tonight with a greater readiness. Let us stand with a greater determination.[13]

Dr. King's words speak to every generation and can be put into two short meaningful words: Go forward. To change unfavorable situations, servant-leadership inspires us to get up on our feet and go to work by leading. The Lord said to Moses and the children of Israel, "Go forward." The promised land, he argued from the mountain of hope, was attainable for every child of God, never to be denied, and our freedom rings from that eternal reality. Like everything else in life, our own ability to move forward with purposeful hope is unlimited and unfinished. When taking intuitive steps forward, the cause of our leadership is faith, as a risk on a vision—a promised land, a significant dream, beyond the horizon of possibilities.

Dr. King dared to trust in the eternal tendency for the good of the whole, which he believed was present in every moment of our lives. While power is narrow and selfish, the beauty of God's love is broad and beneficial. Unconditional love can be discovered by accepting whatever comes our way, intended or not, when we make Christ's pure love our priority. Through our service to others, we realize that love and God's goodness are inextricably woven into the histories of time. The great trick in life is to learn to ascend the ladder of possibility through conceptualizing. We gain the ability to lead in the Lord's way when we learn to see symbolically, to mount in our minds a vision that becomes a reality. A sudden ascent in the road reveals dreams of the promised land, and all the summits become accessible through imagination.

When a visionary leader possesses the attributes of compelling speech, heartfelt persuasion, and the ability to envision bright ideas, their ideals becomes a panoramic experience, where words reveal a picture in a single instant. Leaders traverse the side road, compelling others to join their cause, skillfully outlining an ideal and patiently painting it with words breathing life into dreams. As we envision individuals in our communities adorned in white, we align with the gospel of Jesus Christ,

13. King and Washington, *A Testament of Hope*, 280.

presenting opportunities for redemption. The doors of opportunity will not yield until forcibly opened by our effort and the work we perform. We must learn to stand on our own feet, dream great dreams, and rely on the merits of Christ to improve our lives.

Translating Vision into Action

Jesus Christ, our leading exemplar of conceptualized leadership, used everything around Him and lived experiences for the most significant purpose. Rather than resorting to ambitious speeches or elaborate displays, He focused on the familiar, weaving thoughtful lessons into everyday experiences that resonated with His listeners. The stories of the prodigal son, the Good Samaritan, and the lost coin exemplify how He transformed humble stories into uplifting and beautiful teachings.

In the parable of the prodigal son, Jesus turned the commonplace theme of family relationships into a powerful story about forgiveness, redemption, and unconditional love. When the wayward son returned home after squandering his inheritance, his father didn't react with anger or judgment. Instead, he welcomed him with open arms, threw a feast, and celebrated his return. This simple yet profound example depicted the boundless love and forgiveness that God extends to those who repent, giving hope to anyone who feels lost or distant.

The Good Samaritan took an ordinary travel scenario and transformed it into a lesson on compassion that broke down societal barriers. As Jesus narrated the story, His listeners could picture the dusty road, the injured traveler, and the religious leaders who chose to pass by. But the unexpected twist—a Samaritan, despised by the Jews, stopping to help—challenged social prejudices and redefined what it meant to be a good neighbor.

The parable of the lost coin adds another layer to the theme of seeking and valuing what is lost. Jesus spoke of a woman who had ten silver coins and lost one. Rather than dismissing the lost coin as unimportant, she lit a lamp, swept her house, and searched carefully until she found it. When she did, she called her friends and neighbors to celebrate. Her story underscores the diligence needed to recover what is lost, highlighting the sense of accomplishment that comes with restoring something precious. Through this parable, Jesus conveyed that every soul is worth seeking, and the happiness in reclaiming the lost is immeasurable.

By following the example of Jesus Christ, even the most everyday experiences can become sources of inspiration. The story of Bartimaeus, a blind man from the New Testament, is a prime example of the significance of vision and our capacity to conceptualize it. Bartimaeus, a blind man, sat begging by the roadside outside Jericho's city. When Bartimaeus heard that Jesus of Nazareth was about to pass by, he began calling for Christ to have pity on him. Jesus asked to speak with Bartimaeus, and when the blind man stood before him, Jesus asked, "What would you that I should do unto you?" He replied, "I would that I might receive my sight."[14] Bartimaeus's request was for that which we all need most: vision—both literally and for the ability to envision our ideas before aspiring to lead.

So many of us have eyes that fail to see or witness the many opportunities that could lead to change. The best way to see things accurately and clearly is to attempt to look at them from God's point of view. In revisiting the story of Bartimaeus on the roadside outside the city of Jericho, we remember that Bartimaeus first prayed humbly to God, asking to receive sight. He conceptualized his dream, and then asked directly for its fruition. One of the most telling lines in all the scriptures was spoken by a blind man after encountering Jesus, said, "Whereas I was blind, now I see."[15]

The phrase "now I see" summarizes the moment we conceptualize a vision and plan for success, individually or collectively. One of the most significant accomplishments in life is to develop the ability to clearly see those reflections that have to do with our redemption and accomplishment. Jesus's reference to those who had eyes yet could not see reminds us that we must appreciate the beauties of our individual journeys and realize the diverse ways in which we experience God's blessings in life.

Sometimes, we must close our eyes to see more clearly what is most meaningful in the Light of Christ. A phrase from the song "The Blind Plowman" sings, "God took away my eyes that my soul might see." Physical limitations or hardships can help us gain a better understanding of our spiritual selves. Losing his physical sight allowed the blind

---

14. Mark 10:45–55.
15. John 9:25.

plowman to see the world differently and focus on what was more important than what he could see with his natural eyes.

As Paul stated, "Faith is the [assurance] of things hoped for, the evidence of things not seen."[16] When teaching the poor in spirit, the Book of Mormon prophet Alma said, "Faith is not to have a perfect knowledge of things; therefore if ye have faith ye hope for things which are not seen, which are true. . . . If ye will awake and arouse your faculties, even to an experiment upon my words, and exercise a particle of faith, yea, even if ye can no more than desire to believe, let this desire work in you."[17] By exercising faith, we express our longings for those tender mercies not yet visible to us.

---

16. Hebrews 11:1.
17. Alma 32:5–23.

CHAPTER 16

Overcoming and Leading with Foresight

The greatness of an artist's vision can extract inspiration from experiences before giving it life. Similarly, a leader's vision must be supple and adaptive, anticipating future opportunities. Influential leaders demonstrate two intangible skills: intuition of the unknowable and anticipation of the unforeseeable. Like an artist who uses intuition to bring a vision to reality, leaders leverage intuition to chart a path forward using foresight to sketch their future, creating something unique from only a sliver of possibility. A leader's vision, like the artist's, is a testament to an ability to see beyond the present into the future, revealing the way for those they serve.

While discouragement and opposition will test the authenticity of every vision, a leader who believes that God inspires their vision will develop resilience. A myopic view of life without faith in God's vast presence impairs our vision, limiting our ability to see into the future and encouraging us not to cross a bridge until we reach it. However, history's most visionary dreamers, leaders, and thinkers have always forged ahead, boldly crossing those bridges to success well before they encountered them. Confidence in a leader is partly based on the assurance that they can remain stable, poised, and resilient during times of stress, paving the way for more effective solutions and substantial progress.

Greenleaf defined foresight as the ability to anticipate what will happen by staying ahead of the curve and taking precautionary steps toward collective and individual success. Leaders—teachers, coaches, and mentors working with young people living on the fringes—must be aware that they have grown numb to the pain of setbacks and to witnessing others' successes while themselves falling behind. These losses chip away at their dreams and create towering barriers obstructing their view of new opportunities. These recurring losses introduce the bitter sting of defeat early, but inspired leaders can prompt them to reassess their perspective and find a way to conquer the formidable mountains of failure, unveiling unexplored horizons.

As we faithfully follow the covenant path and strive to uphold our responsibilities to lead, we can heed the words of Book of Mormon prophet Nephi when he said, "I will go and do the things that the Lord has commanded, for I know that the Lord giveth no commandments unto the children of men, save he prepare a way for them, that they may accomplish the things he hath commanded them."[1] His words convey a spirit of "yes" to life, "yes" to God, and "yes" to the opportunity to lead. This spirit of "yes" empowers us to withstand life's challenges and lead in the Lord's way. We can unthinkingly say "no," but before we can faithfully say "yes," we must clarify, organize, examine, and think as follows:

- Get the facts
- Clarify our goals
- Determine the cost
- Appraise the benefits
- Consider the alternatives
- And make the decision

Our ability to lead improves when we plan, organize, motivate and anticipate our aspirations. As prospective leaders, we must be intolerant of forgetting, sidestepping, or delaying opportunities to minister, serve, and achieve. We say "no" by procrastination and indecision. Despite our circumstances, we say "yes" when we foresee our goals and put forth our best efforts to achieve them—knowing that the Lord will prepare a way for our success.

---

1. 1 Nephi 1:7

The Foresight of Survival: Leadership in the Streets of LA

As I peered out the bus window on Imperial Highway, blue Chuck Taylors marked the spot where a tragic youth lay dead on the corner, ignored by the passing cars whose occupants offered only fleeting glances. Amidst the impoverished streets lined with liquor stores, life continued its relentless pace, indifferent to the loss of a young life. Rick Sweat stood at the corner of Slauson Avenue, clutching his brown bag, hiding a worn tall-can of Old English and urging every passing youth to "stay in school." His message, born from harsh lessons learned surviving in the hood, resonated with the weight of experience. In his modest home off Denker Avenue in Los Angeles, Joey Hickman always kept his doors locked tight, cautioning visitors to "keep those roaches out." His words served as a warning for local gangs invading the homes of those who failed to anticipate the menaces of street life.

Joey's admonition was evident on the tragic day when a shooting broke the hard-won but fragile sense of community, when our friend Fred Martin, his eight-year-old son, and Joey were cleaning Fred's garage on 109th Street in LA. We had all grown up together since eighth grade, graduated from Westchester High School in 2001, and played football together from Westchester to LA Southwest. As they stood outside the garage, two unassuming gunmen approached on foot, unleashing a barrage of bullets toward them. Without hesitation, Fred shielded his son from harm, taking the bullets himself, while Joey, too, was struck numerous times as they both hit the ground. In that chaotic blur, bullets tore through lives without discrimination, claiming Fred's life as he selflessly protected his son. Recounting the tragedy, Joey said, "Fred ran straight for his son. . . . He thought of his son before he thought of himself."[2] This harrowing event epitomized the harsh reality many face in the streets of LA, where survival often hinges on split-second decisions. No one can fully comprehend the leadership required to navigate such bleak circumstances.

Fred's sister said, "If what happened on 109th Street had happened in a war, my brother would be receiving a Congressional Medal of

---

2.   Allen, Fatal Shooting sends shudders through a reborn Inglewood.

Honor."[3] But in marginalized populations, a father's martyr-like death goes unseen and unrecognized outside the community. Growing up in Los Angeles, we obtained our strength from our shared struggles outside the margins, relying on our instincts and foresight to guide us through the slow-motion chaos of life.

When the bullets of adversity begin to bombard us, how many of us have the courage and foresight to protect those in immediate danger? Leaders with forethought see danger from around the corner of opposition, like Fred, who gave his life protecting his son. Joey now watches proudly as his oldest son excels as an athlete and an honor student at Inglewood High School. We came of age amongst a dying breed where leadership was scarce. Growing up in LA as Black men often felt like being an endangered species—a joke we made with far too much truth behind it. Words fail to capture the depth of the hardships many of us faced and continue to face. These experiences instilled life lessons of foresight, allowing those who encounter failure or loss to leave disappointment behind and look forward with hope for better days ahead.

The Leader's Time Machine

Looking at the world in the rearview mirror, hindsight is peering into the past, trying to make sense of where I have been. On the other hand, insight gazes at the present, understanding the intricacies of our current circumstances. When I shift my focus to foresight, however, it is as though I am driving ahead, using my headlights to illuminate the path into the unknown future. Focusing on foresight encourages us to navigate the less traveled road ahead of us carefully and deliberately, as we steer through unfamiliar terrain.

Elder Sterling W. Sill foretold that as leaders fail to see in advance and look ahead, foresight could become a lost skill in today's fast-paced world.[4] Jesus, too, encouraged foresight when He said, "For which of you, intending to build a tower, sitteth not down first, and counted the cost, whether [they] have sufficient to finish it?"[5] As Jesus taught, careful planning and forethought are necessary for success in any

---

3. Allen, Fatal Shooting sends shudders through a reborn Inglewood.
4. Sill, *Leadership II*, 68, 373–374.
5. Luke 14:28.

endeavor, whether building a tower or leading a community. It allows us to avoid unnecessary risks and capitalize on opportunities others overlook. Successful leadership invites all to participate in a worthy cause by painting a picture of a brighter tomorrow that connects our deepest identities, excites unlimited possibility, and persuades all toward action.

The routine of noting and writing mental errors on paper may help us develop the ability to lead with forethought. Elder Sterling W. Sill eloquently stated that while reading helps one learn, writing makes a person precise. When we think constructively and journal our experiences, lessons become indelibly imprinted upon our minds. When those experiences recur, we can avoid making the same mistakes. Foresight not only reduces or even eliminates failure; it makes success more attainable. If we can determine what creates success, we can reproduce those factors and embolden future successes.

Leadership foresight was evident in Abraham Lincoln's life. When he prepared for a debate, he spent three-fourths of his time figuring out what his opponent would say and only one-fourth thinking of what he would say. Lincoln knew that one of the predictable precursors to defeat was an unanticipated surprise arising from a lack of foresight. Lincoln strove to prepare himself for every eventuality and to block every possibility of escape for his opponent. When we prepare diligently, we increase our chances for success exponentially.

Successful leadership requires a sense of the unknowable, preparation for the unexpected, and the ability to foresee the unforeseeable acquired through lived experiences. Leaders who lack foresight are reactive instead of leading with anticipation, causing them to lose their authority. In practical leadership matters, where there may be no verifiable evidence of the right actions, it is crucial to assess the potential consequences of every decision. Elder Sterling W. Sill supported the idea of foresight:

> Our minds are equipped to serve us as a sort of mental time machine. In thought, we can go backward or forward across time. . . . The ability to see what is ahead, we call foresight, vision, and imagination. The process of looking back we refer to as reflection, meditation, or consideration. . . . When we desire to recall some important past experience, we let our minds go back to the time of its actual

occurrence. Then we relive this event, its vividness, and influence upon us is rewarded and revitalized.[6]

In an instant, we can return to the past and become inspired by a highlight reel of our most remarkable experiences. Alternatively, we can project ourselves into the future and visualize our accomplishments beforehand. The ideas we generate from that knowledge can enable us to approach unforeseen challenges with confidence.

Drawing in the Sand: Reflect, Withdraw, and Lead

The New Testament story of Jesus and the woman charged with adultery teaches us about the importance of withdrawal and return. The mob challenged, "This woman was caught in the act of adultery. The law of Moses says to stone her. What do you say?"[7] Jesus withdrew and sat quietly, drawing in the sand, reflecting and listening. Through this deliberate withdrawal, He gained the forethought required to respond with compassion: "Let him who is without sin among you cast the first stone."[8] Exercising the confidence and patience to withdraw and reflect before making important decisions allows prospective leaders to tap into their intuition for better-informed choices.

We witness Jesus as a leader. He had a goal—to bring, among other blessings, more compassion to people's lives. A leader must possess an armor of confidence when facing the unknown—more so than those who follow their leadership. Having confidence stems partly from anticipation and preparation but also from the belief that one can maintain composure in real-life situations, allowing the creative process to thrive. We witness Jesus as a leader. He had a goal—to bring, among other blessings, more compassion to people's lives. Jesus's words in the incident of the adulterous women have remained relevant and compelling for over two thousand years and are worth repeating: "He that is without sin among you, let him first cast a stone at her."[9]

Jesus faced a critical decision, one that would define His leadership. The tension was palpable--stoning the woman was the accepted

6. Sill, *Leadership*, 288.
7. John 8:2–10.
8. John 8:7.
9. John 8:7.

punishment, much like how laws are strictly enforced today. What does He do? And, what would you do in His place?Jesus, always the gentleman, did not look at the woman as she stood before Him. Instead, He looked on the ground, busied Himself with His thoughts, reaching beyond time into eternity. Christ used His quiet contemplation to acquire a calm spirit, enabling rational decision-making that eventually benefited and enlightened His listeners. Leading with love made Him less susceptible to the pressures of urgency as He engaged in careful forethought, which required patience and the ability to discover the best solution without immediately choosing or rejecting possibilities.

Jesus waited, one by one, until the crowd went away. The woman alone was left. Hearing no clamor, Jesus raised His eyes, beheld the woman, and said, "Where are those thine accusers? Hath no man condemned thee?" The woman replied, "No man, Lord." His reply was, "Neither do I condemn thee; go, and sin no more."[10] Jesus demonstrated love by meeting the woman where she was and treating her as if she was already where she wanted to be. In His encounter with the woman, Jesus "believed" in her potential and admired her possibilities. He stirred her faith into action, placing a crown over her head that she would keep striving to grow tall enough to wear for the rest of her life.

When faced with a demanding situation, it can be tempting to act impulsively or to give in to the demands of others. Jesus cleared His mind, allowed Himself to be still, and opened Himself up to revelation through the impressions of the Spirit. Achieving an aspired result is not simply a matter of trying harder; instead, it is the outcome of silent, patient, and careful pondering.

With information overload, constantly changing circumstances, and the need to make quick decisions, it can be challenging to maintain a clear perspective and to remain focused on long-term goals. However, we must consider how the actions and decisions of today fit into a larger historical context. Envision a flashlight beam concentrating on the present moment and then following the illuminated path to discover the most relevant action. This beam is strongest in intensity at the current moment. However, it still sheds light on the past and the future. Although history may not repeat exactly, most historical scenarios replicate in some manner, and we must reflect and

10. John 8:10–12.

attend to past patterns that will inform our decisions today. As we immerse ourselves in God's word, our vision expands to encompass a panoramic view of past, present, and future, inspiring us to make the best possible decisions for those we strive to lead.

In the Book of Mormon, Nephi suggests that we remain steadfast in Christ, with a perfect brightness of hope, a love of God and all humanity, continuing to press forward, feasting upon the words of Christ, by enduring to the end.[11] The scriptures are a doorway that leads to paths of immense truth, imparting insights of major significance that allow us to develop the foresight to attain happiness and to accomplish good for our fellow travelers. Like the sand on the seashore constantly moved and rearranged by the waves, the lessons we learn and the knowledge we acquire allow us to leave footprints that may wash away with time but will also continue toward the future, where we will witness every dream and success.

The scriptures allow us to faithfully live the experiences of leaders who have come before us as we travel across the vast ocean of thoughts and dreams. Each word serves as a touchstone, like the standards, weights, and measures that remain consistent over time. Elder Richard G. Scott advocated that "the scriptures are like packets of light that illuminate the mind, providing direction and inspiration from God. They can become the key to opening the channel for communication with our Heavenly Father and Jesus Christ."[12] Learning, pondering, searching, and likening the scriptures to ourselves is like filling a filing cabinet with tools, values, and truths that can be called upon anytime, anywhere. We can compare the scriptures to a mirror that reflects our lives, showing us where to improve and strengthen our weak spots, while also shining into our infinite future, communicating different meanings at different times. All scripture is given by inspiration of God. It can serve as doctrine or as reproof and correction, and also supports instruction in righteousness, communicating different meanings at different times in life.[13] A scripture that we may have read many times can take on nuances of understanding that are

---

11. 2 Nephi 31:20.
12. Scott, "The Power of Scripture," 6–8.
13. 2 Timothy 3:15–16.

insightful as we read with an open heart and mind, ready to learn and apply scriptural lessons to our daily lives.

The imaginative and reflective influence of the mind will determine our success. If we expect to fail in unforeseen experiences, we will surely fail. However, if we foresee success, we will surely try to meet any challenge with vigor toward accomplishment. We can improve the future by improving the present, but to improve the present, we must first refine the model of self in our minds. When we cultivate the characteristic of foresight, our growth knows no bounds. Our spirits expand, life takes on new dimensions, and our personalities ascend to higher levels, reaching beyond the limits of imagination's fingertips. The gospel of Jesus Christ affords us strength, courage, and a venturesome spirit, paving the way for a promising tomorrow. In leadership, there is generally nothing utterly new or groundbreaking. When prospective leaders face familiar experiences rooted in outdated paradigms and recurring challenges, they often need help to address or overcome them effectively. We cannot manufacture success spontaneously out of thin air. Success requires time, effort, and dedication to achieve. Throughout history, storytelling has intertwined the threads of time with the triumphs and stumbles of leadership. The steadiness of these remarkable stories depends on the delicate balance of success within leadership and the skillful use of foresight by those at the forefront of change.

CHAPTER 17

The Sea of Galilee: Stewardship and Service

Jesus said, "It is more blessed to give than to receive."[1] The influence of our service is exemplified in the analogy of the two seas in Palestine: the Sea of Galilee and the Dead Sea. These bodies of water, though sharing a common source, represent opposite approaches to life. The Sea of Galilee is a vibrant expanse, teeming with life. Its waters are a sanctuary for fish, with lush greenery and flourishing trees surrounding its shores. In stark contrast, the Dead Sea is lifeless and exudes an oppressive heaviness. Devoid of fish, its waters are tightly held, allowing no life to grow within or around it.

Both seas are fed by the Jordan River, yet their responses to this shared source differ greatly. The Sea of Galilee, generous in spirit, doesn't just receive its waters—it channels them outward, nurturing the land and supporting abundant life. The Dead Sea's water, however, remains stagnant, unable to flow outward cultivating a harsh environment in which plants and animals cannot flourish. In leadership, exemplary individuals throughout history, like the Sea of Galilee, embody the essence of being both receivers and givers. These remarkable leaders embrace their responsibility to serve, welcoming the gifts and opportunities they receive and using them to uplift others by contributing to the well-being of those around them. By choosing to be like the Sea of Galilee, we can create environments of growth, affluence, and admiration, impacting countless lives through our willingness to serve. With each gift we give, blessings come back to us multiplied.

1. Acts 20:35.

When we fail to serve the beloved other humbly, selfishness hinders our stewardship, like trying to maintain balance on the tilted deck of a sinking ship. Yet, regardless of the times, one of the vital but challenging things we must strive to do is keep serving by listening to that still, small voice. The real heroes and heroines of today are those people who give rather than demand, who are selfless rather than selfish, who share rather than grab, who care about tomorrow as well as today, and those who uphold their responsibilities quietly without the accompaniment of loud cymbals and trumpets.

The purpose of the gospel is to change people, to help the unfortunate see the good in life, and to help good people become better. Amidst the quiet islands of Samoa, we bear witness to President To'afa Iuli, a humble stake president, faithfully tending to his role as a steward over the sunlit shores of Western Samoa, caring for the people of Apia. His visits to the local wards are not routine; they are inspiring encounters brimming with hope in the teachings of Jesus Christ. With each prayer faithfully spoken, President Iuli's love adds to the lives and blessings of the people he serves.

With each journey to the next village, he unpacks and meticulously refolds his clothing, a humble act of dedication to maintain their pristine appearance in the persistent heat. His singular aspiration is to represent the Lord through selfless service. President Iuli instills in his family the timeless importance of families being together forever by welcoming children from neighboring homes, offering them shelter, easing the burdens of other families, and ministering to the youth with loving encouragement. The Iuli family understood the value of hard work and selflessly served villagers with food from their family plantation.

Our service becomes selfless when we faithfully ask ourselves, How can I be an answer to someone's prayer through service I am going to render? President Iuli takes advantage of every opportunity, allowing service to motivate his choices, coloring his perspective with the beautiful hues of Christ's light.

His love is discernible in the beads of sweat upon his brow and the crispness of his attire, even under the shade of each tree. President Iuli's service extends beyond the Samoan people; it sets a timeless example for his own family, as well. His example and love-filled steps instilled the profound meaning of stewardship, laying the foundation of faith and inspiration to serve humbly in various leadership roles within The Church of Jesus Christ of Latter-day Saints.

President Russell M. Nelson advocated that one of life's sweetest returns is the privilege of rendering significant service of worth to others. He encouraged:

> Learn where your talents may be. Each one of us is unique, with special capabilities. We do not look alike and cannot be alike in the share of life's work we are to do. But as [we] lose [ourselves] in service of worth to others, something wonderful will happen to [us]. [Our] life may stand as a monument to greatness, anchored to the pedestal of trust, crowned with the flower of achievement, and glistening with the brightness of [our] own joy.[2]

As we step into the responsibility of faithful stewards, whether of our own talents or those we aim to serve, we find ourselves growing in the process.

The influence of stewardship affords every child of God unconditional love that is reminiscent of a mother's tears—a blend of joy and heartache, just as my own mother felt as she watched her sons survive the hardships of homelessness. Mothers, fathers, coaches, and teachers in every community exemplify immeasurable service and wield influence no less influential than acclaimed leaders. The stories and experiences we acquire from them converge within us, shaping us, as well, into faithful stewards.

Stewardship goes beyond assuming responsibility as a servant; it involves uplifting the least privileged, empowering them to grow taller, wiser, more autonomous, healthier, and more inclined to become servants themselves. Just as my mother strove to raise her sons to become good men, despite the many barriers in her path, we can responsibly lead with love. Her repeated advice—knock down doors—still resonates with me today, conveying a willingness to work hard despite my circumstances.

In his admiration for those like President Iuli and my mother, who uphold the mantle of leadership responsibility, Nelson Mandela stated:

---

2. Nelson, *Teachings of Russell M. Nelson,* 358–359.

I [have] always admired men and women who used their talents to serve the community, and who were highly respected and admired for their efforts and sacrifices, even though they held no office whatsoever in government or society. The combination of talent and humility, of being able to be at home with both the poor and the wealthy, the weak and the mighty, ordinary people and royalty, young and old, people with a common touch, irrespective of their race or background, are admired by humankind all over the globe.[3]

When we steward well, we experience joy and feel a sense of purpose.[4] As I embarked on my journey to discover the hidden path of servant-leadership, I have witnessed and have gratitude for those willing to share with me their talents, touching and inspiring me in the process.

In moments of hardship, the touch of God's tender mercies manifests in an empathetic embrace. As a daughter witnesses her father's battle with cancer, her heart aches with the weight of his struggle. In a humble gesture, the father's caretaker wraps this daughter of God in a fierce, powerful hug, offering unexpected comfort and quietly whispering, "Life can be hard." In these moments, we witness agape love unfolding, evident in the embrace of comfort freely given and gratefully received. Empathy, offered without reservation, strengthens both the giver and the receiver, embodying the love we aspire to see in the world. This gift of empathy transcends mere service and leadership; it embodies the essence of stewardship.

Gifts of Goodness

We should strive to incorporate goodness into every aspiration by recognizing, nurturing, and developing our unique gifts. Ralph Waldo Emerson said, "I have never met a [person] who was not my superior in some particular" vocation.[5] The concept that all people possess unique talents and potentialities, capable of excelling with the right effort, is truly inspiring. When we take the time to discover the distinct gifts God has bestowed upon each of us, we may encounter

---

3. Mandela, *Conversations with Myself,* 354.
4. Matthew 25:14–30.
5. Sill, *Leadership,* 377.

others with abilities that surpass our own, abilities that unexpectedly uplift and inspire us. However, this can become challenging when we fail to steward the gifts God entrusts to us with love and gratitude. The best way to receive and develop more excellent gifts is to use those we already have to the utmost. A good start is to make ourselves remarkable in a talent that can benefit others.

On the path of servant-leadership, we can ponder: What is my gift? How can I excel as intended by God? How does the Lord want me to serve? Am I using my talents to their fullest potential? Elder Sterling W. Sill advised that "first, we must identify the gifts we already have. Second, we need to figure out what we want. Third, we must aspire to acquire the blessings of God. Fourth, we can have faith that we will receive them."[6] Sometimes, gifts, like blessings, come in disguise, and we may eventually excel in what we thought was our most significant weakness.

We may discover that we have the gift of knowledge if we are willing to study and develop a love for learning. We may find the gift of discernment if we practice always thinking clearly. We may eventually find ourselves as leaders when we fully embrace the characteristics of servant-leadership. We will not, however, profit from God's gifts if we fail to receive them faithfully and without aspirations.[7]

In the parable of the talents, Jesus vividly teaches lessons on stewardship, illustrating the importance of using one's gifts and abilities faithfully.[8] In the parable, the master entrusts his servants with his goods and then determines their faithfulness based on the most profitable returns resulting from effective use of their gifts. The servants who could testify they had done all that was expected of them were joyful when told, "Well done, thou good and faithful servant: thou hast been faithful over a few things, I will make thee ruler over many things."[9] We have the agency to receive or reject the invitation to follow Christ, but once we accept, we must commit ourselves to developing our gifts by using them to bring about goodness in life.

---

6. Sill, *Leadership*, 380.
7. Doctrine and Covenants 88:30–40.
8. Matthew 25:14–30.
9. Matthew 25:21.

Jesus instructed His disciples to "feed [His] sheep,"[10] establishing for us a mantle of responsibility. Amidst the people of His day, Jesus's life shone like a glowing searchlight of goodness as He dedicated Himself to ministering and serving others. He gave strength to the limbs of the lame, sight to the eyes of the blind, and music to the ears of the deaf. Jesus walked the path of stewardship, freely imparting His substance and using the gifts of the Holy Ghost to re-bind the least privileged to God's love. Jesus invites us, as His faithful stewards, to let our light shine and to allow others to receive its radiance and glorify our Father in Heaven.

In an October 2014 general conference talk, President Monson recounted the captivating influence of gazing upon the goodness of Christ:

> When Jesus extended to a certain rich man the invitation, "Come, follow me," He did not intend merely that the rich man follow Him up and down the hills and valleys of the countryside. . . All of us can walk the path He walked when, with His words ringing in our ears, His Spirit filling our hearts, and His teachings guiding our lives, we choose to follow Him as we journey through mortality. His example lights the way. Said He, "I am the way, the truth, and the life." . . . Each of us will walk the path of disappointment, perhaps because of an opportunity lost, a [talent] misused, a loved one's choices, or a choice we ourselves make. . . . We, with Jesus, can walk the path of [service]. It will not always be easy. . . . He tells us to be merciful, to be humble, to be righteous, to be pure in heart, to be peacemakers. He instructs us to stand up bravely for our beliefs.[11]

We are not mere spectators of the journey, but active participants along the trek of servant-leadership. The lessons we have learned traversing the steps of Christ allow us to grow because our hearts live united with the Savior's as we walk hand in hand on a path that leads to boundless love.

At the end of President Monson's talk, his voice softened in profound admiration as the stories of service and stewardship unfolded, drawing the listeners into the realm of humble stewards in the Lord's work. He painted a vivid picture of these unassuming individuals

---

10. John 21:1–15.
11. Monson, "Ponder the Path of Thy Feet," 86.

whose appearance was ordinary and unpretentious. However, there was a faithful beat along the path to their doors as people sought to partake of the spirit that replenished their homes.

In those unassuming homes, a profound depth of character resided. The community around them became a glimpse of heaven on earth as a spirit of peace and goodness radiated from every corner. Genuine love and selfless service filled the atmosphere. These stewards held a gift far more valuable than material wealth—they embraced the teachings of Christ. They gave generously of their time and hearts, seeking to uplift and bless others; in return, their homes became places of hope. President Iuli of Samoa is a living example of this selfless service—taking in children from surrounding villages as his own, teaching them the gospel, and offering a place of love within the walls of his home.

President Monson spoke not of the accomplishments or accolades heaped upon these leaders, but of their influence on those around them. Their lives are a testament to the power of simple acts of kindness that exude goodness extending far beyond their front doors.

No Less Serviceable in the Lord's Work

President Howard W. Hunter noted that people tend to focus the spotlight on individuals rather than the many. We quickly identify famous leaders—Dr. King, JFK, and Mother Teresa—while also expressing gratitude for those who are not recognized but are "no less serviceable."[12] As we view stewardship through the lens of history, we must consider all the exciting people who have proven themselves heroic in the lives of the of the people they touched and blessed.

In the Book of Mormon, "Helaman and his brethren were no less serviceable unto the people than Moroni."[13] While Moroni was serving the people with his military strategy, Helaman and his brethren persuaded the people of Zarahemla to defend themselves against their enemies, even to the point of bloodshed if necessary. They swore never to initiate an attack or offend anyone except to protect their own lives. Their faith proclaimed that by following the principles of the gospel, God would bless their service and use them as effectively as those who

12. *Teachings of Presidents of the Church: Howard W. Hunter*, 294.
13. Alma 48:19.

fought with swords. Hence, they preached the word of God to all with faith. Two thousand young men, led by Helaman, entered this covenant and took their weapons of war to defend their country. All the young men were exceedingly courageous and strong, but this was not all—they were always true to Helaman's trust.

Faith is required to do the unbelievable and to prove that something can be done for the first time.[14] Faith empowers us to make a difference even with small efforts. While renowned leaders receive attention, we must also honor those who serve quietly in the late-night hours without recognition but who are no less serviceable. Those who may feel that their contributions are insignificant or unnoticed must remember that their work is opening doors of opportunity into the future. President Howard W. Hunter urged us to focus on *why* we serve rather than where or when.[15]

Clearly, Dr. Martin Luther King Jr. preached powerful messages resonating with the hearts of millions, but the unsung leaders of the civil rights movement understood that their specific location or position of prominence did not confine their purpose. Instead, they were called to contribute to the greater good, to unlock the wooden traps of oppression that weighed heavily on the necks of the downtrodden.

Whether on the front lines of movements for change or in the quiet corners of a community, the heart of service beats with the same purpose—to uplift, heal, and bring hope to those in need, using our service as an influential force to transcend time and place. Stewardship calls for us to embrace the *why* of service—to understand that our actions, no matter how small they may seem, can touch lives and create lasting change. President Monson encouraged those who accept the responsibility to serve their families and communities: "Along your pathway of life, you will observe that you are not the only traveler. There are others who need your help. There are feet to steady, hands to grasp, minds to encourage, hearts to inspire, and souls to save."[16]

Influence is the ability to choose and allow ourselves not to be buffeted by the tides of history. Instead, it is choosing a path, stepping into the ditches that impede progress, and confidently moving toward

---

14. Greenleaf, *The Power of Servant Leadership*, 210.
15. *Teachings of Presidents of the Church: Howard W. Hunter*, 299–300.
16. *Teachings of Presidents of the Church: Thomas S. Monson*, 225–226.

The Sea of Galilee: Stewardship and Service

a destination. We have the choice to follow Christ, and by navigating the path he has marked for us, we will reach our journey's end.

At present, we fight for today and pave the way for others who will come after us. Christlike service is not only in the act itself, but in the transformative effect of love to open doors and trample barriers in the future. When faced with decisions, we should courageously ask ourselves, "What would Jesus do?" and act confidently upon the answer." With a willingness to serve, we become Christ's hands and feet, enriching the lives of those around us and those yet to come.

Our lives are a sacred period, a gift to prepare ourselves and others for the eternal journey ahead. Amid our ever-changing life experiences, we find ourselves at a crossroads where the meaning of leading creates for us a new perspective. Our journey is an opportunity to develop servant-leadership characteristics, become torchbearers of hope, and illuminate the path for those who walk alongside us. We lead not by force but by example, loving unconditionally and following in the Savior's footsteps.

CHAPTER 18

Leadership Growth: Navigating Troubled Waters toward Service

The heap of glass shards piled below what was once a barrier to the boundless sky provides the perfect metaphor for the fragile nature of archaic leadership dogma that historically claimed leadership as the privileged domain of an elite few for personal gain and self-aggrandizing glory. Instead, like a beautiful mosaic, the servant-leadership transforms shards of broken glass into an ideal of stunning beauty with Christlike love. By becoming humble leaders who break the symbolic glass ceiling of possibility, we develop followers into leaders, creating a more promising future for all. As the ancient Taoist proclaimed, "When the leader leads well, the people will say 'we did it ourselves!'"[1] Leaders offer to lead out of inspiration; if valuable, followers accept it voluntarily.

As a formerly enslaved person with no schooling and an inability to read, Booker T. Washington did not allow his challenges to dissuade him from pursuing an education and eventually becoming an educator for Tuskegee. Washington recounted, "Even in those early years I had an intense longing to read, and there was never a time in my life, no matter how dark and discouraging the days might be, when one resolve did not continually actuate my determination, and that was to secure an education at any cost."[2] Like Washington, our lives can be filled with constant and unexpected discouragement, but we can choose to do our best each day.

---

1. Greenleaf, *The Power of Servant Leadership*, 181.
2. Washington, *Up from Slavery*, 37.

In his autobiography *Up from Slavery*, Booker T. Washington revisited his educational journey at Hampton University. He reflected on a pivotal lesson during his sophomore year, where he discovered the all-embracing significance of the Bible, leaving an indelible impression on him. Miss Nathalie Lord, one of his instructors, had entrusted Washington with a Bible that taught him a better way of living. She understood that potential leaders often come from the least privileged backgrounds, and she saw in Washington the capacity for growth. Washington cherished reading the Bible for spiritual growth and its literary treasures, and recounted:

> Looking back over my life I do not recall that I ever became discouraged over anything that I set out to accomplish. I [began] everything with the idea that I could succeed, and I never had much patience with the multitudes of people who [were] always ready to explain why one cannot succeed.[3]

The Hampton educators' selflessness toward the community and their university particularly inspired Washington. A paradigm-shift emerged during his second year: he embraced the idea that those who radiate the greatest happiness are often those who contribute the most to the well-being of others.

We must all seek opportunities to discover our unrealized growth potential, similar to Booker T. Washington:

> Growth not in terms of external achievement but in terms of the [ideals] that are important in the quiet hours when one is alone with oneself; growth in terms of the capacity for serenity in a world of confusion and conflict, a new kind of inner stamina, a new kind of exportable resource as youthful prowess drops away.[4]

Washington gave Sunday lectures at Tuskegee, offering encouragement to students facing immense challenges due to racial segregation and discrimination. During his speeches, he shared personal stories of his own poor upbringing and the obstacles he encountered while attending school without proper resources or clothing. Through these anecdotes, Washington aimed to instill a sense of dignity and optimism in his students, regardless of their circumstances. Washington's

---

3. Washington, *The Booker T. Washington Collection*, 133–134.
4. Greenleaf, *On Becoming a Servant Leader*, 85.

orations inspired marginalized students not to get dispirited by their social and economic plights. In his lecture "Don't Be Discouraged," Washington said:

> The very thing of discouragement, as an element in life, is for a purpose. I do not believe that anything, any element of [our] lives, is put into them without a purpose. I believe that every effort that we are obliged to make to overcome obstacles will give us strength, and will also give us a confidence in ourselves, that nothing can give us. . . . Now it is not a curse to be situated as some of you are, and if you will make up your minds that you are going to overcome the obstacles and the difficulties by which you are surrounded, you will find that in every effort [we] make to overcome these difficulties [we] are growing in strength and confidence. Make up your minds that you are not going to allow anything to discourage you. . . . Make up your mind that in spite of race and color, in spite of the obstacles that surround you, in spite of everything, you are going to succeed in . . . life, and are going to prepare yourselves for usefulness hereafter.[5]

Amid discouraging circumstances, our heads often hang low as we survey the bleak landscape around us. Our bodies move, but our gazes remain fixed as we witness the harsh realities of poverty, violence, depression, and substance abuse that scar our communities. Raised in single-parent households, burdened with the weight of parental responsibilities for younger siblings, we tread through the disheartening atmosphere of discouragement. Life often traps us in our circumstances, and we feel trapped in a room without doors.

Having a friend by your side to help you endure growth challenges allows for unforeseen possibilities as we surpass the barriers of unfavorable circumstances. By leaning on each other, their strength and resilience mirror one another. Eric became my confidant and supported me in my search for growth when progress slowed, and when our backs was against the proverbial wall. As I navigated the darkly shaded streets of Los Angeles, Eric was my light post. While I struggled with a temper that veered between disagreeable and amiable, often leading to outbursts on the football field, Eric remained a steady presence of patience and humility, leading me away from doubt.

---

5. Washington, *Character Building*, 51.

In the book of Proverbs, we read that "a friend loveth at all times, and a brother is born for adversity."[6] Eric embodied the essence of a true friend and brother, never losing faith in me even during our toughest times. We stood by each other, sharing our meager incomes for food, telling each other our goals, and ensuring we traveled safely on the bus. I firmly believe that without Eric by my side during my homelessness, I would not be the person I am today.

While we were in college, Eric and I took those prudent steps toward strength, using football and education as our walking poles, patiently committing to "the process," a philosophy of overcoming each new barrier without using our disadvantaged lives as excuses not to try. The realization that we could exponentially improve our lives emerged when we received scholarships for the University of Idaho. As it did for Booker T. Washington, education led us toward improvement. We were thankful for the reality that we had each other, to lean on making the difference between failure and growth.

Growth is an active characteristic, not one that idly, passively waits and hopes for something good. We must realize that those who strive to grow will suffer no failure except giving up and no longer trying. For Eric and me, our countenance was one of determination. People would ask, "Why don't you smile much?" We would respond, "We don't have anything to smile about." We were on the grind and committed to bettering our lives, although we realized no one could keep us from enduring hardships along the way. Brick by brick, we were committed to the process.

Brick by Brick: Tuskegee's Journey

The phrase "bricks without straw" refers to a task or goal undertaken without appropriate resources. It is challenging to make bricks without straw; we will be fascinated to discover that it is not impossible. We may, indeed, be on the edge of recognizing that making bricks without straw is, precisely, a historical and actual specialty.

In Tuskegee's early days, founders and students baked bricks to build their institution. Booker T. Washington likened it to the

---

6. Proverbs 17:17.

Leadership Growth: Navigating Troubled Waters toward Service

children of Israel making bricks without straw, as they had to make do with limited resources and experience. When it came to brick baking, the students' struggles manifested in their lack of education. The brick-baking process proved a demanding experience for students and Washington alike, as they had to develop unique skills and knowledge, particularly firing the bricks.

At one point, they molded about twenty-five thousand bricks but failed to build a kiln to forge them properly. The kiln became their biggest struggle, and they failed three times. Despite these challenges, Washington, who had undeterred faith in his students, did not want them to be demoralized by failure and decided:

> In the midst of my troubles, I thought of a watch which had come into my possession years before. I took the watch to the city . . . and placed it in a pawnshop. I secured cash upon it to the amount of fifteen dollars, with which to renew the brickmaking experiment. I returned to Tuskegee, and with the help of the fifteen dollars, rallied our rather demoralized and discouraged forces and began a fourth attempt to make bricks.[7]

For the Tuskegee students or anyone who lives life with their backs against the proverbial wall, the impossible is attainable when we believe in ourselves. Faith is required to do the unbelievable and to demonstrate that something can be done—for the first time.

Pawning his watch may have signaled yet another round of their brick-baking experiment, but Washington and his students finally succeeded. Despite failing three times, Tuskegee gained a reputation in the brick-baking industry and discovered an authentic way of serving Black and white communities in the rural South. The bricks literally and symbolically paved the way toward breaking down prejudice and revealing the previously untapped potential of Tuskegee students.

Other Black colleges and universities took up their own brick-backing, among other self-sufficient activities, and the innovation that began with the firing of brick led to the growth of a thriving industry that uplifted the Black communities' economic status in the rural South. Washington recounted:

---

7. Washington, *The Booker T. Washington Collection*, 176.

The making of these bricks taught me an important lesson in regard to the relations of the two races in the South. Many white people who had no contact with the school, and perhaps no sympathy with it, came to us to buy bricks because they found out that ours were good bricks. They discovered that we were supplying a real want in the community. The making of these bricks caused many of the white residents of the neighborhood to begin to feel that the education of Black people was not making them worthless, but that in educating our students we were adding something to the wealth and comfort of the community. As the people of the neighborhood came to us to buy bricks, we got acquainted with them; they traded with us and us with them. Our business interests became intermingled. . . . This, in a large measure, helped lay the foundation for the pleasant relations that have continued to exist between us and the white people . . . and which [extended] throughout the south. . . . I have found, too, that it is the visible, the tangible, that goes a long ways in softening prejudices.[8]

Washington knew that the success of Tuskegee would benefit the larger community in which the students lived and worked. As Tuskegee's reputation grew in the brick-baking industry, the communities in the rural South became more aware of the school's potential and began to realize the value of education. Washington's leadership united white and Black communities.

Tuskegee embodied the idea of growth, which enabled students to recognize the rewards of excellence, regardless of skin color. The brickmaking project made the intangible visible, which softened prejudices and built a road toward shared prosperity, filling in each crack through the promise of service. Washington remarked that the sight of a first-class home in the South built by people of color was ten times more radiant than any words spoken or written upon pages.

Like firing bricks in a kiln, academic rigor developed the Tuskegee students into irrepressible individuals who could form the foundation of society. In the same way that bricks gain sturdiness from the intense heat of the kiln, the students at Tuskegee also experienced a transformative journey that helped them become better leaders for their communities. The long hours spent working in the mud pit honed the students' skills and developed their character. Washington's

---

8.   Washington, *The Booker T. Washington Collection,* 176–177.

leadership, despite the limited resources available, helped shape each student into influential contributors, becoming the mortar that held their communities together.

Washington later aimed to teach the Tuskegee students how to construct their own buildings, stating, "The students themselves would be taught to see not only utility in labor, but beauty and dignity . . . how to lift labor from mere drudgery and toil, and learn to love work for its own sake."[9] Despite doubters, Washington foresaw Tuskegee students constructing their own buildings as an opportunity to develop their unseen abilities by challenging themselves with unfamiliar tasks. Washington recounted:

> The majority of our students came to us in poverty, from the cabins of the cotton, sugar, and rice plantations of the South. . . . I felt that it would be following out a more natural process of development to teach them (the students) how to construct their own buildings. Mistakes I knew would be made, but these mistakes would teach us valuable lessons for the future. . . . Hundreds of Black men scattered throughout the South . . . received their knowledge of mechanics while being taught how to erect [the] buildings.[10]

Despite the odds, Tuskegee undertook this endeavor for nineteen years, constructing forty buildings and graduating hundreds of students. Washington's Christlike love helped Tuskegee students grow and thrive, demonstrating the influential outcome of faith in people's growth.

Greenleaf provided a compelling depiction of the growth process and the intrinsic characteristics of individuals who experience growth. He explained:

> There is a growing sense of overriding purpose in all that [we] undertake. Purpose becomes pervasive in all thinking. . . . [We] become more conscious of effective use of time and more bothered by the waste of time. . . . Whatever [our] work is, there is a growing sense of achieving basic personal goals through it. Those greener pastures on the other side of the fence are not so attractive. [Instead], all of life becomes more unified. All aspects of it seem more to reinforce one another.[11]

---

9. Washington, *The Booker T. Washington Collection,* 174.

10. Washington, *The Booker T. Washington Collection,* 174–175.

11. Greenleaf, *On Becoming a Servant Leader,* 84–85.

With love as a leading belief, we can demonstrate a generational commitment to the growth of all people. President David O. McKay emphasized the far-reaching impact of influence that radiates throughout entire communities:

> No good deed, no kind word can be spoken without its effect being felt for good upon all. Sometimes the good may be insignificant, but as a rock that is thrown in a pool starts a wave from the center which continues to enlarge until every part of the shore is touched, so [our] deeds, silent, many of them, unknown, unspoken, unheralded, continue to radiate and touch many hearts.[12]

Tuskegee students had a ripple effect on community life, spreading goodwill and hope wherever they went, much like the ripples caused by a stone dropped in water. We shape an ideal community through the growth of people, filtering every word through love and seeing others as worthy of trust rather than seeing them as lesser beings, judging them, or trying to compete with them.

Growth from Bethesda's Porch

The Gospel of John offers insights into helping the underprivileged grow. The analogy of the healing within Bethesda's pool mirrors the challenges in life that cultivate growth. Like the angel stirring the water for healing, we, too, must navigate through difficulties to achieve higher goals. We achieve growth by confronting challenges. The story reminds us that opposition will shape us, and we must press forward despite difficulty.

The story of Bethesda recounts, "Having five porches . . . lay a great multitude of [helpless] folk, blind, halt, withered, waiting for the moving of the water. For an angel went down at a certain season into the pool and troubled the water; whosoever then first stepped in after the troubling of the water was made whole of whatsoever diseases they had. And a certain man was there, which had an infirmity thirty and eight years."[13] The man had sought healing in the waters of Bethesda but could not get there in time before someone else entered the pool.

---

12. President David O. McKay. In Conference Report, April 1953, 137.
13. John 5:2–5.

The pool of Bethesda was for those with bodily infirmities. Like the act of the angel stirring the water at the pool of Bethesda to bring forth its healing powers, we can draw a parallel to how God affords us opportunities to gain experience and blessings.

By navigating life's troubled waters, we face challenges that promote growth and higher purposes. Like the man at the pool of Bethesda, some struggle to reach their aspirations and must wait for love's abundance. We all at different times in our lives sit beside the pool of Bethesda waiting for God's tender mercies. We are all climbing our own steps on the porch of Bethesda, and we can reach our goals if we keep moving forward with faith in Christ. Dr. King encouraged us to run if we could not fly, and if we cannot run, we could at least walk. If even that becomes too hard, we crawl on all fours with faith that God loves us.

I recall my personal pool of Bethesda story when I was playing college football. Eric and I had found ourselves awaiting a shift in our quality of life, like the water's movement in the pool, a symbol of God's presence. Amid those trying days, our brother Chris became our motivation for change through his examples of determination. His profound influence enabled us to connect with a belief in God's presence in our lives, aiding us in surmounting our struggles of homelessness; we grew to become resilient.

At a pivotal moment during our journey, we confronted East Los Angeles Community College on the football field. As the game neared its close, with victory hanging in the balance, we sought a means to stop the opposing team's offense during a timeout. Our gazes turned to Chris on the sideline. We asked about a defensive line move he had diligently coached us on throughout the week. A flash of faith shone in his eyes as he encouraged us to execute it for the final play.

Eric and I mustered the courage to apply the maneuver as the game resumed. In a moment of excitement, Eric managed to break through the offensive line and successfully hit the quarterback as he threw the ball, leading to an interception that secured our victory. On the sidelines of the LA Southwest football field we three brothers stood united, grateful for our own transformative event, a result of our brother's teaching and of our courage to try something new. Even though Eric and I grappled with homelessness then, we were united, seizing an opportunity for accomplishment despite the adversities we confronted off the field.

Chris's faith in our ability to shape the game's outcome empowered us to believe in ourselves. LA Southwest recorded that moment, and Chris can be seen in the recording, watching the play unfold from the sideline. As Eric's triumphant hit unfolds, Chris leaps in excitement, fists raised as he cheers on his younger brothers. Chris's encouragement allowed us to make our own walk forward, similar to Jesus saying, "Rise, take up your mat, and walk."[14]

We found solace in Chris's affectionate smile. His love gave us a sense of direction, a faint path to follow. The video recording of the East Los Angeles football game remains one of our final memories with Chris. With every replay, a cascade of emotions overwhelms me—a recollection of us standing together by our own Bethesda waters, awaiting our destined moment of triumph. With the opportunities afforded us, in our own unique ways, we should become like angels who "move the water" for others, helping to heal a spirit by erasing doubt, loneliness, embarrassment, or rejection.

Troubled Waters

Elder Sterling W. Sill advocated, "It is never the peaceful sea that makes the skillful mariner. It was the north wind that prepared the Vikings."[15] The turbulent times we encounter, symbolized by troubled waters, are meant to advance us toward God's love, but we will not make headway simply by standing on the safe shore. As leaders or followers, we help others grow when we approach all challenges as puzzles to be solved or games to be won, leading others to overcome barriers that may initially seem impossible.

Jesus, more than anyone else, spent His earthly life swimming in troubled waters. Though He faced daily opposition, He grew as a leader, man, and servant, uplifting those who needed charity and love. Jesus willingly endured those troubled waters until His final outcry on the cross: "My God, my God, why hast thou forsaken me?"[16] His

14. John 5:8.
15. Sill, *Leadership II*, 349.
16. Matthew 27:37–45.

life exemplified the hard truth that sorrow and difficulty are deeply embedded into the fabric of life.

We produce our best work when faced with demanding situations, and when we find ourselves backed into corners, there is only one direction to focus on—forward. The Lord fits all of our burdens to the strength of our backs. To develop strong backs, we must faithfully embrace greater responsibilities. Like a storm that uproots weaker trees with shallow roots, clearing away lifeless branches, life's challenges expose vulnerabilities and force us to let go of habits or beliefs holding us and others back.

Booker T. Washington believed that we have two directions in life toward which we can grow—backward or forward.[17] Before taking a step forward, we must bring with us the least privileged. As communities, we can grow weaker or more resilient; we can grow smaller or more distinguished, but it will be impossible for us to stand still as individuals or as children of God.

When we reach the threshold of opportunity, requiring only a few more steps, let us remember the inspiring words of Dr. King:

> Keep moving, let us move on toward the goal of [peoplehood], toward the goal of personal fulfillment, toward the goal of a society undergirded by [righteousness] . . . quoting a beautiful little poem from the pen of Langston Hughes, where he has a mother, talking to a son. With ungrammatical profundity, that mother says, Well, son, I'll tell you: Life for me ain't been no crystal stair. It's had tacks in it, boards torn up, and places with no carpet on the floor—bare. But all the time I've been a-climbing' on, and reaching' landings, and turning' corners, and sometimes going' into the dark where there ain't been no light. So, don't you turn back. Don't you set down on the steps 'Because you find it's kinder hard. For I'm still going' . . . I'm still climbing,' and life for me ain't been no crystal stair. Well, life for none of us has been a crystal stair, but we must keep moving. We must keep going. And so, if you can't fly, run. If you can't run, walk. If you can't walk, crawl. But by all means, keep moving.

We can remember that we are all climbing our own steps on the porch of Bethesda. Our service is like helping the underprivileged up the worn steps to the porch of Bethesda, where the waters are

---

17. Washington, *Character Building,* 197.

renowned for their healing touch. Offering a steadying hand on the uneven stone, we ensure they don't trip or lose hope as they ascend the steep steps of life. Along the way, we witness a clear path to help them navigate the crowds gathered for their own reasons. With each step, we share words of encouragement and offer our strength to reach the pool, where the calming waters hold the promises of God's love. As we lift others, we find ourselves uplifted, our spirits renewed by the shared hope that moves us forward with each step toward healing.

CHAPTER 19

Building the Beloved Community

After a youth mentoring event, I spoke with high school students from marginalized communities in the greater Seattle area. When I asked how they might achieve a greater sense of self-worth and how they might more easily achieve their short- and long-term goals, their responses were unanimous. They all emphasized the desire to feel as if they belonged to a community. We receive inspiration and encouragement from the examples within our families and communities, like athletes who elevate their performance to play on a winning team. To support one another is not only our responsibility; it is also one of our most significant opportunities, for we are all on the same journey. In one sense, we all rise or fall, sink or swim together. Within the Beloved Community, everyone feels welcomed, included, and respected.

Reimagined through forgiveness, remade through reconciliation, and imbued with love, "beloved" conveys friendship, respect, and kindness. Deeply felt within people's hearts, "community" means that people are unified without polarities and move forward without being weighed down by struggle. When a community emerges from the abandoned valleys of inequality, false differences in authority and status disappear, fading away bias and prejudice. Civil Rights leader John Lewis proclaimed:

> Consider the two words: Beloved Community. "Beloved" means not hateful, not violent, caring and, kind. And "Community" means not separated, not polarized, not locked in struggle. . . . The Beloved Community is an all-inclusive world society based on simple justice

that values the dignity and the worth of every human being. That is the kingdom of God.[1]

Throughout the scriptures "Beloved" conveys an expression of endearment, reflecting the unconditional love our Heavenly Father and Jesus Christ have for us. "We love [Them] because [They] first loved us."[2] As we walk the path of Christ, we witness His compassionate work alongside the privileged and the marginalized for the good of all people. The love and reverence inherent in the word "beloved" shines through Jesus Christ, who God declared, "My beloved Son, chosen from the beginning"[3] and "This is My Beloved Son. Hear Him!"[4] When we establish our lives and communities upon Christ, the storms of the latter days may come, but as God's beloved, we will stand unshaken.

In his epistle to the Romans, Paul greeted followers of Christ as "Beloved of God, called to be saints."[5] This simple yet powerful greeting was a formal salutation and declaration for all believers who identified and lived the purposes of Christ. Tori Morrison, one of the most renowned writers in the world, emphasized that being the beloved of God means we are fully known and deeply loved by Him. A beloved community, then, follows members of that community as they, too, convey love throughout their institutions, organizations, places of worship, governments, and schools. Paul's religious teachings impart practical advice for people striving to live in a manner worthy of the kingdom of heaven, that wherever one suffers, all suffer; if one rejoices, all rejoice.

The openness of a beloved community creates a safe space for healing and renewal, protecting us from the burden of relationships that oppress rather than set us free. Whenever we encounter obstacles that lift some and oppress others, we recognize the betrayal of the Beloved Community and the removal of our agency to live freely. When articulating the ideals of a Beloved Community, Dr. King said, "Our goal is to create a precious community and this will require a qualitative change in our souls as well as quantitative change in our lives."[6]

---

1. Phillip Mathew, *Finding Leo*, 2021, p. 175.
2. 1 John 4:19.
3. Moses 4:2.
4. Joseph Smith—History 1:17.
5. Romans 1:7.
6. King and Washington, *A Testament of Hope*, 58.

The idea of our being called to be saints is not a theological abstraction; it offers practical implications for how we live and relate to others. The Beloved Community is bound by a shared belief in the transformative influence of love. Greenleaf assured us, "For the servant who has the capacity to be a builder, the greatest joy in this world is in the building."[7]

Dr. King expressed his vision of the Beloved Community, characterized by a profound interconnectedness and mutual respect, following the Supreme Court's ruling to end segregation on public buses after the Montgomery Bus Boycott. He said:

> We must remember . . . that a boycott is not an end within itself; it is merely a means to awaken a sense of shame within the oppressor and challenge [their] false sense of superiority. But the end is reconciliation; the end is redemption; the end is the creation of the Beloved Community. It is this type of spirit and this type of love that can transform opposers into friends. This type of understanding of goodwill will transform the old age's deep gloom into the exuberant gladness of the new age. It is this love which will bring about miracles in the heart.[8]

The redemption that arises when we acknowledge all individuals as the beloved of God transcends the divisive boundaries of in-group versus out-group. It enriches and expands our current concept of solidarity to see beyond *us* and *them* distinctions, recognizing that even those perceived as different or distant from one another share the capacity to love.

When we feel a sense of belonging, we will begin to see the world through a lens of appreciation for one another. In a meaningful moment, my eldest son, Kingston, asked me, "Dad, can I study leadership when I go to college? When did you start studying leadership?" I paused, contemplating the significance of his reflection, and replied, "I have been studying leadership my whole life." On the streets of brokenness, where hopelessness looms and belonging seems like a distant possibility, survival hinges on navigating through the cracks to discover leaders who will lead and help others find their own leadership potential.

For marginalized groups, being part of a beloved community can provide a sense of empowerment, agency, and a space for healing. As

---

7.   Greenleaf, *Servant Leadership*, 261.
8.   King and Washington, *A Testament of Hope*, 140.

we walk toward the place we call community, the sun shines upon us, casting its warm and comforting light upon our shoulders, directing us toward a place of love with each step we take. Elder Phillip D. Rash said:

> Belonging is not simply having a place or fitting in somewhere. Instead, belonging says that this place is my home, that I am needed and have a purpose here, and that these people around me understand and accept me. It is a feeling that my community has my back and wants the best for me.[9]

As the sun provides shade to shield us from the heat of the day, a community of belonging offers reprieve from the battles of life. It is a place where we can rest our weary spirits and allow an oasis of love to nourish our hearts. In a community, *beloved other* allows us to build relationships that provide support and meaning imbuing life with the Light of Christ. In times of need, family members and communities can offer the faith necessary to stay on the path of servant-leadership.

Julia Mavimbela's Journey to Forgiveness and Healing

Dr. King believed in two kinds of faith: the faith that believes despite the evidence and the faith that believes because of the evidence. He explained that the first kind of faith is blind faith, believing without supporting evidence, which is often seen as weak and vulnerable to doubt, as it is not typically grounded in fact. Blind faith is more vulnerable to lack of conviction, where all it would take is for the right person with the right argument to come along and destroy that faith.

The second type of faith is rooted in personal convictions, grounded in individual understanding and experience. It emerges from the both the visible and unseen, strengthened by irrefutable evidence. This faith is resilient, enduring scrutiny and weathering the storms of doubt. Regarding the faith required to persevere through challenging times, Elder Jeffrey R. Holland said:

---

9.   Rash, "Looking to the Margins," 2.

Faith must be unwavering because it will be examined in the refiner's fire to see if it is more than sounding brass, or a tinkling cymbal. . . . It is then, sailing in what Hamlet called a sea of troubles, that it may take all the faith you have to keep your little craft afloat. . . . So, when you are being hammered on the anvil of adversity, when your soul is being refined with severe lessons that cannot be learned in any other way, don't cut, and run. Don't jump ship. . . . When you stumble in the race of life, don't crawl away from the very Physician who is unfailingly there to treat your injuries, lift you to your feet, and help you finish the course. We don't know why all of the things that happen to us in life happen, why sometimes we are spared a tragedy and sometimes we are not. But that is where faith must truly mean something, or it is not faith at all. In such severe circumstances, rare as we hope they are, we can fall back on Alma's reminder that faith and knowledge are related, but they are not synonymous. In some matters you can have knowledge, even perfect knowledge, but in some things, faith will have to do until knowledge comes.[10]

Julia Mavimbela was a South African woman wronged by racism, the police, and the justice system. Her experience exemplifies how faith can transform an individual and impact a community. In 1955, Julia Mavimbela's husband, John Mavimbela, died in a car accident during the racial divide of apartheid in South Africa. At the time, Black South Africans were treated unjustly due to racial prejudice. Unfortunately, local law enforcement mishandled the investigation into the accident, wrongfully placing the blame on Julia's husband, even though a white man had veered into his lane. Following John's tragic passing, Julia felt a deep sense of loneliness. She even inscribed the words "In loving memory/John Phillip Corlie Mavimbela/By his wife and relatives/But the lump remains/May his soul rest in peace" on his tombstone to express the intensity of the pain that continued to afflict her soul. The pain she experienced also impacted her interactions with white South Africans in her community of Soweto.

Julia Mavimbela's story exemplifies the second type of faith grounded in evidence and purpose. Her commitment to love and forgiveness, even during apartheid South Africa, demonstrated the resilience of faith. Julia remembered, "At the time of writing, the lump

---

10. Holland, "A Saint Through the Atonement of Christ the Lord," 2.

that remained was one of hatred and bitterness—for the man who caused the accident, for the policemen who lied, [and] for the court who deemed my husband responsible for the accident that took his life."[11] Fortunately, Julia's mom taught her to swallow the bitter pills offered by the pains and trials of everyday life and encouraged Julia never to look back—only forward.

Julia did not succumb to bitterness. She had a dream years after her husband's death that led to a transformative experience. In the dream, John appeared to her and handed her overalls, telling her, "Go to work." This dream profoundly impacted Julia, and she found solace in community involvement. In search of healing for herself and her community, Julia realized that teaching the children to love working in the soil could be healing, and so she established a community garden to represent hope to people who only knew fear and anger.

Dr. King remarked on Julia's community garden, established during a time of violence and fear, but symbolizing the power of forgiveness to heal deep wounds of the heart. The true focus of revolutionary change is never merely the oppressive situations that we seek to escape, but that piece of the oppressor which planted deep within each of us. That deep piece of enmity impedes our progress toward a beloved community. King reminded us:

> We must also remember that God does not forget his children who are the victims of evil forces. He gives us the [faith] to bear the burdens and tribulations of life. . . . This faith will sustain us in our struggle to escape from the bondage of bitterness. This faith will be a lamp unto our weary feet and a light unto our meandering path. Without such faith, [humanity's] highest dreams will pass silently to the dust.[12]

Faith is an invaluable companion in navigating life's challenges. Julia Mavimbela's story demonstrates our capacity to lead with greater effectiveness and to welcome life through the lens of faith, guiding us toward the blessings of forgiveness and the realization of the Beloved Community.

Loving others—enemies and friends—is like tending a garden. Like a gardener removes weeds, tills the soil, and plants healthy seeds, we can remove from our lives the noxious characteristic of animosity

---

11. Heiss, "Healing the Beloved Country," 42.

12. King, *Strength to Love*, 84–86.

to cultivate friendship through loving interactions. By extending our hands in respect, we nourish the soil of our communities, thereby cultivating an environment where love grows tall and strong. Servant-leaders till with ongoing attention and effort, pruning anything that would choke off the potential for new growth, before finally planting their seeds of love and forgiveness.

God's love can uproot every pain and spirit of anger that persists in our hearts, as in the story of Julia Mavimbela. Her experience with The Church of Jesus Christ of Latter-day Saints significantly influenced her spiritual healing journey. Julia's baptism and subsequent service in the Johannesburg temple taught her the principle of eternal relationships and the importance of forgiveness.[13] Julia's willingness to share her story with others, including her struggles with misunderstanding and prejudice, demonstrated a commitment to building a beloved community, where all find healing. Matthew Heiss, historian for The Church of Jesus Christ of Latter-day Saints, said, "Julia discovered that healing was possible through the gospel of Jesus Christ, not only for herself but also for her nation."[14] Her service in the Johannesburg South Africa Temple taught her that in the temple, "there is no touch of Afrikaner. There is no English. There is no Situ nor Zulu. You know that feeling of oneness."[15]

Blending love with forgiveness becomes an act of generosity and requires us to release feelings of guilt or anguish caused by our personal feelings of outrage or anger. Julia used the metaphor of a hospital to describe her redeeming relationship with the restored gospel of Jesus Christ. Like a hospital that heals the sick, love allows us to confront the negative realities of life in a life-affirming and restorative way, finding healing for spiritual wounds.[16] Julia's metaphor illuminates the importance of having empathy in serving others, recognizing that we are all sick in our unique ways and need healing to recover. The story of Julia's life illustrates how love, forgiveness, and service can help heal even the deepest emotional wounds. Her community garden

---

13. Heiss, "Healing the Beloved Country," 38–43.
14. Heiss, "Healing the Beloved Country," 43.
15. Heiss, "Healing the Beloved Country," 43.
16. Heiss, "Healing the Beloved Country," 42.

is another metaphor for Julia's impact, as the seeds she planted grew and prospered, much like the example she set for others to follow.

The Beloved Community helps break down binary thinking, allowing individuals to see those previously viewed as enemies as members of the same community. When forgiveness is present, love amplifies our ability to connect with others in fellowship. Julia's work in the garden taught the children in her community to dig up the soil of bitterness, throw in a seed of love, and watch what fruits it could yield. She believed that love could not come without forgiveness. Julia recounted, "I knew deep in my heart I was breaking up the soil of my own bitterness as I forgave those who had hurt me."[17] She dissolved the lump of bitterness in her heart, which for anyone else without Julia's faith, may have sprouted into a toxic, noxious weed deep within the soul rooted in sorrow and hopelessness.

Journeying toward the Beloved Community

To my family and those who have read this work: fulfill the purpose that Heavenly Father envisioned when He created you as His child. See everyone as if they are clothed in white. Remember that effort is all that is required to complete the journey.

As we journey together, we will eventually reach the redemptive shores of God's love. Along the way, the stories of others can restore hope and serve as a testament to the true essence of leadership that can build up our communities. We can seek to find stories that vividly illustrate how our reward transcends the worldly differences we experience and leads us to rest in heavenly mansions. In "The Mansion" by Henry Van Dyke, the protagonist, John Weightman, gives gifts only for personal gain and serves himself before considering his neighbor. The story revolves around his life in a luxurious stone house that exudes a sense of tranquility and restrained luxury.

Weightman's approach to life is met with disapproval from his son, causing him to question the righteousness of his actions. While sitting at a table, he notices an open Bible, and his gaze falls upon the words written within: "Lay not up for yourselves treasures upon

---

17. Heiss, "Healing the Beloved Country," 43.

earth."[18] As he continues reading: "But lay up for yourselves treasures in heaven." The book seems to levitate in that instant, and the room darkens. A thought calmly and irresistibly infiltrates his mind, causing Weightman to slump onto the table.

Gradually, his consciousness returns, and he finds himself in a strange land, traversing unfamiliar paths and encountering friendly groups of people dressed in white, both privileged and the least privileged. Among them, he recognizes the old village doctor, a humble yet resolute man who selflessly served the communities of Africa. Another familiar face belongs to a modest bookkeeper who tirelessly cared for his disabled daughter while his wife endured hardships at an early age. Their lives, too, were marked by selfless service.

Among them is a paralyzed woman who had lain for thirty years upon her bed, helpless but not hopeless, succeeding by a miracle of courage in her single aim, never to complain but always to impart a bit of her joy and peace to everyone who came near her. Weightman also encounters a widow who endured hardships to provide for her children and a devoted teacher who dedicated her life to educating the marginalized youth:

> All these, and other persons like them, people of little consideration in the world, but now seemingly all full of great contentment and an inward gladness that made their steps light, were in the company that passed along the road, talking together of things past and things to come, and singing now and then with clear voices from which the veil of age and sorrow was lifted.[19]

It became apparent that travelers were journeying toward the Celestial City (or the Beloved Community) by different paths, and making the ascent, where their mansions awaited them. As the people approached the Beloved Community, a guide clothed in white greeted them with open arms, saying, "Come in, your mansions are ready."[20] They passed him, group after group, talking quietly, not moving in haste but with a certain air of eagerness as if they were glad to be on their way to an appointed place. They did not stay to speak to him, but they looked at him often and spoke to one another as they looked.

18. Matthew 6:19.
19. Van Dyke, *The Mansion*, 44.
20. Van Dyke, *The Mansion*, 44–46.

Occasionally one of them would smile and beckon him a friendly greeting so that he felt like he belonged to their community. One by one, the beloved of God entered their prepared homes, expressing delight as their mansions surpassed their expectations. Sweet voices of welcome, gentle laughter, and melodious songs filled the air within these mansions, creating an atmosphere of warmth and bliss, like the gentle breeze on a summer day.

The journey was across a vast heavenly field, under a tranquil, sunless arch of blue, with an air of peace throughout. The light was diffused without a shadow as if the spirit of life in all things were shining. As they began to walk along the Eternal City, the keeper of the gate, after a moment of profound contemplation, turned toward Weightman and began to share:

Through the mercy of the King, it came softly.

What could I have done better? What is it that counts here? Only that which is truly given, answered the bell-like voice.

It was not earned—it was—given. Only that good which is done for the love of duty, only those plans in which the welfare of others is the master-thought, only those labors in which the sacrifice is greater than the reward, only those gifts in which the giver forgets himself. [Is] there [anything] like that in your life?

Nothing, [John] sighed. If so, they were few, and I have long ago forgotten them.

The guide smiled gently, These are the things that the King never forgets; and because there were a few of them in your life, you have a little place here.[21]

Acts of kindness will not go unnoticed by our Father in Heaven. He is constantly aware of our devoted service toward all people within our communities. The least privileged await our support and comradeship to lift them from their humble positions. Social status, race, color, or creed become irrelevant when God endows us with His eternal rewards. Although we walk miles and miles, toiling with no reward, it will only seem a fleeting moment compared to the tender mercies of God that distill upon us. As we look back upon the hills

---

21. Van Dyke, *The Mansion*, 41.

ascended and the valleys traveled, we will look in awe at what Henry Van Dyke symbolically depicted as the mansions of heaven and the ideal of what Dr. Martin Luther King deemed the promised land.

No matter the length of the journey, unforeseen difficulties can obstruct, detour, and hinder the most determined person. American author and social activist, Bell Hooks wrote in her book *Belonging: A Culture of Place*:

> Life is full of peaks and valleys, triumphs, and tribulations. We often cause ourselves [sorrow] by wanting only to live in a world of valleys, a world without struggle and difficulty, a world that is flat, plain, and consistent. We resist the [authenticity] of difference and diversity. We resist acknowledging that our constraints exist within a [paradigm] where everything is constantly changing. We resist change. When we [accept] the reality of highs and lows, embracing both as necessary for our full development and self-actualization, we can feel that interior well-being is the foundation of inner peace . . .[A] life of appreciation for difference and diversity is a life wherein one embraces [difficulty] as [a companion] to the experience of joy.[22]

Each determined effort we invest in elevating our communities has the power to move mountains. When we trust God, these endeavors return to us as blessings, like faith, that can lead to extraordinary accomplishment. Sometimes, we must travel the valley of ease and ascend the peaks of discontent before we can witness the admiration of God's love.

I love to envision the limitless possibilities of the Beloved Community: the diversity of color and thought, with the shallow fence representing concepts of equality and equity. As the travelers move swiftly and silently through the orchards of the mansions, a sense of reverence lingers, as if everyone dare not speak lest the city vanishes. The city's wall, though shallow, is adorned with precious stones that are inherently small, allowing even a child to see beyond it. As we witness the beauty beyond the radiance of these walls, we can conceptualize our dreams as we witness the reflection of our image from the pearls glimmering with a Christlike image. Unlike traditional barriers of wood or iron, the city gate is marked solely by a gleaming pearl, indicating the end of the wall and the open entrance beyond. The lack

---

22. Hooks, *Belonging*, 25.

of barriers within the city represents the free agency of God's beloved, as He has created no restrictions to our potential. A person of brightness and solemnity stands there, clad not in woven fabric but in a robe resembling the delicate petals of a lily—an embodiment of the living texture of God's love.

"Come in," the figure says to welcome the company of travelers. "You have reached the culmination of your journey, and your mansions await you."[23] Like Christ's clarion call, "Come and follow me,"[24] these words hold profound meaning and symbolize the culmination of a collective journey toward the Beloved Community that celebrates and embraces all its people.

A Gentle Flutter of Great Ideas

As we seek after the ideals of the Beloved Community, the realization of our leadership crisis is evident. It looms overhead like overcast skies, threatening to obstruct the Light of Christ, especially in communities of color, where people struggle against the injustices of coerced power, unearned privilege, and deprivation. The forces for good or evil operate through the thoughts, attitudes, and actions of individuals within our communities.[25] Still, the teachings of Christ provide a moral compass for individuals to follow and a basis for strong, caring communities. To remedy the leadership in his own time, Greenleaf leaned on Albert Camus, who proposed a way for leaders to begin as servants first and create a potential for the emergence of the builders of a better society. In a lecture titled "Create Dangerously," Camus articulated:

> Every wall is a door, Emerson correctly said. Let us not look for the door, and the way out, anywhere but in the wall against which we are living. Instead, let us seek the relief where it is—in the very thick of battle. . . . Great ideas, it has been said, come into the world as gently as doves. Perhaps, then, if we listen attentively, we shall hear, amid the uproar of empires and nations, a faint flutter of wings, the gentle stirring of life and hope.[26]

---

23. Van Dyke, *The Mansion*, 51.
24. See Matthew 4:19.
25. Greenleaf, *Servant Leadership,* 329.
26. Greenleaf, *On Becoming a Servant Leader,* 329.

By drawing inspiration from the subtle promptings of the Spirit and the vastness of God's word, we can create communities that are inclusive, just, and equitable. With this mindset, individuals with a heart for service can work to improve the human condition by eliminating barriers preventing disadvantaged groups from accessing opportunities.

The fusing of beloved and community through the spirit of Christ is an ongoing process of collective discovery. Joined hand in hand, we travel toward the Light of Christ, shining brightly and illuminating the path toward shared abundance. The brightness of the Light of Christ molds together the elements of love and community into a single entity, creating the Beloved Community that is enduring and influential. As we journey together, step outside of our comfort zones to confront social injustices. We begin to greet one another as children of God. Love fuels this transformation, connecting us in meaningful ways to provide a sense of belonging.

With the Light of Christ as its transformative forge, servant-leadership breathes life into the core ideals of agape and the Beloved Community, binding them into an unconquerable force that withstands the most arduous trials of time. As forging requires intense heat and pressure, the journey toward a beloved community also demands unwavering faith and a willingness to embrace potential risks. Love is the impetus that moves our communities forward, establishing connections between diverse individuals and fostering a shared sense of togetherness. We gain a deeper understanding of ourselves and our place in the earthly realm when we strive to build a beloved community that radiates the timeless values of admiration, compassion, and fairness.

Final Words

I have learned that success is evident when we follow the path inspired by Christ, marking a distinct line that leads in the Lord's way. The consistent reinforcement of my hope comes from the unfolding drama of hidden gifts I discovered while journeying along the covenant path. Difficulty impeded my journey toward leadership with missteps and shortcomings. Amid these challenges, through the genuine possibility of failure, I developed into the person I believe God intended me to become. Throughout your servant-leadership journey, you may have recalled experiences when success seemed unlikely and failure seemed imminent, yet you persisted and eventually triumphed. Those moments were when God was calling you to make a difference in the lives of others, perhaps in ways you cannot even imagine yet.

As we reach the end of our servant-leadership journey, my hope is that we carry with us the valuable lessons discovered along the path illuminated by Christ. We can honor His leadership by imbuing our own lives with charity. Then rays of hope will dispel the shadows of disappointment, sorrow will yield to joy, and the feeling of being lost in the confusion of life will vanish with the knowledge that our Heavenly Father is mindful of us. President Thomas S. Monson once said, "Like a bright searchlight of truth, the gospel of Jesus Christ will direct our journey along the pathways of life."[1]

More important than the knowledge we expanded is the impact that the journey had, or should have, on our thought patterns and attitude toward leadership. A journeyer on the path of servant-leadership should expect a broader tolerance, a fairer appreciation of life's experiences, a deeper understanding of community, and a growing

---

1.   *Teachings of Presidents of the Church: Thomas S. Monson,* 168.

admiration for the significance of serving others. Although we encounter fatigue, hardship, and potential suffering, these are insignificant moments, as they will eventually pass; the recollection of opposition will fade away—while our memories will hold the wonder and beauty of the journey with almost undiminished clarity.

Elder Sterling W. Sill once said:

Life was never intended to be merely a leisure trip; it is also a mission, a conquest, a testing. . . . What a thrilling [idea] that if we choose we can present ourselves before God as a generation of fighters, not fighters against anyone, but fighters for everyone, fighters who will dream the dreams and see the visions of eternal righteousness, accomplishment, and then wage an effective war against the empires of injustice, ignorance, hatred, and fear.[2] Therefore, O ye that embark in the service of God, see that ye serve Him with all your heart, might, mind, and strength, that ye may stand blameless before God at the last day.[3]

Presenting ourselves before God as a generation of fighters for everyone is a powerful message. It means that we can choose to be agents of change, servant-leaders who work toward a more hopeful future for those who walk the covenant path after us. Leadership is not authority reserved for the privileged, but rather it is an ideal of leading with a servant's heart.

All my life, I dreamed of setting foot on a path that led me to hope and promise, and now, a fascinating sense of endearment attaches to the names of Jesus Christ: Savior, Great Redeemer, Teacher, Son of God, The Good Shepherd, and the Bread of Life. I think of shepherds abiding in the field, and, unconsciously, I search the sky for one specific star. At the end of the journey, I wish it were possible to join a multitude of heavenly hosts as they praise God and sing, "Hosanna, Hosanna, Hosanna in the highest."

Our walk with Christ is more than a spiritual journey; it is a passage toward a Beloved Community. As I reflect upon the chapters of this book, the concept of leading by serving, which was once only a distant thought, becomes a living truth etched upon my heart. We find ourselves not at an end but at the threshold of new beginnings,

---

2. Sill, *Glory of the Sun,* 335.
3. Doctrine and Covenants 4:2.

with the characteristics of servant-leadership woven into our aspirations, inspiring us to walk a path of love. As He lived and still lives, we also live and shall live. For those who chose to embark on this journey with me:

THANK YOU.

Faith anchors my life in the testimony that God lives, and that Jesus is the Christ.

I find immense joy in my membership of The Church of Jesus Christ of Latter-day Saints, the love that abides in my home, and the eternal love I share with my Beloved.

Every act of love, gratitude, and kindness motivated by the love of God becomes a radiant testament to lead in the Lord's way.

What are the dimensions of a purposeful life? What is the best frame of reference to observe our purpose in the world? There is no formula, no set of guidelines. The truth is, we must each find our own path. Amidst life's trials and triumphs, I have realized that every experience is transformative on the path of servant-leadership, discovering that leading with purpose is not a destination but a continuous, evolving journey. Throughout the journey, I became a student as I took my place at the feet of Jesus Christ, learning that actual change emerges from our shared history and extends throughout eternity, especially when we know to serve first.

What is now proved was once only imagined.[4]

— William Blake

---

4. Greenleaf, *Servant Leadership*, 167.

About the Author

Dr. Ernest Davis, a native of Los Angeles, California, spent most of his life there before earning an athletic scholarship to the University of Idaho, where he graduated with a Bachelor of Science in Communications. Currently residing in Puyallup, Washington, Ernest is married to his eternal companion, Ruth Davis, and they have three children: Kingston, Titan, and Athena. He currently hosts a weekly podcast focused on discussing leadership opportunities within marginalized communities, aiming to inspire change both in his community and beyond.

Ernest earned his MBA from Western Governors University and a Doctorate in Philosophy of Leadership with an emphasis on servant leadership from Gonzaga University. He has been a member of The Church of Jesus Christ of Latter-day Saints since 2005. With over 16 years of leadership experience, Ernest has dedicated his career to leading persons with disabilities at a nonprofit organization. As a follower of Christ, Ernest aspires to inspire change in his community by following the teachings of Jesus Christ.

Bibliography

Allen, Sam. "Fatal shooting sends shudders through a reborn Inglewood." *Los Angeles Times*, April 10, 2012. https://www.latimes.com.

Baldwin, Lewis. *The Arc of Truth: The Thinking of Martin Luther King Jr.* Minneapolis: Fortress Press, 2022.

Becerra, Daniel. "Following the Savior's Example of Empathy and Love," *Liahona*, August 2022.

Bednar, David A. "The Spirit of Revelation." *Ensign*, May 2011.

Blight, David W. *Frederick Douglass: Prophet of Freedom.* New York: Simon & Schuster, 2018.

Bragg, Mark A. "A Master Class in Leadership: One Day with the Savior." BYU Speeches, February 2023.

Branch, Taylor. *At Canaan's Edge: America in the King Years, 1965-68.* Simon&Schuster, 2006.

Children's Songbook. Salt Lake City: The Church of Jesus Christ of Latter-day Saints, 1989.

Church Educational System. *Church History in the Fulness of Times: Teacher Manual* (Religion 341–343). 2nd. ed. Salt Lake City: The Church of Jesus Christ of Latter-day Saints, 2001.

DeMello, A. (1990). *Awareness: The Perils and Opportunities of Reality by Anthony De Mello.* Image Books.

Douglass, F., & Blight, D. W. (2022). *Frederick Douglass:Speeches & Writings (Library of America, 358).* Library of America.

DuBois, W. E. (2017). *The Talented Tenth.* CreateSpace Independent Publishing Platform.

Eig, Jonathan. *King: A Life.* New York: Farrar, Straus, Giroux, 2023.

Faust, James E. "Spiritual Healing." *Ensign*, May 1992.

—————. "The Power of Self-Mastery." *Ensign*, May 2000.

Flynn, Jack. "35 Amazing Advertising Statistics," 2023, https://www.zippia.com/advice/advertising-statistics/#Advertising_Statistics_by_Marketing_Tactics.

Fujimura, Makoto. *Art and Faith: Theology of Making*. Yale University Press, 2021.

Greenleaf, Robert K. *Life Style of Greatness: A Personal of Donald John Cowling, Third President of Carleton College*. Carleton College, 1966.

——————. Don M. Frick, and Larry C. Spears. *On Becoming a Servant leader: The Private Writings of Robert K. Greenleaf*. Jossey-Bass, 1996.

——————. *The Power of Servant-Leadership*. Berrett-Koehler Publishers, 1998.

——————. *The Servant as Leader*. The Greenleaf Center for Servant Leadership, 1995.

——————. *Servant Leadership: A Journey into the Nature of Legitimate Power and Greatness*. Paulist Press, 1977.

——————. *The Servant-Leader Within: A Transformative Path*. Paulist Press, 2003.

Greenleaf, Robert K., Anne T. Fraker, and Larry C. Spears. *Seeker & Servant Reflections on Religious Leadership*. Jossey-Bass Publishers, 1996.

Hafen, Bruce C. *The Broken Heart*. Salt Lake City: Deseret Book, 1989.

Hawthorne, Nathaniel. *Passages from the American Note-Books of Nathaniel Hawthorne. Vol. 2*. Smith, Elder, and Co., 1868.

Heiss, Matthew K. "Healing the Beloved Country: The Faith of Julia Mavimbela." *Ensign*, July 2017.

Henson, Josiah. *The Life of Josiah Henson: An Inspiration for Harriet Beecher Stowe's Uncle Tom*. Dover Publications, 2015.

Hinckley, Gordon B. "And the Greatest of These Is Love," BYU Speeches, 1978, https://speeches.byu.edu/talks/gordon-b-hinckley/and-the-greatest-of-these-is-love/.

——————. "The Light within You." *Ensign*, May 1995.

——————. "We Walk by Faith." *Ensign,* May 2002.

Holiday, Ryan. *Ego Is the Enemy*. Portfolio, 2016.

——————. *Stillness Is the Key*. Portfolio, 2019.

Holland, Jeffrey R. "A Saint Through the Atonement of Christ the Lord," BYU Speeches, January 18, 2022.

Hooks, Bell. *Belonging: A Culture of Place*. Routledge, 2009.

Horsman, John H. "Perspectives of Servant-Leadership and Spirit in Organizations." Diss., Gonzaga University, 2001.

Hunter, Howard W. "The Great Commandment." *Ensign*, October 1994.

———. "The Lord's Touchstone." *Ensign*, November 1988.

———. "True Greatness. *Ensign,* May 1982.

Kimball, Spencer W. "Humility," BYU Speeches, January 16, 1963.

King, Coretta Scott. *My Life with Martin Luther King Jr.* Puffin Books, 1994.

King, Martin Luther Jr. "The Drum Major Instinct." Sermon delivered at Ebenezer Baptist Church, Atlanta, GA, 1968.

———. *In a Single Garment of Destiny: A Global Vision of Justice (King Legacy)*, edited by Lewis V. Baldwin. Beacon Press, 2014.

———. "Loving Your Enemies." Sermon delivered at Dexter Avenue Baptist Church. Montgomery, AL, 1963.

King, Martin Luther Jr. "A *New Sense of Direction.*" *Worldview.* New York: 1958, 15(4).

———. *Strength to Love.* Beacon Press, 1963.

———. *A testament of Hope: The Essential Writings and Speeches of Martin Luther King, Jr.,* edited by James M. Washington. HarperOne, 2003.

LAWT News Service. Los Angeles Southwest College names new football coach; Henry Washington steps aside. Nate Turner, former college standout on the gridiron and in the classroom, to lead Cougars. *Los Angeles Wave*, April 20, 2017, http://www.lawattstimes.com.

Lund, Steven L. "Flashes of Light." BYU Speeches, September 20, 2022.

Mandela, Nelson. *Conversations with Myself.* Farrar, Straus and Giroux, 2010.

———. "I Am Prepared to Die." Speech, Rivonia Trial, April 20, 1964.

———. "I Therefore Place the Remaining Years of My Life in Your Hands." Cape Town, South Africa, February 1990.

———. *Long Walk to Freedom.* Little Brown Book Group, 2013.

Mathew, Phillip. *Finding Leo.* Wipf and Stock, 2021.

Maxwell, John C. *Developing the Leader Within You 2.0.* HarperCollins Leadership, 2019.

Maxwell, Neal A. *All These Things Shall Give Thee Experience.* Salt Lake City: Deseret Book, 2007.

———. "But for a Small Moment." BYU Speeches, September 1974.

———. "Endure It Well." *Ensign,* May 1990.

———. *A More Excellent Way.* Sale Lake City: Deseret Book, 1967.

———. "Patience." BYU Speeches, November 1979.

———. 'Plow in Hope." *Ensign*, May 2001.

———. *A Time to Choose.* Salt Lake City: Deseret Book, 1972.

Middlemiss, Clare. *Cherished Experiences: From the Writings of President David O. McKay.* Salt Lake City: Deseret Book, 1955.

Monson, Thomas S. "Finishers Wanted." *Ensign,* May 1972.

———. "Go for It!" *Ensign,* May 1989.

———. "The Paths Jesus Walked." *Ensign,* May 1974.

———. "Ponder the Path of Thy Feet." *Ensign,* November 2014.

———. "Your Jericho Road." *Ensign,* February 1989.

Munrose, Myles. "The Most Important Aspect of Leadership: Passing It On." https://youtu.be/9XGp8iPvXHM.

———. "Ponder the Path of Thy Feet." *Ensign,* November 2014.

Nelson, Russell M. "Embrace the Future with Faith." *Ensign,* November 2020.

———. "Love One Another." *Ensign,* May 2018.

———. "A More Excellent Hope." BYU Speeches, January 8, 1995.

———. "Ponder the Path of Thy Feet." *Ensign,* November 2014.

Nelson, Stanley and London, Nicole (directors). *Becoming Frederick Douglass.* PBS Documentaries, 2002.

Nelson, *Teachings of Russell M. Nelson.* Salt Lake City: Deseret Book, 2018.

Obama, Barack. *Speeches.* Canterbury Classics, 2020.

Packer, Boyd K. (1981). "The Mantle Is Far, Far Greater Than the Intellect." Brigham Young University Studies, 21(3), 259–278. http://www.jstor.org/stable/43040959.

Rash, Phillip. "Looking to the Margins: Creating Belonging." Brigham Young University devotional. Provo, UT, June 4, 2019.

Ratcliffe, Susan, ed. Oxford Essential Quotations (5 ed.). Oxford University Press, 2017.

Scott, Richard G. "The Power of Scripture," *Liahona,* November 2011.

Sill, Sterling W. *The Glory of the Sun.* Salt Lake City: Bookcraft, 1961.

———. "Great Experiences." *Ensign,* June 1971.

———. *The Laws of Success.* Salt Lake City: Deseret Book, 1980.

———. *Leadership.* Salt Lake City: Bookcraft, 1959.

———. *Leadership Vol. III.* Salt Lake City: Bookcraft, 1978.

———. *Leadership Vol. II.* Salt Lake City: Bookcraft, 1960.

———. *Making the Most of Yourself.* Salt Lake City: Deseret Book, 1971.

Bibliography

Sill, Sterling W. "The poetry of success." *Ensign,* May 1978.

Sill, Sterling W. and Dan McCormick. *Lessons from Great Lives: Learn To Be Rich In All Areas of Your Life.* Aylesbury Publishing, 2011.

Talmage, James E. *Jesus the Christ.* American Fork, UT: Covenant Communications, 2006.

Teachings of Presidents of the Church—David O. McKay. Salt Lake, Utah: The Church of Jesus Christ of Latter-day Saints, 2003.

Teachings of Presidents of the Church—Ezra Taft Benson. Salt Lake City: The Church of Jesus Christ of Latter-day Saints, 2014.

Teachings of Presidents of the Church—Gordon B. Hinckley. Salt Lake City: The Church of Jesus Christ of Latter-day Saints, 2016.

Teachings of Presidents of the Church—Howard W. Hunter. Salt Lake City: The Church of Jesus Christ of Latter-day Saints, 2015.

Teachings of Presidents of the Church—John Taylor. Salt Lake City. The Church of Jesus Christ of Latter-day Saints, 2001.

Teachings of Presidents of the Church—Joseph Smith. Salt Lake City: The Church of Jesus Christ of Latter-day Saints, 2007.

Teachings of Presidents of the Church—Lorenzo Snow. Salt Lake City: The Church of Jesus Christ of Latter-day Saints, 2012.

Teachings of Presidents of the Church—Spencer W. Kimball. Salt Lake City: The Church of Jesus Christ of Latter-day Saints, 2006.

Teachings of Presidents of the Church—Thomas S. Monson. Salt Lake, Utah: The Church of Jesus Christ of Latter-day Saints, 2020.

Teachings of the Presidents of the Church—Wilford Woodruff. The Church of Jesus Christ of Latter-day Saints, 2004.

Tutu, D. *No Future Without Forgiveness.* Doubleday, 1999.

Van Dyke, H. *The Mansion.* New York: Harper & Brothers Publishers, 1911.

Washington, Booker T. *The Booker T. Washington Collection: The Negro Problem, Up from Slavery, the Future of the American Negro, the History of Slavery .* Ancient Cypress Press, 2019.

Washington, Booker T. *Character Building .* Independently published, 2022.

Williams, Lea E. *Servants of the People: 1960s Legacy of African American Leadership.* Palgrave Macmillan, 2009.

Wirthlin, Joseph B. "Never Give Up." *Ensign*, November 1987.

Woodruff, W. *Deseret New: Semi-Weekly*, December 21, 1869.

Zepel, Barry. "Washington Can't Tell a Lie: Southwest Is Good." *Los Angeles Times.* September 7, 1990. https://www.latimes.com.